REALITIES OF SOCIAL RESEARCH

REALITIES OF SOCIAL RESEARCH

By

Jennifer Platt
The University of Sussex

A HALSTED PRESS BOOK

JOHN WILEY & SONS
New York

Published in the U.S.A.
by Halsted Press, a Division
of John Wiley & Sons Inc.
New York

ISBN: 0 470–69119–0

Library of Congress Catalog Card No: 75–30275

Printed and bound in Great Britain

CONTENTS

101580

For Alice, without whom the work might never have been started, and Charles, without whose help it could not have been finished.

PREFACE

As with most social research, this book could not have been written without the co-operation of many other people. My respondents could, and did, offer me not merely raw data but also many sophisticated sociological insights into it; I have drawn on these freely and with gratitude. Beyond their purely intellectual contribution, they also gave me much welcome encouragement, a high level of co-operation even at considerable personal inconvenience, and an extraordinary amount of hospitality. Unfortunately, it is unlikely that they will all want to interview me in the future, so I shall not be able to make repayment in kind, but I would like to express my very warm thanks here. There is a practical and ethical problem arising from the fact that my respondents are members of the group most likely to read this book. This makes it harder to preserve their anonymity, where this is necessary, than in most research reports. I have, therefore, gone to some lengths to make it difficult to identify individuals or projects in the text, though I have always been conscious of the danger of concealing relevant information by doing this. All names have been changed, and sometimes sexes; institutional affiliations and research topics have been changed or described in general terms, and other potentially identifying features have been treated in the same way. If the same name happens to appear in more than one place, it does not refer to the same individual. (Some projects are, however, named in Appendix B; the reason for this and comments on the issues involved are given at the end of Appendix A.) It is galling to have to make such efforts to preserve the anonymity of a sample to whom I owe even more than is usually the case. I can, however, thank by name the people who gave me help in some capacity other than that of respondent. Colin Bell and John Wakeford in particular encouraged me at early stages to develop my ideas, and they and David Oldman, Susan Budd and Frank Bechhofer gave me practical help later on. Stella Shaw of the Social Science Research Council had several helpful discussions with me, and provided some useful background information; she has also contributed a note on S.S.R.C. policies and practices, which appears as Appendix D. David Oldman, Martin Bulmer, Colin Bell, David Webb and Stella Shaw read parts of the manuscript and gave me the benefit of their comments; the usual disclaimers of course apply. The Arts and Social Studies Research

7

Fund of the University of Sussex made grants that covered my expenses for travelling and subsistence while interviewing, and some extra secretarial costs. Several gallant typists struggled with the problems of transcribing my tapes, and of them I should like to thank particularly Kathy Thorp, Joan Robson and Madge Sirett. Finally, my husband struck a blow for men's liberation by looking after our daughter more than he would otherwise have done while I was away interviewing; that debt will be repaid in kind.

Jennifer Platt
The University of Sussex
December 1974

CHAPTER 1

Introduction

This is a book about the sociology of the social research process. Most books about the social research process are textbooks on method; most books about the sociology of sociology are discussions of the published end products of research; this book arises from a dissatisfaction with the general failure of sociologists to fill the gap between the two. There is an established tradition of methodological appendices telling the history of particular projects, and relating them to the intellectual autobiographies of their authors, but inevitably these tend to be sophisticated versions of the ordinary material of professional gossip; there is a striking absence of more systematic study of such topics.* It is strange that such a methodologically self-conscious discipline as sociology should produce many books on the techniques and the philosophy of social research but almost none on its sociology. There are obvious difficulties in approaching the subject, but nonetheless it seems worth attempting.

The social history of this book is told in the appendix; here its intellectual background is relevant. My own research experience, conversation with other people about theirs and the reading of methodological appendices all showed that there are practical social contingencies in the doing of empirical research that have consequences for its progress and outcome. Everyone who has done any research knows this already, but somehow it has generally stayed at the level of gossip, anecdote and the folklore of research units. Perhaps this may be partially explained by the feeling that such divergences from the normative philosophical picture of pure scientific method should not be publicly admitted; perhaps also there is a more respectable feeling that it is intellectually parochial to study oneself. My comment on such attitudes would be, firstly, that I see no reason to assume that social research is ethnographically less interesting, or theoretically less relevant, than other work situations, and, secondly, that in so far as methodological norms are valued there is a special need to study the circumstances that make it easy or difficult to follow them.

* A partial exception to these generalisations is ed. Richard O'Toole, *The Organization, Management, and Tactics of Social Research,* Schenkman, Cambridge, Mass., 1971. This contains several chapters very relevant to the themes of this book, although they are based on reflection on experience rather than research.

9

Although there have been two very distinct intellectual traditions in the sociology of sociology, they have had in common that most of their research has consisted of the study of published works, and the variables used to explain their characteristics have commonly been ones, such as the social background or institutional affiliation of the researcher, that existed before the process of producing the published works started; the nature of the process, the mechanisms by which the observed correlations came about, have been relatively neglected. The two intellectual traditions referred to are the empiricist, and the sociology of knowledge approach. The empiricist tradition produces works such as the plethora of citation studies and measures of the relative productivity of leading sociology departments which have appeared in recent U.S. journals; these studies report very large numbers of facts, but are usually of limited sociological interest. The sociology of knowledge approach addresses itself to far more significant problems, but often at a macroscropic level; its tendency to pay little attention to the extent to which there is (or is not) precise evidence to support its conclusions has become vulgarized, in some contributions to recent controversy, into a propensity to make assertions for which there is no evidence. It will be clear that, for both substantive and methodological reasons, I am not entirely happy with either of these traditions.

What has been attempted in this study is a detailed empirical investigation of the nature of the process of doing social research, its causes and its consequences. The purpose is threefold: to satisfy a simple ethnographic curiosity; to provide data and suggest interpretations that may help to advance theory in such areas as the sociology of work and of education; and to suggest sociologically realistic prescriptions for the conduct of successful research which may supplement the usual methods-textbook formulae, which tend to ignore the social factors in research.

The crucial weakness of the study reported here is that it has very little to say about the character and quality of the publications of the social researchers whose work was investigated; in a sense the dependent variable is missing. There are practical reasons for this. One of them is that some of the projects studied have not yet reached publication, and a few of them never will. Another is that to have given proper attention to the publications too would have been to embark on a whole separate study, and would have taken very much longer. A third is that one of the main points of interest of such a study would have been to judge the intellectual success of the works, in order to relate this to the manner in which they had been done, and to devise an acceptable criterion of success that represented more than personal judgment would be a task of enormous difficulty. These difficulties have been skirted by discussing results only in terms of whether research was completed at all, whether it was completed on time, and whether it reached publication in some form or not. The main focus, however, is on process rather than product; much as I regret the omissions, they must be justified by the need to focus on a manageable problem area. If this line of research were to be developed further, it is very much to be hoped that it might prove possible to find ways of linking the research process with the nature of its eventual product; there are a variety of interesting lines along which publications might be classified.

The project has been conceived as essentially exploratory in nature; although from the beginning there were some ideas about what was relevant and likely to prove significant, the design was not planned to test hypotheses. The data collected came from long, unstructured interviews with research participants about their experiences. In principle it would have been preferable to proceed at least in part by direct observation, and to conduct interviews at different stages in the progress of each project in the sample. In practice this could only have been done over a much longer period of time, and would probably have entailed studying considerably fewer projects. What has actually been done is to interview the participants at a point as near as possible to the end of the research period, sometimes just before the end and sometimes after it.* The disadvantages of relying on memory are evident, but seemed to be outweighed by the advantages of being able to ask about the whole course of a project. Where more than one person was involved in a project, the aim was to interview at least one person from each hierarchical level of the team. The interviews covered such topics as how the individual came to be involved in that project and its role in his career, the nature of the division of labour and hierarchy within teams, the institutional setting and funding of the project and their perceived consequences, the ways in which the course of the research and the private lives of researchers influenced each other; all this in the context of a general history of the project and its social events.

* In some cases it was rather longer after the end of the project than one would have liked. In 4 cases this was because I thought that the project, from what I knew of it already, had some special interest. In some others a problem of definition arose, because it is not clear when a project is to be regarded as finished; a number were over in the sense that their grant had ceased and the team dispersed, but not over in the sense that publications were still being worked on.

11

The ways in which the sample investigated here was chosen, and other details of method and methodological problems, are described in Appendix A. The broad principle followed was to look for research projects with these characteristics: (i) the project was done in Britain; (ii) it was near completion, or had been completed fairly recently; (iii) the topic was sociological, taking 'sociology' in its most broad and catholic sense; (iv) it involved the collection of empirical data, taking 'empirical' to include the application of systematic techniques to documentary sources. The sample has no formal claim to representativeness of any defined population, and I have attempted in the analysis not to make claims to generality of a kind that it cannot support; however, there seems to be no reason to believe that it is particularly *un*representative of recent British empirical research in sociology, especially that done within the universities. Although the effective sampling unit was the project, it is also a sample of individuals, and so can be described in either set of terms. Originally the project was seen as the unit of analysis, but after a very few interviews it became clear that any one project needed to be understood as one stage in the life of the individuals concerned, and that a team project was the point of intersection of several careers; thus the individual also became a unit of analysis. The interviews were with 121 individuals, and refer to 55 different projects; the number of individuals seen from any one project varies from 1 to 8.* Forty-four of the projects were based at universities, and 11 had no university connections; of the university-based ones, 18 were commissioned. Some of the projects had more than one source of finance, but if each is classified by its main source this is the breakdown: Social Science Research Council (or, earlier, Department of Scientific and Industrial Research), 11; Nuffield Foundation, 7; other foundations, 3; British government departments, 14; commissioning clients, 7; university or research unit funds, 5; Ph.D. students' grants, 6; other sources, 2. Project teams varied in size from 1 to 16, hierarchically divided into from 1-4 ranks. (Full details are given in Chapter 5.) The method of data collection most frequently used was the survey, which played some role in 43 of the projects; other common methods used were observation, usually participant (19), depth interviews (16), and study of documents (12). Among the individuals in the sample, there were 96 men and 25 women;

* In a small number of cases where there had been acute conflict with clients, or administrators outside the team had played a significant role, it seemed important to get their perspectives too on the situation, and so some clients and administrators were included among those seen.

they included 9 graduate students, 23 university lecturers, 5 readers or senior lecturers, 6 professors, 31 research assistants, 26 research officers, 13 holders of senior research posts, 4 research administrators or clients, and 3 in miscellaneous other jobs.*

The plan of the book is to start by considering the nature of the institutional framework within which social research takes place, and the nature of the external influences to which it is exposed; it then goes on to describe what happens within the research team, and finishes by considering the characteristics of the individuals involved and the ways in which their separate lives affect and are affected by the research. Particular emphasis is laid throughout on the importance of social factors in determining the events of research and its likely outcome, and thus on the extent to which what really happens departs from textbook norms, or can only be understood when the social context is also taken into account.

* These are the occupations held at the beginning of their projects; a number had been promoted or changed job by the time I saw them. The classification here is by main occupation, and so the numbers do not always correspond with those given later on; at some points individuals are distinguished by their ranks in the hierarchy of a particular project, and then titles such as 'research officer' are used with a different reference.

CHAPTER 2

Research Grants and Timetables

A key institution in the social research system is the research grant; almost all the projects studied were financed by research grants from a funding agency. The grant is normally given for a predefined number of years, with the possibility of extension if application is made by a prescribed deadline; it consists of a fixed total sum, often allocated to specified subheadings of expenditure. To obtain the grant an application must be submitted an appropriate time in advance of the start of the project; the application gives an outline of the subject and methods proposed, the timetable, and a costing of the resources required. In some cases funding bodies give a grant for a pilot study on the understanding that, if it is successful, a further application for the main study will be favourably received. A final report on the results achieved is expected, and interim reports may also be required.

Most of these conditions are obviously required to meet the needs of funding bodies, who operate in a situation where their resources are limited and there is competition for the grants available. They cannot enter into open-ended commitments and must be seen to administer the competition for grants fairly, and they want to ensure that the money given is spent responsibly and that they get the best possible return for it in terms of results. In order to achieve their objectives they have to set up bureaucratic procedures to process applications and monitor the progress of projects under way. The inherent uncertainty of research suggests procedures that have to be to some extent externally imposed, and the competition for scarce resources probably makes it seem wise to prefer the risk of rejecting good proposals to that of accepting bad ones; when proposals judged weak are accepted, conditions and reservations are particularly likely to have to be made. Funding agencies acting under these constraints are faced by grant applicants, with their own ends in view, who may be interested in manipulating the situation to suit *their* needs.

Almost all the projects funded by government departments or private clients were commissioned by them, and so were 6 of the 10 funded by foundations. None of the projects funded by D.S.I.R. (the old Department of Scientific and Industrial Research) or S.S.R.C. (the Social Science Research Council) was commissioned by them, and this must be the reason why the discussions of 'grantsmanship' and the politics of application all come from these.

This is a rich area of folklore, to which my data can make only a modest contribution. Only one person claimed to have made deliberately false representations to the S.S.R.C.; he said that his application stated the intention of interviewing one group to which he knew it was in practice impossible to get access, though it would have been desirable to see them. Members of two projects said that they had asked for less money than they really needed because, within the S.S.R.C.'s rules, this meant that they could get a quicker decision:

"[. . . we seriously thought very hard about costing, and we came up with I think £30,000. [Senior official of S.S.R.C.] then came in and said, 'that size would have to go to too many committees, if you want to get it in a hurry cut it in half,' which was politics, and a nod from [senior official] is as good as a bloody wink, isn't it? but it wasn't enough.]"*

The project from which this quotation comes was one of a fairly topical nature, so there was an intrinsic need for speed. One consequence, however, of starting an ambitious project without enough money was that several of the things planned did not get done; another is that, several years after the original target date, most of the material has still not been written up and published, and it has lost its topical interest. The other project was less dramatic, but again the shortfall of money in relation to planned tasks caused serious delays. A third project had similar difficulties because, knowing the rule, they asked for a smaller amount of money than they would otherwise have wished, but they lost both ways: they were applying

* Here and subsequently, the conventions followed in the presentation of quotations from interviews are these: (i) square brackets round a passage indicate that I did not succeed in recording it entirely verbatim, or that I have substituted a description for a name or added an explanatory comment; (ii) . . . indicates, as is usual, that a passage has been omitted; sometimes, however, it indicates that the respondent's sentence tailed off without being completed, and these cases can usually be identified by the syntactical oddity of the resulting phrase; (iii) J.P. indicates a comment made by me; these have been recorded with less care for verbatim accuracy than those of respondents. Occasionally a third person was present at the interview, and when they are quoted this is indicated by putting e.g. (wife) : . . . ; (iv) all names have been changed; government departments are referred to as DoX; (v) (etc.) indicates that the respondent continued on the same lines and I did not record what was said because it was essentially repetition or elaboration of a point already made.

for a grant extension, and had not realized that the rule does not apply in that case, so they did not get speed of decision either. There was also a fourth one, where no particular need for speed was felt, but a young and inexperienced director was advised after the rejection of his first application that a small application was more likely to be accepted; he ended up applying for, and getting, £3500 to interview 300 respondents, which turned out to be not nearly enough. On another project the directors felt that they had a legitimate grievance against the S.S.R.C.'s irrational cheeseparing:

" . . .we put in for this money, and what it boiled down to was the S.S.R.C. said lovely project, we adore you both, but we're going to reduce the size of the project. . .the important thing to grasp is that the original costing was for more labour than we eventually got. . . .S.S.R.C. quite arbitrarily chopped one of these [research assistants] out, they wanted to save money I think, they didn't even think about it. . . .Now there is no doubt at all, I think, that if we had had the third assistant we would be a hell of a lot further along with the project. It would have been cheaper. . . .They had never heard of inflation. . . ."

(The last comment refers to the fact that in the end an extension had to be granted, and by that time research assistants were more expensive than they would have been at the start). This complaint may presumably be taken, retrospectively, to have been justified, since more money was given in the end; whether the S.S.R.C. could reasonably have been expected to anticipate this is a subject on which the director can not be regarded as an unbiased witness. It seems likely that a funding organisation (particularly a governmental one) will more often be blamed by outsiders for wasting money on a project that turns out to be relatively unsuccessful than for not giving it enough, because it will always seem reasonable, at least to those who do not know the details, to blame the researchers for their failure; this gives the funding organisations an incentive to keep grants down. But, looking at this from the other side, it will always be easy and comfortable for researchers to blame shortage of funds for their own delays and inadequacies. (For further discussion of funding, see below.)

In addition to comments on strategies of application to the S.S.R.C. there were a number of references to its internal politics. Four respondents mentioned 5 projects for which there was, by their account, some difficulty in getting a grant because the research topic had some connection with the spheres of interest of two or more of the S.S.R.C.'s subject committees. Sometimes this just caused delays as the application went through several committees, perhaps complicated by disagreements as to which committee should make the final decision. In one case the director felt that committee disagreements had more substantive implications:

"...the application was part sociology, part [other discipline], so it went to 2 committees. [Other discipline committee] were very keen, but they wanted a pretty large study; they thought that a necessary condition of a sample on this kind of work was that one should be able to generalise to the national population, and they were less concerned with the number of variables...The Sociology Committee wanted me to go for depth rather than for representativeness. It was fairly clear they only talked to each other through me as it were."

Another director, working in a substantive area not clearly associated with any one traditional academic discipline, found that his proposals usually went to more than one committee, and felt that this was representative of a more general situation:

"This is one of the problems of this area of research. It doesn't have an institutional base, so if you want a reason for not supporting it it can very easily be found. It's a problem to me in that it is outside the main stream of sociological research."

Given the disciplinary division of the social sciences, such difficulties are inherently likely to arise; when the funding organisation is, for excellent reasons, internally divided along the same disciplinary lines, the bureaucratic structure tends to exacerbate the difficulties.

Two references were made to other kinds of internal political issue. One respondent had been told that an application of his was turned down because one person on the committee was against it and he happened to be a friend of the chairman. Another respondent said:

"I had asked the S.S.R.C. for money for a market research agency to do the fieldwork....They said no, flatly. The reason was that there was a big battle going on over the establishment of their own survey research centre, and it was fairly clear that those who wanted such a centre wanted to show that there was a demand for it by showing that there were people doing projects on their money who were getting on in an amateurish sort of way."

17

Whether these discreditable imputations were correct I cannot judge. They refer to events of a kind that are possible in any organisation; on the other hand, the formal secrecy of the process for deciding on grant applications provides ample scope for paranoid interpretations by those whose proposals are rejected. However, for as long as getting research grants is important to social scientists they will speculate, on the basis of whatever fragmentary information is available, about the internal political processes of the S.S.R.C. and other funding organisations, and the nature of their speculations will affect the type of applications submitted and the manner in which they are presented. Their folk beliefs thus have some practical significance, and would do even if wholly incorrect. This is an area which might profit from some more systematic research.

Shortage of money was not always blamed on the funding organisations. For 5 projects (4 of them funded by the S.S.R.C.) which had found themselves short of funds participants specifically said that the initial costing had been bad. There were a variety of ways in which this had come about: (i) the heavy cost of transcribing taped interviews had not been anticipated; (ii) the poor initial response rate to a survey had necessitated putting in more resources than originally planned; (iii) a large number of interviews had originally been planned, even more were actually done, and the consequent sample size was so large that standard computer packages could not be used on it; (iv) the high cost in time of participant observation, and the technical difficulties of combining data from it with survey data, had not been anticipated; (v) the application in effect only allowed time for the collection of the data and not for its analysis. Some of these problems arose because directors had no previous experience of the particular techniques involved. In an ideal world the experts at the funding organisations would have spotted their excessively optimistic assumptions and corrected them; in the actual world of British sociology at the time they were probably not sufficiently expert to do so, since they too could not yet have had much practical experience. Perhaps they were also too tempted by apparent economies to consider whether they might be false ones. Another way in which this sort of situation might come about is suggested by this comment:

"We went to [funding organisation] and put up our application; it was very specific, saying how many interviews etc., and [organisation official] said it didn't matter, we're giving the money to Bernard Smith and he is a good chap — that's the way we work. . . . In retrospect it was a horrendously vague outline. . . ."

[Organisation official] might well be embarrassed by this now, in the light of the exceedingly prolonged history of this project. It is no doubt not accidental that, in the two cases above where it seems more reasonable to have expected the proposers to anticipate the difficulties that actually arose, the directors were well-known academics whose reputations probably made it seem superfluous to quibble over the details of their proposals. Even distinguished academics can err, or lack experience in some fields.*

Sometimes shortages of funds arose for other reasons than poor initial costing. One researcher, holding a research fellowship at a university financed by a private client, found himself in this situation:

> J.P. "How did you process the first survey?"
> "My wife and myself were at home . . . .We used the dining room over the Christmas vac, working an 18-hour day doing a straight count and cross tabulations, acting like punched-card machines: a colossal task. . . ."
> J.P. "Did you have any money for research assistance?"
> "Yes, there was money available. [Client] did include provision for expenses, which could have been for assistance on an *ad hoc* basis, or to subsidise the publication of a hardback tome, and this was what they really wanted to save it for. They were very parsimonious in granting expenses of any kind. . . ."

* Detailed costing can be a very complex matter, and can only be properly carried out when the research proposal goes into sufficient detail. This is shown by a recent publication of the S.S.R.C. Survey Unit (Donald Monk, *The Use of Survey Research Organisations and the Costing of Survey Research*, Occasional Papers in Survey Research I, 1972) which explains how it is done by survey organisations. This publication is designed to meet the need created by the fact that "there are an increasing number of people who find themselves in the position of requiring the facilities for conducting a survey. In the majority of cases the situation will be a new experience . . ." (p.2). It suggests one reason why costing may be poor, which is that the vaguer the plans on which the costing is based the more difficult it necessarily becomes to make accurate estimates of cost. I think that many research proposals do not go into the details on such matters as sampling that would be needed for accurate estimates. Perhaps it would not be reasonable to expect them to do so. One well-known methods textbook has an appendix on "Estimating the Time and Personnel Needed for a Study", which says: "It appears to be an almost universal rule that every operation takes longer than one would anticipate if everything went smoothly", and goes on to suggest as a rule of thumb that 50% or more should be added to initial estimates to allow for contingencies. (B. Selltiz et al., *Research Methods in Social Relations*, Revised One-Volume Edition, Methuen, 1971, p. 503, Appendix A.)

J.P. "Did you raise the possibility of assistance on the analysis?"
"Yes, I did. The reaction was, the phrase used was something
like: 'we're doubtful about committing any more money when
nothing is coming out.' It became money on a sale-or-return
basis, though they were committed on paper to give the university up to £5000 a year for 5 years. The university liberally interpreted this as being a total sum of £25,000, all of which [client]
could keep except for the day-to-day expenses of my salary plus
whatever expenses [client] was prepared to offer."

Obviously this situation was an unusual one. The researcher eventually
concluded, too late, that what his client really wanted was something
quick, cheap and unscholarly which would not have raised these
problems. Another research team had only a small grant from their
own university (to study an aspect of its operation) and so found
that they were forced to do data processing by hand themselves. A
third study was financed by a government department which could
not legally anticipate the vote of the coming year, which meant
that the grant ran from year to year and could always be affected
by national cuts. As a consequence, the director said,

"I became obsessed by what I think I can get the DoX to grant
you. If we'd had a super-secretary to coordinate the 3 or 4
people working more or less in isolation, and needing a central
person to keep trace of everybody, it would have cost £1000 a
year but shortened the project by a considerable amount".

Perhaps he could have got more money if he had asked for it, but
perhaps the guesses he made at the time about what was practical
politics were right.
Whether or not funds are adequate depends on the nature of the
project which they support. Participants said of a number of projects, including most of those where there were complaints of shortage of funds, that they had been too ambitious in conception or
had collected too much data. Sometimes the excessive ambitious-
ness had become obvious at an early enough stage for the whole plan
to be changed, and those projects had managed reasonably well; it
seemed commoner to realize that too much was being attempted
only after the data had been collected and it was evident that there
was too much of it to cope with. There were 3 ways in which there
could be too much data: (i) too many cases were studied; (ii) too
many items of information were collected on each case; (iii) too
many different types of data were collected. When (i) or (ii)
occurred, this could lead to problems of quantity in simply fitting

such bulk onto the computer; when (ii) or (iii) occurred, the problems became more intellectual ones of grasping and interrelating such a large mass of information, and knowing where to start on analysing it. One project managed to collect 250 items of information on each of 15,000 cases! A participant said that eventually this had to be used as a sort of data bank rather than a coherent single project. Sometimes it made a significant contribution to the problem that the coding was far too detailed:

"...one was not sure what one wanted to explain, and because of this, and because the questionnaire contained a large number of open-ended questions, there was the immediate problem of how to code it...we took out as little as possible; we were going to assume the existence of large and powerful and also free computer facilities, and have to use those to construct higher-order codings. This decision was very much influenced by the fact that we had excellent computer facilities, and also the fact that I had become very interested in computers...And so we adopted the strategy of coding which was fantastically diffuse and general, and an immense number of punched cards, so that for instance question [27] became 3 punched cards!... So then we put an enormous amount of labour into producing these descriptive tables, so we had an immense amount of descriptive bumf lying around....It's not finished now, and it doesn't seem likely that it ever will be finished."

"...there were 5 different categories for no answer, answer not relevant, question misunderstood etc., you could go from 0 to 99, 2 column coding, and the 90s was the no answer...it went absolutely haywire because it meant there were great areas of print-out taken up with exhaustive reports on a string of individuals who had answered 'not relevant' or 'misunderstood'...."

(It is interesting that these 2 cases both arose in part because one team member became fascinated by computer problems — see the discussion of this in Chapter 5. In one, however, it was also felt by others that the member quoted above had made his own contribution by going through an ethnomethodological phase that made him reluctant to lose any details.) A large part of the lack of anticipation or adaptation to available resources can be attributed to inexperience, and some of the things that were done would have been desirable in a world of infinite resources; in the actual world an over-ambitious project whose funds run out may never get finished, and so the net result is worse than that of a more modest one. However, infinite resources would not solve all problems. The largest of the projects with an excessive amount of data had collected it in part because they had an unusually large grant, which enabled them to get data from many sources and to collect information on whole populations rather than samples.

The broad nature of the problem seems clear, although there are two radically different ways of presenting it. The first way is to say that if research directors had made more detailed plans in the first place, costed them properly, and anticipated the consequences of research decisions made as they went along, the difficulties experienced would not have arisen. The second way is to say that if funding agencies' procedures did not attempt to bureaucratize the essentially unbureaucratizable, and if they did not require a degree of anticipation of contingencies that could only realistically be expected in an area where no further research was needed, and furthermore, if the agencies showed real commitment to the emergent needs of projects once they had taken them on, the difficulties experienced would not arise. It is obvious that both these statements are true: if either factor had been different, the situation would have been changed. It is also obvious, however, that on at least some of the projects a level of experience and professionalism on the part of the directors, which it would not be unreasonable to expect, could have reduced the extent to which the inherently surprising and emergent character of research gave rise to difficulties. (One of the reasons why they did not always fully apply the expertise they had is discussed in Chapter 3.) It is possible, though less obvious, that funding agencies could, without undue risk, operate more flexibly and responsively even within the unavoidable financial constraints.

There is one research context within which the practices of the funding agencies have a special importance: independent research units can be wholly, or almost wholly, dependent on *ad hoc* research grants. For them it is of crucial importance to have the right number of projects running at any one time, and appropriate new projects starting as the current ones finish; how far this ideal can actually be achieved depends on the current state of intellectual fashion, and of funds in the bodies that commission or finance their projects. They cannot hope to be able to offer tenure to most of their staff, though the opportunity may arise to move on from one short-term contract to another; perhaps paradoxically, this is easier for junior staff whose skills are not highly specialized. It was reported that it was not uncommon for highly qualified senior staff to be forced out, against both their own wishes and those of the unit, because no project appropriate to their skills and interests could be arranged to run

22

end-on with the last one. From the unit's point of view this meant that the high turnover of staff created administrative problems, that there were difficulties in getting staff, and that experience was not shared and passed on as it could have been. (The staff's point of view is discussed in Chapter 6.) Staff who are about to leave are under great pressure to tie up all the loose ends, sometimes on several projects, before they go. If they get another job that starts before the end of their existing contract, if seems unethical to hold them to a contract which could spoil their occupational chances, and so they are released early. Since no funding agency pays for the preparation of research proposals, this has to be done from general funds or in time paid for by another project. This, together with the tendency asserted by some research workers for grants not to be great enough to allow adequate time for analysis and writing, helps to create a pattern where each project lags a little behind its timetable; once one has done so the waves spread outwards and create a general feeling of pressure, without any of the leeway provided by tenure in university posts which are not tied to projects. Timetables were much more often adhered to than in university projects, both because it was financially essential and because it was necessary to maintain a good reputation with the funding agencies in order to get further grants. But this was not always achieved without substantive non-monetary costs, as is shown by this comment from a senior member of a leading independent unit:

"I asked that a certain thing be stopped, and because of the power structure asked should be in quotation marks. [If we go over schedule it costs us money, so we can't explore all possible avenues. Further analyses after the end of the month would not be authorized] . . . ."

J.P. "Was this decision made on financial or intellectual grounds?"

"Denis has a very good mind, and what he was doing was forming damn good ideas and chasing them, but we had a deadline to get in, you can't go to DoX a year later. . .We'd been given the terms of reference to do a certain thing on a certain budget, everything else is jam, though it's difficult to get this across to good research people. . . ."

Denis, his junior colleague, was quite embittered by this experience and by the emphasis on the need for good public relations that he saw pervading the unit's activities. He felt that the shortcomings of the sample and instruments of data collection were such that the only legitimate conclusion to reach in their report was an inconclusive

23

one; his senior colleague, however, rewrote the draft:

> "The way he changed the report was to tone down the apologies or the rubbishing of the [instruments], he used words like 'caution', 'professional judgment', 'educated judgment' to try and assess the effects of the distorting factors."

This followed an internal memo commenting on the draft which concluded "...The approach was so negative that a more balanced picture should be presented if the [unit] is ever to be funded again!" Denis also said that in this unit

> "The press officer seems to me to have assumed too much power. The image men have moved into [unit]: the idea that it's image that wins contracts and funds, and you need as much publicity as possible. I was told by the press officer, and so was the deputy director and everybody, to be careful not to say too much [at the press conference to launch the report]; 'let's pull together to give a favourable impression of [unit]'."

Denis was a young man in his early twenties and of left-wing views, and the research findings seemed to run counter to left-wing beliefs. Charles Brown, his senior, was rather older and held a position in the unit where he was responsible administratively for the planning and finance of a group of projects; although he sympathised considerably with Denis' views on the project on which they worked together, from his perspective it was simply not practical to act on them. Denis made his case to me fairly dramatically, but it seems evident that it had some validity. Reactions of the kind he describes are a rational response to the environment in which independent research units find themselves, if they want to survive. Perhaps it is too easy to compare this sort of response with a hypothetical ideal world in which the course of research is influenced only by the perceived intellectual demands of the topic, and there are no external constraints. Universities are nearer to this ideal world, but at least one pair of directors of independent research did not see it as without disadvantages:

> A: "Partly what I'd say, if we get very blunt, is that if people in the universities want to collaborate with research institutes that are more applied in orientation, there's got to be a shift in their time orientation!" [A university colleague had just failed to meet their deadline.]

> B: "... the fact is that people in university departments, because they have another agenda, teaching, administration and so on,

and don't have the time pressure of funding substructure, they have a different time span of getting things done. . . . [You've got to write it up even if it's not quite finished.]"

A: "[it tends to be treated as negative by academics, but our experience is positive. The impact on us as people is another matter, but in terms of work production it's good.]"

We may conclude that the situation of the independent unit encourages some valuable kinds of professionalism*, but that meeting deadlines and keeping to budgets can entail distortions or incompleteness in the research.

The whole question of timetables and deadlines is one of some importance, and merits further exploration. Sometimes the timetables that people doing commissioned research had to work to were amazingly tight by normal academic standards — 6 months or less for a fairly large-scale survey for a Royal Commission, 3 months for a policy-related survey for a government department. These deadlines were met, as in effect they had to be if the research was to be used. Even when there was no rigid external timetable to conform to government researchers, for instance, could find that embarrassing questions were being asked in the House of Commons about the progress of their report, and this created heavy pressures. One researcher employed by a large voluntary organisation had to produce some findings in time for the annual conference, in order to demonstrate that its money was being usefully spent and to justify his continued employment. (Unfortunately his effort was wasted. One member of the executive was responsible for the matter:

"In the event, when that particular chapter of the report was called he was missing, presumed in the loo, so there was no reply forthcoming from the top table, so they passed on to the next business!")

Quick results, however, were not achieved without costs. Various respondents reported that pressure of time had made it impossible to have a large enough sample to generalise to subgroups; that it had meant that a survey was the only possible method of data-collection

* Sophisticated and elaborate procedures for scheduling projects and allocating resources among them had been developed in these units. In at least some respects, however, these procedures would not be applicable in the ordinary university faculty project, since they depended on making economies of scale (e.g. in the use of statisticians) which could only occur where there were several projects running more or less concurrently under one central administration.

25

when participant observation would have been more appropriate, and that it had made it necessary to start data-collection without adequate preparation, and had forced the analysis to stop at a fairly superficial level.

The normal academic project was scheduled to take 2 or 3 years. Whatever the intrinsic needs of the research, it was almost always felt necessary to make the starting and finishing points fit in with the academic year, since if they did not it might be impossible to recruit suitable research workers in the first place, and it would create difficulties either for them or for the project (if they left early) at the end. This probably meant some rounding of numbers, and may have been a factor contributing to the late completion of university-based projects, since applicants would probably be more likely to round the number of years down in order to increase the chance of getting a grant, and so underestimate the likely duration of their research. When the work looked like running over time, extensions of the grant could be applied for; when a grant had been given for a short period for a pilot study, a further application was needed for the main study. Either of these contingencies could create considerable difficulties. There is a basic dilemma: if a further application is made early on, a pilot study will not yet have been carried very far and so may not provide a convincing basis for an extension, and it may not yet be clear that a main study really is going to need more money; if a further application is delayed until the last minute, continuity of employment cannot be guaranteed to research assistants and they are forced to start applying for other jobs. Some projects lost workers in this way even though their grant eventually was renewed, and this caused great inconvenience. (A similar situation could arise in institutions operating under an annual vote.) Thus directors had difficult decisions to make about the timing of applications. Some resentment was felt about the implications of the funding agencies' policies for pilot studies; in one case the time allocated to that phase was disproportionate to the role envisaged for it in the whole project, and as a result once the main grant was received it was put aside and not analysed. This was possible because the lead time for reapplication made necessary by the agency's procedures was such that it could not have been analysed before the reapplication anyway. In general, a requirement to base a further application on a pilot study tends to lead to an artificial separation between pilot and main study, and the pilot may be treated simply as a bureaucratic requirement to be got out of the way. (Even where reapplications are not involved, pressure of time sometimes leads to pilot studies being put on one side without real analysis.)

Researchers sometimes felt that their grants allowed inadequate time for some stages of the research, normally of course those at the end. Two people, each with considerable experience, asserted that grants never allow enough time at the end for writing up, especially given the likelihood that some workers will have to leave before the end of their formal contracts. For one, who usually worked on commissioned research, this meant that although the main report for the sponsors got done, because it had to be done, potential journal articles never got written. For the other, whose experience was more in university research, it meant that analysis was not done as thoroughly as he would have liked and that some interesting data was left unanalysed. No-one ever reported having time in hand before a grant ran out.

Such problems could arise because the timetable originally proposed by the directors turned out, in the light of hindsight, to be inappropriate. One director said that 2 years from a 3 year grant had been too long to spend on fieldwork, and that it would have been better to spend more time on preparation and analysis. Others pointed out the difficulty of anticipating how much time one was going to need for participant observation, and the sheer time that it took to integrate participant observation and survey data.

Part of the difficulty of working out a good timetable arises from the inherent nature of some kinds of research. Several research assistants reported marked lulls in activity at some stages:

"It seemed to come very much like that – drop everything and do this, for a minute or a week or a month, like the questionnaire, and in the meantime go along to [research locale] or a [key episode to be observed] came and drop everything and go along to that, which meant that the work was interesting and varied [but at other times we were stuck for work to do – we threw paper aeroplanes at the window.]"

That quotation comes from a rather disorganised project, but nonetheless depicts a situation that can be hard to avoid. The total amount of work to be done often cannot be completed in only the time it takes to do that amount of work; timing is affected by the subjects of the research. If there is a questionnaire, there is a lull while one waits for the replies; if there is participant observation, particularly of special events rather than day-to-day behaviour, it can only be done when the relevant events are taking place. If such an event occurs when another part of the research is planned to take up time, both cannot be done adequately unless there is slack in the team. In some areas of research there are institutional constraints on research timetables. Studies of university students must avoid the summer exam season as well as the vacations. One study of universities planned a before-and-after design, which meant that if the pilot year was to be of use a "before" survey had to be done within a month or two of the research team's first meeting; inevitably it was fairly rough and ready. Research in educational institutions for these reasons also suffered particularly from such external contingencies as an extended postal strike. For example, one survey was scheduled to go out to schools when the postal strike started, and eventually questionnaires had to be delivered by car; if they had been left until the strike was over some of that year's school-leavers would already have been gone, and that would have meant waiting until the next year; as it was, the response rate was affected. Several studies were delayed by student protest activities, when directors were academics who were either caught up in the political turmoil or physically prevented from using their offices and other research facilities. Finally, among external delaying contingencies that researchers could not have anticipated, one man's computer was struck by lightning! Less dramatically, there could also be internal contingencies, as when a research assistant left in the middle for another job, or was fired for incompetence, and it took time to replace them.

Even when such contingencies did not occur the dynamics of the research process could mean that things did not go in accordance with the plan, because the plan was necessarily made before the team was really into the situation they were to study. There were two cases where people said that in practice the research had diverged from the plan laid down in the grant application, though without there having been any initial intention to deceive:

"[S.S.R.C. official] kept saying 'where's your hypothesis?' and so on. I think other people have had this experience, being expected to formulate the thing in natural-scientific terms when we wanted to do something much more open-ended. But as a result of this catechism we came up with [2 guiding ideas] and we spelt out in some detail what the implications would be. . . . I think it wasn't a bad document as it went, and in some senses we followed it fairly closely. What really happened was that by the time we got a year or so into the ground the whole terms of the debate began to change, and it no longer seemed the most relevant problem, so though we wrote a report to the S.S.R.C. we're not going to write it out eventually in those terms."

". . .the purpose of the research and the scheme itself. . .was a matter that we were considering all through the pilot year. . .

and of course it was always changing during the pilot year. All this is confidential, it is partly due to the fact that the aims of the research that there were and the purpose and outline that was accepted by the S.S.R.C. was a very bad one and we all realized it. . . .I'm sure Angus would agree that it was a bad design and idea. So we were trying to deal with this and somehow change it without letting the S.S.R.C. see that we were changing the whole thing drastically."

The first quotation is self-explanatory, and shows the characteristic difficulties of attempting to stick to a prearranged plan even when, as was (very unusually) so in this case, there had been the opportunity to do some preliminary research before putting in the application. The second quotation refers to a situation where Angus, the working director employed full-time on the project, had had to put together an application fairly hurriedly while still at another university and before he had had the opportunity to familiarize himself with the research milieu; under those circumstances it is not very surprising that plans changed when he was employed full time, and other research officers, who had not been involved at an earlier stage, joined the team. Such changes seem almost inevitable when fairly detailed proposals have to be submitted in advance, and there were undoubtedly others; they need not invariably affect the planned timetable, but are quite likely to do so.

More than half of the university-based projects in the sample studied were not completed by their deadline, so it is not surprising that many respondents regarded lateness as normal, if deplorable. In principle, one "solution" to the problem of lateness would be for researchers to improve their timekeeping, and another would be for grants to be open-ended. The latter solution would not necessarily produce the desired results. Two projects had had grants with no definite timetable, and both took an inordinate length of time and, although in the end there were some publications, were not altogether satisfactory to the participants, who might have worked better with the discipline of a deadline. On the other hand, one respondent who worked in a government research unit thought that it had been very valuable to him not to be forced to commit himself too far ahead:

". . .this would only possibly have been done from a government research thing. All field work was done in 2 years. The steps never committed me more than 6 months ahead. I was able to be very flexible about the extra help I had. When I needed extra clerical help, I could get it for 3 months. So I could do a lot of things that, if I needed to indent in advance for 3 months,

I could never have done."

Such flexibility could also be achieved, with luck, by academics who were not in a hurry and whose research only needed small sums from time to time which they could get from their own universities at short notice. There was one project of this kind; the participants enjoyed it a lot, and didn't mind that it took a long time – indeed one said that this was an advantage, because it meant that she was able to learn more from it. These experiences suggest that the former solution to the timekeeping problem would not be unequivocally beneficial either, even if it were possible.

When projects do take a long time there are intrinsic problems, whether or not deadlines are being missed:

> "We'd originally really planned to write articles as we went along. . .It would have concentrated our thoughts and sustained interest to produce them. It was a tremendous effort and strain writing this up a decade after it was thought of."

> ". . .the real difficulty is that you make certain decisions on what questions to ask and so on at points of time, and it takes a very pigheaded individual not to change at all over time and maintain the validity of the data in relation to their ideas over time. To do it you have to be someone like Jones who just shuts his eyes and ears and plods on. . .So it's a real problem, the development of self and the discipline is faster than one can complete a long-term research project."

Ideas could change even during a 2 or 3 year research project, and numbers of people reported that this had caused difficulties. The quotation above gives the main themes: individuals' ideas change (both in response to what they learn from doing the research and as part of their general intellectual development) and there are changes in the nature of the discipline to which it seems necessary to respond. One more quotation illustrates these themes further:

> "Every project starts where the previous project ends; by the time you get to the end you're no longer there, and if you were it wouldn't be worth doing it. . . .I understand what is going on in this sector of society better than 4 years ago, and because I understand better I'm not happy with the way I was looking at it. . . the fact of finding it out changes you, so you can't do a neat testing job. The other thing is, theory changes. We've been doing the project in the middle of the rise of symbolic interactionism. . . the intellectual climate does affect the way you look at the

30

research you have got; anybody doing a large scale survey research in 1972 is under attack from colleagues in a way he wasn't in 1968."

The swing of fashion to phenomenology and symbolic interactionism was specifically mentioned by several respondents, as something that had either directly affected their own intellectual development or affected what it seemed relevant and necessary to relate their own ideas to. There were other developments, or single publications, that had the same effect in particular fields, and the same consequences followed for policy-orientated research when the direction of public discussion on policy issues changed. It is possible that the youth of British sociology, and most British sociologists, at the time, contributed to the tendency for ideas to develop and change and respond to fashion in the course of one project; I have no way of knowing whether this tendency went farther than is usual in situations where sociology is more established. Intellectual fashions are not always changing equally fast, and those caught in mid-project when they are on the turn are likely to experience some discomfort, whether it is internalized or merely responded to as external criticism. Some, however, are part of the change of fashion, not just among those who respond to it once it has started; perhaps the issue is why it should be that the research experience does not drive *most* people to take up a critical standpoint about the adequacy of their own efforts. (One possible answer to this question, not wholly without plausibility, is that those whose research is technically worse are more likely to have its defects forced on their attention. But this does not explain why they should blame the technique, instead of or as well as their own application of it.)

Implicit in this discussion is the possibility of making value judgments of certain kinds about research projects. The earlier part of the chapter tended to assume that it was self-evidently desirable to finish a project, and to finish it on time. So perhaps it is, other things being equal; the later part of the chapter hints that perhaps other things are not always equal. There are two rival conceptions of the purposes of research involved. The first sees a sociological research project as a finite task, definable in advance, which is entered into as a commitment to a sponsor and/or to the testing of a hypothesis; the research is successfully completed when the original task has been fulfilled as planned. The second sees the project as a perhaps arbitrarily delimited part of the continuous stream of interrelated interests and ideas which goes to make up the intellectual career of the participant; such research could hardly be completed, except in a tentative and provisional sense, and could be judged successful to the extent that it stimulates new ideas and carries forward the participants' intellectual development. Although these alternative conceptions were not made explicit, it seems to me that they represent conflicting norms which many of those I interviewed found themselves torn between. The formal structure of the system of grants and contracts and deadlines creates moral obligations which imply and support one norm, while vague humanistic conceptions of the proper activity of a member of a university support the other. Careers can more easily be built with the blocks of neat completed projects, but the desire not to commit oneself and to procrastinate may conveniently be rationalized. I do not intend to imply a preference for one of these styles over the other; the point is simply that both exist as diffuse norms, that there is a tension between these norms, and that the funding bureaucracy is virtually compelled to adopt the norms of one style while there are numbers of factors pulling many of those who take their grants towards the other style.

Given the practices of the funding agencies and the characteristics of their clientele, many projects do run out of funds and time and there are dysfunctional consequences. Research teams split up; this always means that members are busy with new jobs, and usually also means that they are geographically separated and so further communication is complicated. Even before the money runs out the knowledge that it is going to do so can be disruptive: research assistants have to take time off for job interviews and may eventually leave early, and the sense of insecurity before people have got their next jobs weakens concentration and commitment. Subsequent collaboration at a distance takes longer, and the longer the whole process takes the more chance there is for ideas to move on beyond the original starting point and for team members to grow apart. Thus some projects are completed late or never. The continual dispersal of research teams combines with a number of other factors discussed later in the book to create difficulties in building up a satisfactory tradition: those who have learnt from experience are disillusioned, or combat-weary, or no longer directly involved in empirical research, and so are less likely to transmit to others or to put into practice themselves what they have learned.

CHAPTER 3

University Organisation

Of the 55 projects in my sample, 44 were in one way or another university-based; that is, they were Ph.D. theses, were directed by teaching members of university faculty, were based in university research units or were commissioned by outside bodies and carried out by specially appointed university research fellows. (The sample may well be biased towards university-based research). For those projects that are university-based, the way in which the social system of the university operates has important consequences for the research.

Twenty-four of the projects were directed by teaching members of university faculty,* and in most of these at least one faculty member was actively involved at some stage of the research. (The others were non-working directors). In almost every case it was mentioned that teaching and related commitments interfered with the progress of the research.** These other commitments meant that there was just a general shortage of time to devote to the research; sometimes the lack of time might have been anticipated, because it stemmed from routine teaching and administration, while in other cases it arose from unexpected events like the illness of the Professor or an outbreak of student unrest. In several cases senior people were involved in setting up new sociology departments or new universities from scratch, and this was enormously time-consuming. Whatever the reasons, this lack of time had specific consequences for the research projects:

> "[Autonomy is good if you can take decisions, but we had difficulties with firms, who typically took the line that if we were to do the research they wanted to speak to the organ grinder not the monkey, and then we were embarrassed that the organ grinder would say he was too busy to see them and perhaps they couldn't even see him. We would have to ring up or catch him on the stair, and he would say 'I've just got to rush to Senate' and so on.]"

> "Bruce Wiggins was nominally in charge of us, but he was very

* Here only those people who were faculty members at the beginning of the period of the research are counted as such.

** Notionally full-time research workers were also often heavily involved in teaching to the detriment of their research; see the discussion of this in Chapter 7.

busy doing teaching and many other things besides the project, so if you wanted to see him about something he would say 'don't just tell me about it, write it down', and it was very difficult to keep up with him."

"Conrad and I, as you might guess, have been involved in one thing or the other . . . and that is the major reason why none of this damn stuff has yet seen the light of day. I've done 4 or 5 quite substantial working papers, only 2 of them based on the actual research data because to get to work on those things depends on finding 2, 3 or 4 weeks in the vacation period to do it. I cannot do it in term, it is absolutely unthinkable, we have the worst staff/student ratio in the faculty, we're teaching like buggeree and all these other commitments . . ."

Other people said that directors' lack of time meant that they were too busy to see that the research was kept moving along (while research assistants didn't feel that it was their place to take major decisions), that research assistants did not like to ask directors for their help when needed, and that the directors were too busy to think about what they were actually doing. All these things meant that communication between directors and assistants was hampered, and that the whole research process was slowed up.

However, the problem was not simply the total amount of time available, but the way in which it was distributed. The distinction between term and vacation meant that the possible work flow was uneven, and there was no guarantee that the phases of the research that most needed directorial attention would occur in the vacation:

"Dilys and Erica carry the burden of the project during term, but I go berserk in the vacation, and this leads to a very uneven flow of work. It's almost impossible to carry through a line of thought; you find yourself going back and saying 'what the hell was it all about?' . . . "

If, moreover, a careful plan had been made to ensure that the director had a sabbatical or was on vacation at key points, the whole plan was vulnerable to any hitch in the research; sabbaticals, let alone university terms, could not be changed around at short notice, and the director found himself back teaching again when he was needed. (Some who had had sabbaticals – and they were in the minority – felt that they had timed them badly, and they would have been more useful at the start of the project when detailed plans were being made and research assistants being launched). Similarly, the specific timetabling of teaching during the term could make it difficult or impossible to engage in some kinds of research activity:

> "Last year we tried to so arrange our timetables that we could
> have a series of points when we could meet, and we found it im-
> possible to get more than one hour. In any event, term after
> term has gone by getting incredibly frustrated that it isn't
> possible to sit down for more than half an hour and simply talk
> about the project. This has meant that the supervision has left
> much to be desired."

> " . . . she was so bloody seldom there – then in the latter stages,
> interviewing 4 days a week, the fifth day was a get-together;
> Helen sometimes had other university things to do on that day,
> and we resented this. We didn't see much of her because of other
> commitments, and then she'd turn up and tell us she'd done
> something. Whether she'd mucked up something she'd done, or
> we just didn't think she should in principle, I don't know . . ."

> " . . . it was then that they started coming over to me and saying
> they heard I was all right and why the hell didn't I come . . . and
> see a different side of the job. So towards the end of November
> I started to . . . then, having established the relationship, I had
> to come back here and start teaching and preparing things and
> the fieldwork was curtailed, but at weekends I occasionally went
> in on Saturday night but this wasn't always fruitful because
> [group members] who had approached me weren't always
> working . . ."

(This speaker was doing participant observation on a group to which
it was hard to gain access; if they had not done some weekend work
his eventual success in getting in would have borne even less fruit).

But even when teaching and other unavoidable commitments might
have permitted academics to spend a fair amount of time on their
research, they did not necessarily do so. For at least some people
there was a marked tendency to take on further, optional commitments. One senior academic gave a splendidly graphic account of the
process as he had experienced it:

> " . . . this, as with every other piece of research I've been con-
> cerned with or tried to do, takes about 10 times as long as one
> thinks . . . I'm not trying to make excuses about this, a lot of
> other things have happened, including other research projects
> one gets involved in . . . [there is an exponential curve of commit-
> ments. In the early years you're busy teaching, you start giving
> papers and you get other commitments and hope for the time
> you really are wanted. It's terribly nice to be asked to do things;

you eagerly say yes, though you're discreet enough not to appear too eager about it. You take on jobs . . . on the editorial board, publishers ask you for books, it's very nice to go on an S.S.R.C. committee, to feel you've got recognition . . . wonderful when you get asked to organise an international project] and you go on until you find that you just haven't got any time to do any-thing but answer letters in connection with all these things . . . If you write a research proposal 10 to 1 you get away with it, do it, you can't be without a research proposal, that would be a terrible thing, and long before you realize it you're hopelessly over-committed."

More junior people had not yet managed to acquire commitments on quite this scale, but some were at least kept extremely busy within their own universities. For some, teaching and student counselling were a prior moral obligation and therefore took priority in any clash with research; for the rest, most other kinds of commitment were more likely to occur at fixed times scheduled by other people and therefore took priority simply by the fact of having been already arranged. Thus what, in principle, is an essential part of the role of the academic, in practice often had devoted to it only the residual time left over from other activities. There were some deeply-felt com-plaints made about the assumption, imputed to the powers that be, that it was really possible to do social research properly under these conditions – for example:

"I was involved in 3 areas of teaching at various levels . . . a very general teaching load spread over a wide area. So how did it fit in? Well, absolutely not at all. One of the things which, if I had any say in the management of the department, I should stress very emphatically is that people undertaking research should pass through hoops to do so, that is, things with a large budget . . . Having done this, the institution, the department, must then be prepared to pay the price in terms of what they expect out of one . . . Running a £25,000 project is a full-time job, after all; one cannot operate major research with a continual outflow of expenditure for which one is held accountable by the grant-aiding body and at the same time be expected to do one hun-dred per cent teaching."

It does seem possible that the needs of the characteristic large-scale sociological research project are not met by the usual provision made by universities, which is more suitable to traditional research in the humanities, requiring only a solitary scholar and his books. The provision made by funding bodies, on the other hand, implicitly assumes either that the academic has plenty of time left over from his other tasks, or that his role will be that of the non-working director who will need (and wish) to contribute only the occasional word of guidance to his research workers. Perhaps the funding bodies' assumptions would seem more reasonable to those on the spot at a time when sociology departments were not expanding fast and university finances were not so tight; at the time of interviewing they were often unrealistic. But there is an element of circularity in the situation, since directors would not so easily feel able to give their research low priority if they did not know that other people were employed on it full time; in some ways the customary division of labour enables the academic to have the best of both worlds. In other ways, however, a choice is forced upon him: do the research vicariously, at least at the fieldwork stage, or neglect other tasks and potential commitments. This situation probably encourages people either to start on the kind of research project that it is conventionally acceptable to do vicariously (especially surveys), or not to attempt empirical research at all.

Another aspect of university life that is important for the research project is the nature of the department in which it is located. The occasional project has no departmental location:

"For a long time we floated, completely unattached – we had a very long string floating to the Vice-Chancellor . . ."

This director, an established academic in his field who had come from a teaching post and did some teaching while employed on the research, found that it was a year before he was invited to the home of any member of faculty of his new host university. His juniors reported that it took some time before they were able to borrow small things they needed like calculating machines from other parts of the university, and that one of them was not accepted by the relevant department as a Ph.D. student and so had to register at another university. This degree of organisational isolation was rare, but it seemed common for full-time researchers to be regarded as academically marginal; this marginality was both expressed and emphasized by the practice of allocating them to geographically distinct offices, sometimes in a separate building. This exaggerated the cleavage likely to be produced in any case by the different work patterns of research and teaching staff, and the frequent absences of research staff on fieldwork. The low status of research workers could also be shown by making them share offices, or move offices frequently, which caused some resentment. When research and teaching staff's offices were physically segregated, even when the distance between them was objectively small, it could reduce communication between directors and research workers:

> "At times I certainly thought I saw less of him here than in [other university], because he did have definite reason to come over every week in [other university], whereas he didn't have definite reason to come upstairs every week and see me in [new university]. It was partly because the research staff were on the top floor, and the teaching staff on the floor below, and people tended not to come up very much . . ."

Another research worker suggested that the absence of a departmental common-room used by both groups had the same effect.

Where researchers had any significant contact with the department, its intellectual climate affected the research, not always helpfully. One research assistant found it very much helped the writing up to move back when fieldwork was completed into a department where there were a number of other young people in similar situations who supported each other socially and intellectually. There was another department which obviously had a very strong character at the time, since it was commented on by people from 3 projects there independently; here are some of their comments:

> "[Professor] started a series of seminars, the first seminar at [university] for anyone interested in sociology, and this was a new world for me. It's marvellous to hear people talk and argue about things that I was becoming interested in. . . ."

> "To be in that department, where the phenomenology thing was going on, and [Professor's] phrase rings through my mind, 'crass empiricism', and we lived in a separate building with the post-graduates and somehow [Professor], although we were all fairly theoretically oriented as people, used to refer to us as crass empiricists and assumed that we all spent our time crouching over pages of numbers and this tended to create difficulties for us because we were constantly trying to compete with the phenomenologists on their own ground, writing theoretical papers etc. . . . . If I wanted to do a paper on the research no-one was interested, but if they did a paper on explanation and we said something about somebody it had to go towards the whole philosophical thing, how can we know the sun will rise tomorrow etc."

> "[Most discussions in the department were of a theoretical character rather than detailed research advice, which came out

of books of the standard sort.]"

This was a fairly extreme situation; lack of interest in empirical research is probably commoner than definite attacks on it, and intellectual ferment does not go on all the time. The extreme situation, however, indicates some of the ways in which a departmental climate can encourage, influence and undermine projects. Strong departmental character was often affected by particular charismatic individuals, and a number of people mentioned the importance of such individuals in determining the direction their research had taken. Where charisma had been conspicuous, disillusion had tended to follow on closer contact, or on finding that the great man himself didn't actually take much detailed interest in the research. Closely associated with the purely sociological tone of the department, and of key individuals within it, was its political atmosphere; this seemed more likely to affect the choice of topic and initial approach than the way in which the research was conducted in detail. At the level of university politics rather than of ideological issues research could also sometimes be affected by departmental politics; posts were created or jeopardized to promote the ends of powerful people, and in one case ten minutes of an interview schedule was put in for the benefit of another department as a peace-offering to heal a historical breach.

So much for the internal affairs of the department; departments also had relationships to the larger world of sociology which were consequential for their members. Several people from very small departments reported that for them being cut off from sociological discussion had meant that they mixed with, and were influenced by, members of other disciplines; this could be very stimulating, but could be professionally disadvantageous if it influenced the research to go in a sociologically marginal direction. Other people realised after the event that they had been very cut off from the central tendencies in sociology, even completely ignorant of significant recent developments:

"So it was conducted and written up, not as part of any dialogue, which I now regret very much, the fact that it was done virtually in isolation. I'm amazed that I imagined . . . that I had the audacity to do it, now, in such isolation, but I do now realise, looking back, just how isolated it was from the main stream, well, some of the central elements in British sociology."

" . . . this was really before I got hold of Goffman . . . That would have completely changed my stuff if I'd got it sooner. It shows

39

how parochial we were at that point. If I'd been in a university department [rather than a research fellow with an office in another building and doing no teaching] people might have called my attention to what I should have been reading sooner."

Sometimes, however, there were other institutions which helped to counterbalance this kind of isolation. Being invited to give conference papers spurred some people to action, and a research student in a provincial department of anthropological inclinations was one of several who found the British Sociological Association's summer school very valuable:

" . . . my only contact with other post-graduate students was going to the first B.S.A. summer school; that esablished a very strong peer group. That was very important; it didn't help about [project topic], but it did help about sociology . . . that exposed me to sociology for the first time, and I realised that what went on in [Redbrick] wasn't quite like that! The preparation for that summer school, for the first time I read Lazars-feld!"

Probably such isolation is less common now that British sociology, and individual departments, are larger and more established.

Another aspect of university organisation which is relevant is the division of the social sciences into distinct disciplines, usually organised into separate departments. The sense of career insecurity that people could feel when working outside a sociology department is discussed elsewhere. Fifteen of the projects studied were inter-disciplinary in their personnel — that is, some members of the team were by training and/or identification not sociologists. Sometimes this had come about because a director had deliberately set out to recruit a team with a variety of skills and interests appropriate to the problem to be studied, and sometimes it was accidental. Whatever the reason, it introduced another element into the total research situation. A few people found it valuable and stimulating, and felt that their intellectual development had been permanently influenced by it or that they would want all their future research to be inter-disciplinary. This was relatively uncommon; in 10 of the 15 projects disciplinary differences were a source of conflict or dysfunction of some kind. In one case a sociologist and a statistician both said that they often simply could not understand what the other was talking about! More often the problem was not one of literal understanding but of divergent approaches and intellectual styles. Here is another statistician talking of his collaboration with a sociologist:

" . . . she wrote the first draft [of a chapter, which] . . . I felt was not at all acceptable, it would really have to be a lot rewritten, though using a lot of the material she had drawn on, but not drawing such extreme conclusions. . . ."

J.P. "What was it about it that you objected to?"

" . . . it went too far . . . for a book like this, which is very statistically based. There was too much hypothesizing and guessing for my taste."

And here is a very interdisciplinarily-minded psychologist:

" . . . I became the only psychologically-trained person in the group . . . I like to think the tension between me and the others was more due to me being a psychologist . . . and not to me being [senior within the group]. So I personally would be very concerned in an interdisciplinary group to make sure that there are at least 2 of each discipline. I felt a certain amount of difficulty . . . with the really socialized sociologists, because I was not prepared to become a sociologist like them."

In these sorts of circumstances people who were not committed to an interdisciplinary approach could become very concerned to preserve their disciplinary identity. Here is another psychologist who found himself outnumbered by sociologists:

"Dan and I get on very well except for occasional outbursts on the personal level, but from the point of view of academic backgrounds and interests, they are totally opposed . . . Gill's intellectual and academic . . . point of view is very different from me, and to some extent from Dan, but as Gill and Dan are sociologists they're able to talk about it with each other. To be perfectly honest I thought Gill had a prejudice against psychologists, so we don't get on as colleagues should really to make a good sort of general atmosphere in which the research can take place, and this was equally due to both of us. I have, perhaps, I think, a prejudice against sociologists . . . I disagreed to such an extent with the positions taken, just the research positions taken by Dan and Gill, that I developed my own side of the research. . . . I feel from the point of view of the research as a whole this is not a good thing I did, but it was the only way I could preserve my identity as a psychologist. . . ."

Dan, however, was one of those who thought that the experience of working with someone from another discipline had been very valuable.

41

Another researcher, who had experience of both successful and unsuccessful interdisciplinary work, drew a moral:

"I think the emphasis of the division of discipline . . . encourages the departmentalisation thing. It may be all right in institution-building in universities, but it's counterproductive when you try to have an interdisciplinary approach to something . . . When you have teams with a strong sense of territoriality, you'll have a report with separate sociological, economic and psychological bits. There are areas which get left out in that way."

However evident the moral may be, there are strong institutional forces pulling people towards distinct disciplinary approaches; the pressure to disciplinary conformity is probably particularly strongly felt by younger people who do not yet have a securely established base or identity in any particular field. To the extent that this is so, the effects of different patterns of intellectual training and socialisation are reinforced by personal needs, and conflicts and disagreements are likely to follow; sometimes these conflicts and disagreements may be resolved, and even bear fruit, but in other cases they can be pointlessly disruptive or lead to an unplanned fragmentation of the project. The data in hand are not sufficient to support an analysis of which kinds of interdisciplinary arrangement are more successful. It would seem, however, a plausible hypothesis that such arrangements are more likely to be successful when entered into deliberately; junior researchers of diverse backgrounds may have formed part of a director's plan, but even if they were aware of the plan when recruited none mentioned that this was an attraction to them.

Finally, universities as opposed to other institutional bases for social research seem to have some distinctive characteristics or influences of a less tangible kind. Of the projects in the sample, the university ones tended to use a greater number of different modes of data-collection, and more often used participant observation. They were also, as is mentioned elsewhere, much more likely not to meet their deadlines. It seems plausible to suggest that these findings all follow from a less bureaucratized ethos in university research: there is probably more willingness (and opportunity) to follow ideas where they lead. This is encouraged by the choice of research topics for their intellectual interest rather than their value for practical applications; the interest is not of a kind that suggests urgency. Most professional research organisations outside the universities seem to be set up primarily for survey-type work, which employs a fairly

42

standardized basic technique and can benefit from economies of scale in the staff employed; the lesser professionalism of most university projects may sometimes have advantages. Researchers working to contracts with a serious deadline several times mentioned the need to stop thinking and exploring further ideas as the deadline approached; they met their deadlines, but at some intellectual cost. The university ethos, as well as the academic's employment situation, encourages neglect of deadlines.

Thus, there are a variety of respects in which the character of the university setting affects projects located there. Teaching commitments complicate research timetables and communication within teams, and for a variety of reasons tend to take priority over research; departmental character can give intellectual support and stimulus to the research team or sap its morale; disciplinary divisions create divergences of intellectual style and reference group that are hard to overcome; the relatively unworldly pursuit of ideas for their own sake leads to research styles with special strengths and weaknesses. The outcomes cannot be understood without taking the setting into account.

CHAPTER 4

Outside the University

Every piece of social research depends to some extent on the co-operation or compliance of some people outside the research team, and is influenced or constrained by a variety of external factors. This chapter is concerned with a range of such factors which had consequences for the projects studied, affecting stages from the initial gaining of access through to the final publication of results.

At the stage of gaining access a variety of problems and responses were experienced, but this will not be discussed in much detail because it is fairly familiar ground in the literature; a few selected aspects only will be reported. First, a number of respondents said that for them it had been easy to get access to organisations because their institution had established contacts and good relations in the area; these were usually people at upgraded colleges of technology needing access to local industrial firms. People at universities, on the other hand, several times reported some hostility to universities as such, especially in industry, either because of their general image as hotbeds of radicalism and student unrest or because their interests were seen as frivolously academic and of no practical use. Several experienced research workers referred to an idyllic past age when access was much easier:

"... one of the reasons we got co-operation so easily was that no-one had done research there before. By 1965, of course, it was entirely different."

"... unlike today, co-operation was very good. They were the good old days when people let you do research because it's a good thing to do research, and didn't ask awkward questions like 'what's in it for us?' and 'what's it going to cost us?'."

"Sociological inquiry wasn't the great bore it's become now, people hadn't been saturated with it."

Another researcher who had suffered a poor response rate gave a detailed example of one reason for refusing:

"... it was a time when educational research was just in its mush-rooming period and the schools were getting fed up with it ... One school in Birmingham, a big comprehensive, had been approached 50 times by research workers in the course of the year."

One person, faced with difficulties in getting access to an institution with governmental connections, adopted a course of action unfortunately likely to be open to few of us: he organised an M.P. friend to arrange for a junior minister to make a strong speech in the House of Commons urging the need for more public information on the issue, and when this had been publicized in the newspapers doors were suddenly opened. It is interesting that some of the most politically complex situations seem to have arisen for those studying aspects of their own universities; the dedication of the institution to the pursuit of knowledge did not extend unequivocally to knowledge of itself. A number of people doing research in other contexts, however, mentioned that they had had no problems in getting co-operation because the research was sponsored by the administration of an organisation rather than any outside body; this did not necessarily imply that every individual was co-operative in spirit, but at least technical co-operation with the research was in effect an order transmitted through the usual chain of command. In some governmental or government-sponsored research in industry the issues were complicated by the fact that firms receive many official government questionnaires to fill in; there is some resentment of this, and objections to "acting as unpaid civil servants" could spill over onto the research. One institution found an ingenious way of not co-operating without actually refusing: it deliberately took on no clients of the relevant type during the month of the survey!

Some gatekeepers did not totally refuse access, but would only permit it on condition that certain proposed modes of research were not used. Two headmasters objected to sociometric tests on semi-ethical grounds. In one case it was proposed to do them on the children, and the objection was that

> " . . . I was a bloody fascist, they were spending all this time teaching the children the Christian virtues of love thy neighbour etc.";

in the other case it was proposed to do them on the teachers and the head turned it down because he said he knew the staff would object,

> "because it involved one member of the staff rating another, because there were questions not just about liking but about things like who would you go to for advice and therefore it would be treated as a breach of professional ethics."

(My impression is that schoolteachers in general are peculiarly sensitive subjects of social research; the reasons might repay investigation.) In another case a ministry made it plain that unless 3 questions were deleted from a schedule they would not give the necessary permission to approach the local administrations of the institutions to be studied; the objectionable questions were ones which asked clients of the institution how often a procedure was carried out, and if it had not been very often this might have laid the institutions open to public criticism. There was another study in which the government Social Survey was not prepared to let its interviewers ask a group of people about an embarrassing medical condition to which they were vulnerable; presumably fear of public criticism was involved here, as it would not have been for a commercial agency. Sometimes there was no overt censorship, but research workers simply found that in practice they didn't have access to the higher echelons of the organisation, although at a lower level they had more or less a free hand; this was particularly so if they were perceived (usually correctly) as having fairly low status within academia.

After formal access was obtained, where appropriate, there could still be many difficulties at a more personal level — and also corresponding advantages. Some people found that they had strategically located friends or former colleagues whose help was vital to the research, or that their sex was an important asset. One woman, who did fieldwork in a very masculine setting, said:

"I think probably if I was asked the largest asset of the whole research project I would say being female. A lot of men I don't think would have been willing to be interviewed by a man ... . to frilly a female couldn't have been able to get the men to talk, and too professionally aggressive a one wouldn't have done either. They didn't equate me with [hierarchical superiors] or with the professional people like doctors or lawyers."

Perhaps not many women would have managed to survive as well as she did in that setting*; she got a lot of jokes about her sex, and remarked that

"One of the obvious ways I was known there was by my knickers, because they saw them when I was going up the

* There were a number of projects in my sample where it seemed reasonably obvious that either men or women could more appropriately do the fieldwork, e.g. because it entailed participant observation in a very masculine subculture. There were only 2 cases in which at the recruitment stage it had been specified that a woman was required and one where it was implicit that there should be a man; there did, however, seem to be a higher proportion of women where what one might call the gender context of the research was less masculine.

stairs. If I was wearing a long skirt they would say 'Take if off, dear, take it off!' . . . I was treated a bit as a mascot is treated, given a special position and treated with joking affection."

There were other personal characteristics, besides gender, that could also affect ease of access. In two cases fieldworkers could not or would not join or become actively involved in the Conservative Party. Social drinking was very important in some groups of subjects, and anyone who did not want to join in was handicapped. ["There was a [group] wine and cheese party. I was with a group who disliked [leading figure] roaring drunk and flaked out. The point was that after that the key bastard of [group] would then talk to me; I'd become one of the lads."] Some felt conscientious qualms about the extent to which they could legitimately participate in religious activities when they were non-believers. Two young men reported that their working-class backgrounds had given them particular difficulties which were not fully appreciated by their colleagues:

"I'm very worried I'm going to tread on their toes or do something I shouldn't have done unwittingly . . . I don't know how much this is a general problem for the working-class kid who comes up in the world, and even in research it can get you into situations where you meet people of high status and haven't had any experience of this, and that experience you have had has not taught you what you need."

There were 2 instances in the sample in which researchers had initially got access, but eventually were more or less thrown out, and these are of some interest as case studies. In the first case, a researcher was commissioned to undertake research into the operation and effects of an institution on those who passed through it. When a report was submitted on a few pilot interviews it was evident that there was potentially damaging material, showing that the institution (which depends heavily on public support) did not always operate as those in charge intended and had assumed. The researcher was asked to end his research, and offered money instead to work on a quite different topic. But he had registered the subject for a Ph.D., and did not want to drop it. Shortly afterwards there was a change in the occupant of a key position, and the researcher asked permission of the new man to continue the research; this was given, on the condition that he confine himself to the history of the institution rather than the present, and that the institution should have a veto on publication. The material he subsequently produced was felt by the members of the institution to show his basic hostility to their ideas, and lack of understanding of what they were trying to do, although outsiders who read it thought that it was quite fair. To cut a long story short, the veto on publication was exercised, and there has been a long drawn out controversy as the researcher attempts to get some of the material published and he and the institution try to negotiate an acceptable form of publication. He sees it as an academic freedom issue; they see it as irresponsible to allow the publication of something they feel is biased, but which would do their institution (to which they have a moral and emotional commitment) harm in the eyes of outsiders who do not have other sources of information on it. A senior manager of the institution summarized what had happened like this:

"... at some stage along the line the idea that the research should become a Ph.D. project, and this would help in his academic career, had been injected, and I can't now remember how, and probably the [board] did agree to this formulation, and if you like innocently wanting of course to help Frank Brown personally, but I think very inadvisedly, and not realizing the implications of such approval, because when the Ph.D. in draft was shown us a great deal of exception was taken to it. Frank Brown, of course, for his part said that we didn't like being told the truth about ouselves, whereas we said this is in fact not the truth ... Frank Brown tried very hard to be detached, impartial, objective, whatever the words mean, but underneath all that was a discernible hostility to the [institution] and what it represented ... he didn't have the knowledge, the background understanding ... to put the [institution] in a meaningful context ... There then was raised the question of academic freedom ... was it right to prevent publication of research in any shape or form? Well, we considered that the spirit of the understanding at the beginning had been that of consultancy to us, and it should be left to us to draw the inferences."

Frank Brown's point of view is summarised in quotations from 2 letters that he wrote to this manager:

"I was not writing for [institution] or solely about [institution], but was making a contribution to knowledge ... surely the point of employing a sociologist is precisely to use his insights to take a fresh look at routine social behaviour? ... I'd agree that the researcher must respect the values of his subjects, and that is why I've leaned over backwards to be

sympathetic to what [institution] was trying to accomplish.
I, of course, shall be writing for an academic audience with my
remarks qualified by painstaking research for all available
evidence. ...''

"From a career point of view I need publication of my work in
an acceptable academic form; but, more importantly to me
personally, is that I feel deeply committed to seeing my work
in print, as I do not feel that I can sit back and let 5 years'
work be shunted into a siding."

The clash of interests and perceptions, and the divergence of purposes
in the initiation of the research, is obvious, and with hindsight it
does not seem very surprising that serious disagreements arose. It
seems likely that they could only have been avoided if the researcher
had become socialized into the norms of the institution, and/or had
not been at a career stage where publication and recognition was
particularly important to him. Not every institution is so sensitive,
and indeed the researcher remarked that he had known of other
institutions of the same kind which had made no objection to the
publication of material about them which was more damaging and
equally inconsistent with their formal ethos; these other institutions,
however, had more confidence in the solidity of their social support,
and relied less on favourable publications to recruit clients, and so
did not feel so vulnerable.

   In another case, where a researcher was commissioned to do research into the problems of an organisation, the organisation had
few statistical data about its flow of clients, so it was agreed that
some fact-finding should be done in this area. It was put in writing
at the beginning that the researcher should do some work for the
organisation and also do his own Ph.D. He did an observational
study in which he discovered that large numbers of clients were in
effect being dealt with by unqualified staff as an unintended result
of administrative arrangements, and wrote a report on this. He
showed the report to a deputy manager, who said the senior manager
would be very interested to see such fascinating stuff; indeed he was,
as his subsequent letter showed. The letter expressed dismay and in-
dignation, and accused the researcher of having abused his position to
compile a document based on gossip which was likely to provoke a
great deal of ill-feeling within the organisation. It demanded a
written assurance that all copies of the paper and of the notes on
which it was based had been destroyed as a condition of permitting
any continuance of the research.

   The researcher judiciously stayed away for a few weeks. It was found that the letter was libellous, so he got the head of his department to write pointing that out and suggesting that something should be salvaged from the research, which is what was done. Large parts of the planned research depended on a confidence which no longer existed and had to be abandoned, but he was allowed to return for long enough to complete a survey which was nearing its end; the Ph.D. thesis had to be changed to compare that institution with others, and to consider more limited aspects of each than had been intended. He had no difficulty in getting access to the other institutions, despite the fact that the word spread about what had happened; numbers of junior managers thought that he had said the sort of thing that needed saying. He was able to publish the material eventually, suitably revised, because his initial contract had carefully specified that he should be allowed to do so. (His supervisor, who had considerable experience of such research, had seen to this.) I did not in this case try to interview the senior manager concerned, because the researcher asked me not to. However, the researcher suggested some reasons, apart from individual personality, why the senior manager reacted as he did. His institution was in the throes of a major reorganisation, in which many individuals' posts were affected and careers were at stake; thus any public criticism of the way in which his branch was run aroused acute personal and political sensitivities. He had left day-to-day liaison with the researcher to a deputy, and so had not known any of the details of the direction of the research; the initial commission had been extremely vague, and left open what should be done, especially in the parts intended primarily for the thesis; thus he was taken by surprise by the results. It also happened that he was just about to go on holiday when the paper reached him, and so could envisage things getting out of control while he was away if he did not act quickly. The author said that a lesson he had learnt from this experience was that it is unwise in the interests of pure research to feed back results before you have finished your research, although as a reformer, practitioner or employee one may feel that it is ones duty to pass on information with practical implications as soon as possible.

In both these cases the tension between the needs and motives of the researcher, and of those who commissioned the research, is evident. When a commissioning relationship works out happily it is mutually beneficial: the client gets his practically useful information, and perhaps a little prestige for being so enlightened too; the researcher gets his data and the publications based on them and makes his contribution to public knowledge. If initial intentions are not made clear by both parties, or if the outcome of the research is unexpected or the situation being investigated is a politically delicate one, ructions can easily follow; the effect on the research depends on the stage that it has reached, the nature and formality of the contract, and the ethical position taken by the researcher.

But the question of the relationship between researcher and sponsor or client does not arise only over matters of access to data, as indeed the case studies given have already shown, and other matters must also be discussed. First there is the question, already touched on, of the client's motive or purpose in having the research done. Unfortunately there are very few cases in which I interviewed clients, so that in general the only available data are the imputations made by the researchers; these are inevitably biased in various ways, though the note of surprise in many of the comments suggests that people did not simply go in with biases against clients. In two projects commissioned by governmental bodies, the researchers concluded that it was not so much the findings that were wanted, as being seen to be initiating research. In the first, there was an issue which aroused strong public feelings and the eventual decision was bound to affront some groups:

> "We felt we were going to be a surrogate for public opinion — they were worried about it and wanted to be seen to take it into account. . . ."

In the other one, the possibility of giving a new kind of welfare benefit to a particular group could have arisen:

> "It was so dubious, why should DoX want to finance social research? The formal line they gave me was 'we have a conscience too'; in fact over the years there have been questions in the House on 'why not give [benefit] ', etc. Cheaper than action always is research, and for 2 years I was there whenever the question came up. They could say 'we are financing research on it."

In fact the researcher here was specifically told by the department concerned that they would not have the money to finance such a benefit. When a new minister took office he summoned him to say that he did not want anything that would embarrass the department, and was so horrified to find that the contract did not provide for a veto on publication that he took legal advice about it, and added a clause allowing the minister to comment before publication. It may seem surprising in these circumstances that research had been commissioned at all; the researcher's explanation was that the Professor who negotiated the contract was a friend of the previous minister.

51

The contract was very vague about the precise topic to be studied, and the researcher found he could get no positive guidance from the department about what would be of interest to them. The Professor said he should just go ahead and do what he wanted to do himself; he did this in part, but in a way that was connected with the presumed interests of the DoX.

In another small group of cases the researcher thought that the research had essentially been conceived as a public relations exercise:

"But, frankly, the reason I was there was because it was a politically important time to have someone there doing research [nobody was interested in the results – my name appeared on committee documents and a lot of paper was circulated to tell them I was there doing research – it was politically expedient as much as anything.] "

J.P. "How did they approach [university] ?"

"They wanted someone to do research, it didn't much matter what it was . . ."

J.P. "Did they have anything in mind about the form it would take?"

"No, that's the main reason I say they just wanted someone doing research . . ."

"As to why they did it, I don't know. There was a general idea of good publicity out of it. My book is coming out generally favourable to the company and they aren't taking any great interest in it. It makes it somewhat puzzling in retrospect why they financed it. In the managing director's office I noticed that he had a framed Senate vote of thanks to the company for [a donation], and they had got a couple of dinners at [College] out of it and obviously enjoyed that . . . they hoped there might be something useful in terms of general industrial relations policies, but again they are not taking any great interest in that subsequently."

"[local branch of clients] saw research purely as having a ratifying role. This gradually became evident to me. They didn't see research as throwing light on what they actually did, but as an illuminated manuscript to their greater glory . . . instead of sharing interest in it, one's general scientific curiosity . . . the wonders that the computer had produced, there was this tremendous resistance."

In this last instance the research had been commissioned at headquarters. The research design entailed studying a case of good practice, as exemplified by the local branch, so that when an investigation of their records revealed that in reality practice fell short of their ideal standards it is perhaps not surprising that they objected and refused to believe that the results could be accurate. This instance was also one of several where the researcher concluded that at least part of the client's purpose was to use the research to confirm a decision that had already been made, rather than to base a decision upon the findings. Another was a project commissioned by an industrial pressure group from a market research agency on a topical issue. The director said that the pressure group deliberately chose a respectable agency because they wished to appear objective: "They wanted to prove a point – they didn't want to do it at the expense of invalidating the object of the exercise itself." Unfortunately from their own point of view, this is just what the pressure group inadvertently did:

"We did this report quite objectively . . . They took the report exactly as it stood and reproduced it, and then on different coloured paper a foreword for which they claimed responsibility – and there was in fact only one thing wrong with that, which unfortunately was the first sentence . . . [Few people knew of the key proposal at that time, so only those who did were asked their opinion of it; of them, 80% were in favour or didn't know.] What they put in the foreword was that 8 out of every 10 people in London now favoured [proposal]. Everybody saw through it – it completely destroyed their investment in the research because nobody took it seriously."

That was perhaps a bizarrely extreme and open case, but there were others where bodies whose main function was not as a pressure group nonetheless seem to have had similar ideas, and indeed did not feel the same need to produce objective research to support them. A researcher within a government department writes of the reaction there to her fairly strong findings:

"I said I thought they ought to do something, and they all said this is fine, have a working group which will consider the implications of the report . . . The structure of the Civil Service is that you have administrators who are impartial etc. who sit there and have power, and they're advised by experts of various sorts . . . Research workers do research and they don't advise . . . [the key administrator] knew what he wanted to do in certain respects, and he wanted to use the report to support what he wanted to do . . . [I found that there was a greater demand for [facilities for one group] ; DoX wished to expand

[facilities for other group] , so a paragraph about that was rewritten, in keeping with the evidence but deemphasising it. A
reference to a theoretical example in Scotland was added while
I was on holiday!] "

In another case a university researcher was working on a project for a
semi-governmental body investigating the need for certain facilities:

"It was leaked to the *Finanacial Times* that we were going to
say [facilities] are largely irrelevant, and it became obvious that
it was totally unacceptable to the [working party]. The reaction to the initial thing was to commission someone else to
investigate the need for [facilities] and publish that before
ours. . . . I certainly felt . . . under tremendous pressure to produce what was wanted rather than serious findings."

It was not only governmental bodies that behaved in this way. A researcher sponsored by a private organisation found that his relationship with a key official broke down when his findings suggested that
the organisation was not attaining some of its valued goals as well as
it had assumed, and when he recommended that one function for
which the official had been responsible should be taken over by a new
department – as indeed it was later. As he remarked,

"It was quite logical in sociological terms . . . In those days I
wasn't a political animal; I still believed that facts were facts!"

It is somewhat ironic that one of the few cases where the client unequivocally wanted guidance on the formation of policy should be
the first of the longer case studies given above, where the data produced were exceedingly unwelcome – and indeed, as the senior
manager interviewed himself pointed out, the board had in effect
taken a decision anyway before the research was well under way. As
some of the quotations above have already shown, clients did not
only want things to which research seemed inappropriate but sometimes seemed not to know what they wanted at all. One researcher
for a semi-governmental body sought guidance in vain, and eventually
had to write his own terms of reference – which were then approved.

Even clients who were not sure what they wanted substantively
could nonetheless have definite expectations in some ways, and
sometimes these expectations showed a lack of understanding of the
research process. For instance, they would exert pressure for quicker
results than were feasible in an academically respectable project, or
make objections when researchers wanted to change their original
plans in ways which the investigation so far suggested would be

54

appropriate. (One project was commissioned to explore the nature of an effect that turned out to be so small that the problem was to detect it at all.)

So far this account may suggest virtuous researchers and vicious or ignorant clients, but the researchers too were not without vices that sometimes contributed to a divergence of interests and purposes between the parties. On one lengthy project one of the directors found it embarrassing, and said that it caused bad relations with the sponsors, that they came to believe that delays were being caused because the researchers were only interested in techniques and in playing with the data instead of getting out the facts; he thought this was a misunderstanding. But perhaps the sponsors were right, for a co-director said this:

> "I think in terms of the survey the purpose was two-fold — it was both to make estimates and explicate theory. It was necessary to make estimates because what paid for this is what [sponsor] conceived of as research, they were very interested in estimates; our own interests were probably in the development of theory. . . ."

and he went on to express regret at the lack of opportunities for using the newest and most sophisticated statistical techniques; part of his motive in taking the project on had been that he hoped it would give him data on which these techniques could be used. The director of another project described how it was clear to him from the start that what he wanted to do was to pursue his own interests and not simply to serve the needs of the client:

> "I wrote up a very very vague proposal, 2 sides of paper saying I might look at [topic] ; in fact it was complete bluff, in that it allowed us to do anything at all we wanted . . . part of the early contacts were with [client's liaison officer] and took the form of him saying that they had all these problems and how we ought to look at them, and me saying all kinds of incomprehensible things so we didn't have to look at them."

A report has been written for the client, but it is very brief. Cynicism was encouraged by the director's belief that whatever the contents of the report no action would be taken on it, but there may be an element of the self-fulfilling prophecy in this; the client organisation is one which he finds very alien and towards which he has an ideological hostility. But even when there is no such hostility and the researcher is honestly anxious to do a job for the client he has his own interests as well, and this can lead to giving different impressions to

55

different people:

> " . . . very subtle controls can be exercised in this kind of situation. . . [there is] the tendency I have to describe the project in different ways to different people; slight schizophrenia sets in when you're writing things simultaneously for the company and the trade unions and academics."

Here the anxiety felt is more that the company is exerting too much pressure on what is said at the end, but the same point applies at earlier research stages when the researcher's need to serve several masters simultaneously can create practical and ethical problems. Sometimes the issue is really only one of verbal descriptions, but sometimes it is one of a deeper divergence of interest. It is not surprising, even if it is ethically deplorable, that when there are structural pressures on researchers to have interests that diverge from those of clients they should sometimes become involved in deception. Nobody has to take a client's money, but both the money and the research opportunities can be very tempting. Moreover, it may well not become clear until late in the research how far client's and academic's perceptions and standards differ; each subculture can be so alien to the other that they do not even realize that their taken-for-granted assumptions about the aims of research differ.

Whether or not assumptions differed, clients often affected the way in which the research was done. The choice of sample was affected in several cases by the sponsor's insistence on the inclusion or exclusion of certain groups. Sometimes this did not make much substantive difference, except to the expense of the project: a semi-governmental body insisted that Scotland be included, although there were few instances there of the kind to be studied, and another wanted wives of a group of employees being studied to be interviewed too. In other instances the effect was more serious: it was insisted that a whole population be approached rather than a sample, or that comparative samples relevant to assessing the impact of a measure be not included. The questions asked in surveys could also be influenced: a private organisation asked for the inclusion of a lot of detailed questions in one area, the main effect of which was a large increase in the bulk of data to be analysed without a corresponding increase in the interest of the results; in a project commissioned by a governmental body questions on politics and religion were not allowed to be included. When it came to analysis, the only effects reported were of a different sort: the data of special interest to sponsors were analysed first (and the rest left until later and used much less), or a simple computer package was used that looked as though it would give something quickly to show to the sponsors (but turned out to be unsuitable and to deliver more or less undigested data).

The stage of most interest to sponsors or clients, however, was the presentation of the final results, and here a variety of modes of influence and intervention are reported. Sometimes the influence was primarily editorial, as when a sponsor interested in affecting general public opinion urged the deletion of a theoretical chapter that they thought would be an obstacle to the lay reader; some of this material reappeared elsewhere in the book, but some was just cut. A similar alteration reported was this one, where the motive was political in a different sense:

> "At one point. . . there was in the opening a critique of tests of statistical significance much on the lines now advanced, but this was thought in the state of the [unit's] affairs at the time a bit too much and so was suppressed."

The occasional researcher in effect censored himself out of a feeling of obligation to give the sponsors more or less what they expected and had paid for. ("The biggest problem was the sponsor in our heads rather than any real. . . obstacles that they put in our way.") Thus one tried to emphasize facts rather than theories; another left out some potentially sensational episodes in a group studied because they were not the main focus of the research and notoriety might affect the credibility of the sponsors (who were in no way connected with the group studied) in relation to the main issue. It was the usual practice when the research was done on the client organisation to submit the text for vetting; sometimes the understanding was that corrections should only be on matters of fact,* but sometimes it went rather beyond this:

> ". . . the company tended to adopt a line of objecting to every little item that reflected anything unfavourable on it. . . There is one particular incident where they fired 3 people. . . and that's still in the book and they object to it. . . There was a

---

* One established unit had a standard policy on this that enabled it to maintain its integrity:

> ". . . we reserve the right that it shall be published. . . What usually happens is that a draft is prepared, sent to the sponsor and saying we would appreciate comments, and it was also sent to readers; comments are collated, and if they say 'God, you can't publish that' [if it's an arithmetical mistake we are glad they spotted it]. If they say you can't say that because it's against our policy, our standard phrase is 'is it in any way erroneous in fact? If so, would you please specify'."

57

quibble that went on for some time about work conditions in the [product] plant. I wanted to comment on Blauner on process production [conditions good, gleaming, no dust etc.] the [product] plant wasn't like that, there was [product] dust in the air, and the company and I went toing and froing on how bad the conditions were and I think I probably did give a certain amount of ground on that. . . They like to have this propaganda about being one big happy family etc. [So I say there is intermanagement rivalry and make 6 small criticisms and say there was trouble with the trade unions when first established and they don't like that.] . . . I think they will be surprised when it's reviewed in the journals, they'll read 'this presents a favourable account of Product Co. as a good company.' . . ."

This author felt that there had not been great problems because in general he had said favourable things about the company. Despite this, at one point the question had been raised of whether they wished to go ahead with publication, at which stage their attention had to be drawn to the fact that the contract did not give them a veto. Sensitivities were aroused by any comment that could be construed as unfavourable, and what was expected seemed to be a consultancy report or PR job. Although there was no formal veto, the author felt exposed to informal pressures on which he commented interestingly:

". . . the kind of control that was very slightly a problem was the informal one of wanting to please people who were doing things for you, whose time you were taking up and so on. . . . It's interesting that I haven't found at all the same problem in subsequent research. . . when I was securely established in a research team and not involved in fieldwork [and no longer a graduate student]. The more you are involved in the fieldwork, the more involved you start getting. . ."

In another instance, where the research was commissioned by a semi-governmental body, the pressures were not subtle at all:

"there was one entire chapter struck out after the first draft. This was the chapter written almost entirely by me, and it was trying to pick out what I thought were the issues that ought to be debated and were tending not to be — in other words it questioned some of the things that people seemed to be taking for granted. I was told that there was no place for this because it was opinion and didn't arise from the data, and therefore was not suitable."

58

In this case the pressures were successful, though the author said that on other issues he had managed to be sufficiently elusive not to have to conform to the suggestions of the London-based civil servant appointed as liaison officer to the project. It is striking how often it was reported that when there was an objection to the content of a research report it took the form of a demand for greater 'objectivity':

"The internal report was resisted on the grounds that it was too technical by the editorial board. . . so then we put in all the sociology. The first report, the ministry liked. . . so draft 2 got all this internal history in, because it starts getting interpretative and explaining things and no longer bald in letting facts speak for themselves. The ministry wanted us to take things out, and then it got really unpleasant. . . we were in their grip, because it was so full of statistical tabulations that we needed a substantial subsidy to be published. . . and they used the purse strings to get the plain unvarnished account."

"[Chairman] particularly didn't like any kind of speculation or attempt to widen out the discussion to interpretation of the data. If you said 'this finding was surprising' he would say 'how can you say that? That suggests that you have preconceptions' or 'you're supposed to be doing an objective survey'."

In the first of those 2 cases the government departments concerned were working with an outside organisation whose interests were being defended, and the researcher thought that they had a shared motive to favour a policy which his research suggested was going to be more expensive and less efficient than the existing arrangements. The need for a subsidy made censorship possible despite the fact that the research contract carefully specified a right of publication whatever the outcome. In the second case the research was done on an institution in a state of internal political turmoil, and the researchers were perceived as having a political position. The pressures for 'objecticity' normally seem to imply simply leaving out all the sociology and publishing nothing but a list of facts. (The publication from the second project is indeed rather like that, and although on an interesting subject is one of the most boring things I have ever read.) Only one case was reported of total suppression of research, and this was where the research was on a controversial topic of great political interest, and the results did not favour the political position taken by the sponsors, or at any rate could have been used against them, and moreover would have been likely to cause difficult relations with some of the groups to which they referred.

59

So far the process of formal vetting of research produced by government departments has not been mentioned, because it appears to be so elaborate and institutionalised that it can hardly be compared with what happens elsewhere. A detailed description of the process as it was carried out in one instance is given by someone who did research for a government department, on a topic that to the uninitiated would sound as though it could hardly have political implications:

"We had to send it to more than 100 people for comment. . . It is continually impressed on you that you are not able to establish anything too damning about other government departments, and everything is checked for libel and so on. We've got one chapter at the end. . . which was written partly as a result of observations,and some more general information; it concluded that[certain] facilities are not useful. This had to be very carefully cleared with the DoY and DoZ; there were several interdepartmental meetings discussing it. An appendix at the back sets out what [special] facilities are available; it looks pretty straightforward, but it was quite incredible how every word has been vetted. There isn't a single word there that DoY and DoZ didn't agree with. [The original version said that some private facilities are less satisfactory than state ones, but DoY would not let that go through and it now says that some are similar to state ones.] Where our own research was concerned we were able to hold out and say this is what our findings are and it cannot be dropped, but when it came to things like this it was not our own findings and putting our own interpretation on them was more difficult to hold out. [Apart from government departments it was sent to the managers of all the institutions on which data was collected, to interested voluntary associations and even people who had contributed photos that only appeared on one page.]. . . During the course of the research the DoX [which sponsored the research] were amalgamated with the Do Topic, and this therefore meant that we were not able to say anything at all critical of the [Topic] side because in effect we were criticising ourselves. With the DoY and DoZ, when the chips were down, if our own administrators supported us, we could criticise them, but you can't say something to criticise yourself!"

He goes on to point out that many of the comments made were about statements with policy implications, and drew attention to relevant aspects of policy questions for which other departments were responsible. It was important that nothing unequivocal be said on a policy issue unless it really was official policy, since once published it could be construed as a policy commitment.

Another government researcher mentions far fewer complications, presumably because her results were published in a format intended to be less policy-relevant and did not involve areas for which other departments were responsible. But censorship still operated; one point has been quoted above. No difficulty was made over a reference to the incidence of homosexuality among a group of employees working with children. However, a direct quotation from a report had to be put into indirect speech because it might inhibit those who wrote them if they thought they were likely to be quoted in research, she was not allowed to acknowledge the help of clerical staff on the ground that this was not Civil Service practice, and a reference to an employee liking Scottish children better had to be deleted. The report took a long time to clear, so presumably it was vetted by a number of people.

Those two cases are the only ones in my sample where the research was done internally to a central government department, and they were both destined for publication. Clearly there are special constraints in that situation; the distinctive characteristics of governmental research are discussed further below. When research was commissioned by the government from universities or outside units the same vetting process did not seem to be applied, although there was great anxiety that no individual or organisation should be identifiable in the report.

All this concern among private and public sponsors for the detail of what is published might suggest that there is great interest in the results of research, and that immediate action will be taken on its findings. This, however, is far from the impression that the researchers usually had. Of the 12 projects in my sample that were commissioned by sponsors who in principle were themselves responsible for acting on the results, and had already received the results at the time of my interviews, 5 positively objected to them; 3 showed almost no interest in them or inclination to act on them; one was acted on only to the extent that local managers chose to do so; and 3 presumably did have the consequences intended, or at any rate were not overtly rejected.*

* One might well suspect that these results are due to the way in which the sample was recruited. Only one of the projects concerned, however, was definitely drawn to my attention because it had had difficulties; 2 more might have been — I can't clearly remember — but could easily have come up for other reasons, in that I knew of the people and saw others in their departments. Among those about which I knew absolutely nothing before I approached the researchers (except that they had taken place) were 4 which had had severe problems of the kind described.

One reason for lack of interest was suggested by this comment:

> "[liaison officer] is very enthusiastic. 'Just the sort of stuff we want' he says, which is not true at all. The man who set it up has left [organisation]. It was his baby. The man who comes next, it was just something on his file."

In a number of cases where research was sponsored by large organisations, private or governmental, the individual responsible had moved on by the time the research was finished and so there was no-one left to take an interest in it; in theory the organisation was the sponsor, but in practice it was an individual, and there were no administrative mechanisms for feeding in research results and so no practical likelihood that action would be taken on them.* The fact that the officer responsible had changed was also another reason why results tended to be criticised or rejected, since the person concerned had had no involvement with the earlier stages of the research. But sometimes there were other reasons for lack of interest or action. One project had been to investigate the need for a then highly fashionable nostrum; by the time the results were in (suggesting that the nostrum was not of much relevance) the fashion was over in any case. On another project the researcher suggested that the nature of the Civil Service was a key factor:

> ". . . one makes a mistake if one views administrators in the government as being burning to improve the things they are administering. They're quite willing to improve things if it can be proved to them how it can be done, but the context in which they work is one which directs their attention to things like scandals, political things basically, and they haven't got the sort of contact, the sort of careers which would motivate them to improve [nor would it further their careers if they did improve things, because it's not clear who's responsible and they have moved on by the time it happens.] . . . Nobody knew there was a general scandal because nobody collected figures until

* The lack of interest shown could also be discouraging when research was not sponsored:
> "We drafted an 8-page summary of the findings and sent it to all schools that took part in the survey; so far only one has even acknowledged receipt of it. We also. . . selected a sample of 24 to take part in a third phase [and. . .] sent them a copy of the book for £2.50, and that was the one that acknowledged receipt, and she basically only acknowledged it because she was retiring and wanted the copy of the draft we had promised sent to her home rather than the school. So one can get a bit disillusioned."

I did. . . [if one client commits suicide and it hits the *Mirror* they worry about that.] "

It seems evident that there are many excellent reasons embedded in the structure of bureaucracies and the contexts in which they have to operate why research should not be taken very seriously as research. It has a role to play in image-building and the management of impressions, both internally and externally, but this means that its results cannot be permitted to be too inconsistent with the desired image. It does seem that, even bearing this in mind, some sponsors are unrealistically sensitive about what may be said, and pay little attention to the likely interest in it of the audience to which academic publications are addressed. When it comes to action on the results, there are many considerations other than the "facts" or an isolated rationalistic calculation of the relation between means and ends to be borne in mind. Issues that, to the researcher, look fairly straightforward, for the member of the bureaucracy have histories and ramifying political implications. It may be shocking, but should not be sociologically surprising, that personal careers and departmental rivalries are salient among these. To the naive outsider like myself it was extremely striking to find how often researchers working for government departments mentioned the internal political significance of inter-departmental rivalries, which could have real consequences for the research, as when one department withheld information in its possession from another. A further special characteristic of government work, in no way discreditable but often just as inconvenient for research, follows from the fact of public accountability. Any aspect of the research may be picked on by someone and made into a stick to beat the government with; there is particular sensitivity in the Civil Service to the possibility of questions being asked about it in the House of Commons. This means that pre-censorship has to be exercised to avert possible objections, even if the research procedure might seem quite innocuous to any professionally competent person; consequently certain questions are not asked, exceptional emphasis is laid on the preservation of confidentiality and anonymity, and so on. Thus some of the practical advantages that one might expect from access to governmental sources of information are not available. (Obviously this can be argued to be ethically desirable, even if it hinders research, though it is not clear how far it is done as a matter of ethical principle rather than political expediency. In some of the instances described, however, the confidentiality that might have been breached was entirely notional — as, indeed, was the breach — some people with no interest in individual cases had access to the

63

information anyway, and using it for research purposes would have meant only that other people with no interest in individual cases also had access to it.)

The usual method of control in governmental projects done by outsiders was a project steering committee representing the relevant interests and/or a departmental liaison officer. In general these seemed to have offered advice and engaged in discussion rather than given orders, and sometimes they played an important facilitating role in contact with other government departments. One left-wing researcher, working on a topic of overtly political relevance, was delighted by the cooperation and helpfulness of his liaison officer, who was an active member of the International Socialists! Not all relationships were quite so happy, and this next speaker states an evident underlying norm:

> "[. . . he struck me as a very intrusive person, so I got a feeling that I was being monitored rather too closely. He's a government servant and has to watch where the money is going, but I see myself as an independent research worker who shouldn't be scrutinised too closely.] "

Such an attempt at close supervision was unusual – and unsuccessful. One director mentioned that she had not even been told when her liaison officer was changed; but this was one of the cases where an established relationship had been built up with the department over a number of projects, and in these less need seemed to be felt for formal controls. Both governmental and non-governmental steering committees sometimes imposed constraints which were cursed at the time, but which turned out in the end to have been valuable because they forced a clarification of objectives or refinement of methods.

Some of the variation in relationships with sponsors or clients described in this chapter depends on the type of "sponsorship" involved; this distinction has been blurred so far. In fact there are several different types of sponsorship: (a) research is commissioned by the sponsor into an outside topic on which it wishes to influence and/or inform opinion; (b) research is commissioned by the sponsor, usually into its own operations, primarily as a guide to internal policy; (c) a contract is agreed between researcher and sponsor, on the researcher's initiative, in which the researcher offers findings in return for funds or cooperation and access to data; (d) research is submitted to with more or less resignation by the "sponsor" on the understanding that it will have some right of comment on or control over the findings. Which of these relationships hold, affects who is doing whom a favour by the research, and this, together with the details of the formal contract made and the degree of financial independence of the researcher, determine the balance of power in conflict situations. The cases of conflict have been those in which the research results are in some way unwelcome to the sponsor, and the sponsor was able to enforce its opinions to the extent that it had legal or financial control over the research or bureaucratic authority over the researcher. Conflict was, of course, much more likely to arise in some situations than others, and there were some groups, probably those to whose subculture the idea of objective research as an end in itself is most alien, who seemed particularly sensitive to any hint of criticism. (It was notable, however, that even universities could be very sensitive when the subject of the research was themselves.) Normative controls are involved as well as naked power, but norms are not always shared by researcher and sponsor, and their disagreement may itself be a source of conflict.

The data presented in this chapter show that the course of research could be quite strongly affected by external factors. Access to data was problematic, and depended on the cooperation of those who controlled it and the personal characteristics of fieldworkers; sponsors could have reasons for influencing the sample studied, the methods of data collection, the questions included in a schedule, the depth of the analysis, and above all the content of what was finally published. Researchers did not always feel that the pressures exerted were improper or intellectually inappropriate, but there was a strong tendency for them to do so because they tended to hold norms and have career interests that were inconsistent with the guiding purposes of sponsors or clients.

CHAPTER 5

Team Organisation

A key aspect of the sociology of the research project is the way in which the actual research tasks are organised and divided, and that is the subject of this chapter. We shall start by describing the nature of the division of labour adopted in different kinds of project and its rationale, and go on to consider some of the consequences of different arrangements. Hierarchical divisions and horizontal task differentiation are both relevant and, as is shown below, often interrelated.

The personnel of the projects studied varied considerably, ranging from one person doing all the research tasks himself to teams of 12 or more members arranged in a hierarchy and recruiting further temporary employees for tasks such as interviewing and coding. The "team", as defined in the choice of the sample, is in effect the graduates involved on a relatively permanent basis; this omits secretarial and clerical staff, the normal interviewers and coders, and a small number of people in miscellaneous roles. But there is usually information on whether such other employees were involved, so their presence can to that extent be taken into account although they were not interviewed. The table below shows the basic distribution of teams by size and rank:

Size of teams* [number of people in the team]	Number of ranks in team				N
	1	2	3	4 or more	
1	16	-	-	-	16
2	2	5	-	-	7
3	1	7	2	-	10
4	1	2	8	-	11
5	-	-	1	-	1
6	-	2	3	-	5
7 or more	-	-	3	2	5

The commonest types of project in the sample are those with a 'team' of one, or of 3 or 4 members occupying 2 or 3 ranks; how

* In a few cases two team members who were not present at the same time have both been counted; the number is a total of those ever participating rather than present concurrently.

representative this is of the whole population of projects that could have fallen into the sample cannot be known, but my impression is that it is not atypical. The numbers alone are somewhat misleading about what was going on in the projects in the sample, since teams falling into the same category could be organised in rather different ways. The first misleading factor is that there were some team members who played a very small part in the actual research, either because they dropped out early on or, more commonly, because they were directors who construed their role as minimal. In some of these latter cases, it was hard to decide whether they should be classified as part of the team at all, but since levels of participation seemed to form a continuum with no natural breaks they all were. The concept of the research entrepreneur, as distinct from research worker, took on a greater meaning as I contemplated these cases. Even "entrepreneur", however, has too active a connotation for some, and terms such as backer or broker might be more appropriate to describe what they did. The second misleading factor is that some projects involved far more people than the members of the "team", either because interviewers, etc., were recruited *ad hoc,* or because the director(s) belonged to research organisations with a permanent staff, not allocated to particular projects, to do such tasks. There were also occasionally other people of a rather different sort involved: these were, for instance, representatives of clients who took part in some of the research decision-making; research unit administrators who took part in administration and politics, and operated financial constraints; or senior academics who played an introductory or political role for their juniors. In view of these complexities, a typology of projects has been devised; it makes intuitive sense, and the categories distinguished do broadly differ in the appropriate ways when the data are looked at systematically. It is as follows, with the number of cases falling into each type in brackets:

A 1-3 team members, director(s) working, no other resources used (13)

B 1-3 team members, director(s) working, small other resources used (8)

C 1-3 team members, director(s) working, large other resources used (8)

D 3 team members, advisory director(s), no or small other resources used (3)

E 3 or more team members, advisory director(s), large other resources used (5)

F 3 or more team members, non-working director, moderate or large other resources used (4)

G Complex project, team of 4-5 members (6)
H Complex project, team of 6 or more members (8)

Notes:
(i)   The distinction among working/advisory/non-working refers to the degree of participation by the director once the project had been initiated; "advisory" means that the director may have been quite active in early stages, and taken part in writing up, but played only an advisory or consultative role in between.
(ii) The distinction among no/small/large other resources used refers to the extent to which the team depended on non-members to do a share of the work. The resources used were counted as large if most of the interviewing, coding and data processing were done by other people, and as small if others were brought in on only one of these, or on more but team members still did a substantial proportion of the total.
(iii) Projects classified as complex were ones where there were at least three different ranks within the team, and often some role-differentiation within one rank. In every case but one, large other resources were also used; in the one exception the team's boundaries were unclear, but it had at least eleven members.
(iv) Type E looks ambiguous, because its definition leaves some overlap with G and H. There are two cases in it that might have been placed elsewhere, but they seemed to have more in common with that type. One consisted of 6 or 7 junior academics working part-time under the direction of a senior; the other used not very large external resources but had 4 team members at 3 ranks, and so is placed here as a sort of compromise between D and G.
(v)   There is one anomaly in type C. A project with 4 members at 3 ranks has been placed there because 2 of the members were really undertaking almost independent minor pieces of research, so that for practical purposes the team on the main body of the research was two.

Obviously, the numbers of cases in some types are so small that categories would need to be collapsed for some purposes; the distinctions are made initially because they seem theoretically relevant. The types given are not logically exhaustive of the range of possible types distinguished by the dimensions used, but they are exhaustive of the patterns actually found in the sample studied.

It will also be useful to look at the details of the horizontal division of labour; vertical or hierarchical divisions will be considered later. How, then were the various research tasks divided among the different categories of people involved? For tabulation purposes some basic research tasks have been listed, in roughly the order in which they become relevant in a typical project,* and it has been noted who participated in them: design, politics, administration, questionnaire design, pilot interviews, training of interviewers, main interviews, depth interviews, observation, coding, data processing, analysis and writing.** The tasks chosen are not all those that were actually performed, but the main fairly standard ones. Every task was not required for every project; methods of data collection varied, some small or very straightforward projects in effect had no politics or administration, not all data were formally coded, and so on. The number of cases available in relation to any given task also varies because (i) occasionally there is no information in the interview about who had been responsible for some tasks, and (ii) in two cases the interviews were about a complex of inter-related projects and the different parts of the programme could not be disentangled.

The division of tasks among different categories of research worker is summarised in the following table. Broadly, it shows that in the typical project directors are heavily involved in design, politics, administration and questionnaire design, and then again in analysis and writing; somewhat less involved in depth interviews and observation; and rather little involved in other tasks. Junior researchers are heavily involved in interviewer training, observation and analysis; somewhat less involved in administration, questionnaire design, pilot interviews, depth interviews and writing; and rather little involved in other tasks. Non-members of the team are heavily involved in main

* The list of tasks has a bias towards those of survey research. There are 3 reasons for this: (i) survey tasks fall most clearly into distinct stages, (ii) survey procedure is the most standardised, and so provides a generally understood terminology; (iii) more of the projects in the sample used surveys than any other single method.

** A little further definition of some of these categories might be helpful. "Design" means establishing the basic intellectual strategy of the project. "Politics" means the negotiation of grants and access, public relations, and in general the management of the project's external relationships. "Administration" means running the routine of the project's bureaucracy, particularly non-academic aspects such as salaries. "Observation" usually means participant observation, but includes three cases where it was non-participant. "Coding" means actually doing the coding, not just compiling the codebook or supervising coders. "Data processing" means being concerned with the mechanics of getting the data on to cards or tape, programming and seeing it through the counter-sorter or computer, though without necessarily doing the physical tasks oneself.

69

Proportion of projects in which each task listed was
participated in by each group

	Directors	Junior Team Members	Non-Members of Team
Design	100	32	10
Politics	94	26	21
Administration	82	69	13
Questionnaire	79	76	5
Pilot Interviews	17	65	42
Interviewer Training	35	88	25
Main Interviews	30	27	87
Depth Interviews	63	70	6
Observation	53	83	16
Coding	28	42	63
Data Processing	25	42	69
Analysis	83	88	0
Writing	90	75	2

All figures are percentages. The number of cases on which the
figures are based is the number of projects in which that task was
done and there was information on who did it.

interviews; somewhat less involved in coding and data processing; rather little involved in politics, pilot interviews and interviewer training; and hardly involved at all in other tasks. (Note that the total participation recorded in any one task often adds to more than 100%, since more than one group could participate substantially in the same task).

These gross figures, however, are slightly misleading, since there are some variations in the pattern with projects of different kinds and sizes. In the smallest projects, directors were heavily involved in every task; senior team non-members might play some part in politics and administration, and junior team non-members were sometimes recruited for such tasks as interviewing and coding; where there was only one rank, there were by definition no junior team members. In a few projects, of varying sizes, non-working directors were barely involved at all after the first stages; their role was simply that of sponsoring and launching the team who did the work. In the largest teams, directors could devolve even their more distinctive tasks; only 65% of directors, as compared with 88% of juniors, participated in administration in teams with 3 or more ranks. Junior team members (who may be academically quite senior) have a fairly high level of participation in most tasks across all types of project. Their relatively low score on design and politics is partly because research assistants had frequently not yet been recruited at that stage; at other points their participation appears relatively low because non-members were employed and they were primarily involved in supervising these. The label 'junior', however, includes team members who were virtual equals of the directors as well as others mainly confined to the hack work. The latter tended to exist only in the largest and most differentiated teams, where the more specialized and mundane tasks that smaller teams farmed out to temporary employees could be kept within the team. (Some 'one-man' teams were in fact directors using agencies that could provide a package service for standard research techniques; the division of labour was then very similar, though coded differently in terms of my categories.) In the smallest projects (sometimes Ph.D. theses) strategically-placed powerful outsiders could sometimes give needed sponsorship or assistance, and so an unusually high proportion of these teams had team non-members participating in their politics.

Within teams there is another aspect of division of labour that can be discussed: teams used different principles for allocating work among themselves. (These 'principles' were probably, though not necessarily, deliberately chosen; they record the way things happened in practice.) The main principles followed were these:

(i) members had different skills, and tasks were allocated to whoever had the most relevant skill; (ii) the research topic was subdivisible, and different aspects of the topic were allocated to different members, perhaps in terms of their interests and experience; (iii) the research was to be conducted in different geographical areas or institutions (e.g. industrial firms), and each member was made responsible for one or more areas; or (iv) the research topic was to some extent inter-disciplinary, and members came from different disciplinary backgrounds, so each was responsible for the aspects to which their own discipline was relevant. Obviously, these principles cannot always be clearly distinguished from each other, and sometimes more than one of them was used simultaneously, as when, for instance, each research worker had primary responsibility for the part of a questionnaire relating to his interests and they then divided the responsibility for administering it by area. If the information available is classified by the principle(s) followed, counting twice where two were followed in the same project, the numbers of projects using the different principles were: skill $-$ 18; topic $-$ 17; area $-$ 10; discipline $-$ 8. There were also 5 cases where no discernible principle was used, and 3 on which there was no information. The commonest combinations were skill and topic $-$ 7, and skill and area $-$ 4.

How was it that these differing patterns of division of labour came about? This was not a topic on which I commonly asked direct questions, nor was it one that respondents spontaneously discussed much; it is perhaps interesting in itself that both they and I took many common features for granted. However, on points that were perceived as unusual or controversial, comments were made and norms asserted, and from these and the general patterns described some reasonable inferences can be drawn. But one of the problems of discussing these matters is that the direction of causation is not always self-evident. A team of a given size may have been recruited because it was already planned to collect data from that number of areas; on the other hand, it may have been decided to select a certain number of areas because that was what the team could conveniently cope with. We shall piece together the available fragments and see what emerges.

One obvious possibility is that the methods of data collection determined the structure of the team that was set up, and individual directors mentioned such considerations; at the level of the whole sample we can look at the correlations, though the issue is complicated by the fact that many teams used more than one method. There is a slight tendency for teams using a greater number of different methods to be larger and to have more ranks, but the type of method is of more interest than the number. The table below shows, for each major mode of data collection, what proportion of the projects using that method fell into the different types.

Method of data collection*	Project type				
	A	B,D	C,E,F	G,H	Total
Observation	37%	16%	26%	21%	19
Depth interviews	29%	29%	6%	35%	17
Documentary	43%	25%	9%	25%	12
Institutional	-	-	(2)	(1)	3
Survey	15%	20%	33%	33%	40
Tests	(1)	(1)	(2)	(1)	5

Observation and documentary research favour the smallest teams with no outside resources, surveys favour the larger teams and those with more outside resources, and depth interviews virtually exclude the medium-sized teams using outside resources. This pattern makes obvious sense in terms of the kind of resources one needs for different strategies. The largest teams have the capacity to do whatever they want, while smaller ones have more limited resources. It seems probable that the correlations would be more clearcut if no team had bitten off more than it could chew; intuitively it seems plausible to suspect a "Woodward effect"* by which the more successful projects would show an organisational structure appropriate to their technology. Obviously the scale of the data-collection is also relevant; surveys carried out by the smallest teams were of smaller samples than those done by the larger ones, and so on.

Where there was an initial plan that determined who should be responsible for what, it had necessarily to be made by the director(s), and affected the nature of the team that they recruited and the impression they gave at job interviews of the work to be done. Such plans could be very broad and vague: young Smith appears to be numerate, so he can be responsible for the computing; Ms. Brown is female, so she can do the women. Very precise plans could hardly be made when, as was often the case, the details of research design and methods had not yet been worked out; anyway, there were always many tasks not covered by the initial plan. On projects where there was not an initial plan, there usually seemed to be either a

* J. Woodward, *Industrial Organisation: Theory and Practice*, Oxford University Press, 1965, Chapter 2.

consciously egalitarian ethos, or an actual equality of status between participants, which meant that the appropriate mode of allocation of tasks was seen to be either group negotiation about who would rather do what, or the following of a norm of equity by which everybody shared equally in the main tasks. Sometimes grievances arose about the allocation of tasks. Where the norm of equity was followed, the grievances were more likely to be about how much was in practice done by the team as a whole: qualitative equity cannot ensure quantitative equity, and when directors were busy teaching in term-time their research assistants were still likely to get landed with more of the drudgery.

Behind the more or less formal decisions made, some latent criteria for the allocation of tasks may be inferred. I list the major ones:

1. Directors may decide which tasks they wish to take part in, and other people have to do what is left;
2. Directors are allowed to have other commitments which take priority over the research, and this can effectively limit the tasks they are able to participate in;
3. Researchers of high general academic status do not take part in participant observation;
4. Researchers of high general academic status conduct unstructured interviews with their equals (e.g. other academics, industrial managers); unstructured interviews with their social inferiors (e.g. industrial workers) are conducted by junior research workers;
5. Non-members of teams do not take part in participant observation (although they may do non-participant observation);
6. Survey interviewing, coding and data processing are normally done by people of low status: team non-members, junior team members, and directors themselves only when they are of low general academic status;
7. Team members who have taken part in fieldwork participate in analysis and writing *unless* there is at least one rank in the team above them and below the director, when they may not;
8. Directors (and only directors) may participate in writing even though they have played a negligible part in fieldwork, coding, data processing and earlier stages of analysis;
9. Researchers of low general academic status only take part in politics and administration on the smallest projects.

The most general idea underlying these criteria is that there are some types and phases of research that require skill, theoretical understanding and the exercise of discretion, while others are relatively standardised and mechanical; the first can only be done properly by trained sociologists with some involvement in the project, while the second can be done by any reasonably competent person with some *ad hoc* training, and where possible should be. These assumptions are absolutely routine; most sociologists take it for granted that survey interviewing, coding and data processing are normally devolved upon other people. The other general ideas are to do with rank; there are high and low-status tasks as well as high and low-status people. Writing, the non-routine parts of analysis, unstructured interviewing and research design are high-status tasks; participant observation perhaps ought to be, but it is too time-consuming for men with other commitments, and men of high status have other commitments. Moreover, there are few opportunities for participant observation in high-status groups, and another apparent norm is that social interaction even for research purposes, should, as far as is possible in the circumstances, be confined to equals. (There are of course good sociological reasons why it might be wise to follow this principle even if it were not consistent with one's personal preferences). Some hierarchical principals that might otherwise operate become less practical when low-status people come, by the nature of the division of labour, to possess crucial information that cannot easily be summarised, and they are then naturally involved in the high-status tasks of analysis and writing.

Finally, research politics often involves contacts with high-status outsiders, and is therefore normally done by the highest-status person available; research administration varies in content, but is generally organised as far as possible so that equals deal with equals and superiors supervise inferiors.

The cases where these general criteria notably do not apply are, a few idiosyncratic ones apart, those where the directors held specific norms that ran counter to them. These norms were of two types: (i) the norm of equity among researchers, and (ii) the norm that closeness to the data is desirable. We shall say more about norms of equity shortly. The norm of closeness to the data is most commonly applied only to certain kinds of data-collection, namely, those where a standardized structure has not been imposed on the process in advance.* Some directors, however, felt that they should at least do a few of their survey interviews to get the feel of the thing; it is not clear what distinguishes these directors from the others, except that

* Where the data had been collected by participant observation, depth interviews, or documentary or institutional methods, it was overwhelmingly the case that at least one of those doing the writing had been in direct contact with the data; where the data had been

there is some tendency for them to be among those who on the basis of experience have developed ideas of their own about the best way to run research teams. Whether or not the greater closeness to the data that they have improved their understanding of it, the policy is good for the morale of other members of the team.

It is plainly necessary to consider some of the issues to do with hierarchy and authority in research teams directly at this point. The first thing which is very clear is that, in teams with more than one rank, only the director can decide that they should be 'democratic'; juniors may wish they were, and their behaviour can affect the outcome, but policy is determined by the director. To that extent, no team is completely non-hierarchical. Some directors did have a very definite policy of this kind:

> "I wanted to establish the fact that though I was nominally director, I regarded myself as a working member of the team, and regarded them as autonomous researchers . . . . Graham came from a very hierarchical organisation and always tried to play it that way. He couldn't easily fit into the sort of structure initially that I had created . . . . immediately they arrived they started to have their own view of what could be and should be done, and these views I wanted them to nurture and insisted that they did nurture them − even though they were frequently in conflict with what I thought should be done . . . ."
> J.P. "Did you ever exercise authority or influence disproportionate to that of one out of three?"
> "Oh yes, I certainly did have that, for a number of reasons. There was a tendency for both Graham and Pauline to expect me to have it, and if I did anything it was to try and undermine that. I expected them to argue and to get them to state openly with a properly constituted discussion . . . ."

As this quotation suggests, juniors were sometimes taken by surprise, and indeed a little disconcerted, to find how much they

collected by survey or standardized testing, in a majority of cases none of the people writing had been in direct contact with the data. There was a noticeable tendency for direct contact to occur most often in pure university projects, least often in non-university ones, and to an intermediate extent in externally commissioned projects at universities. ("Direct contact" was operationally defined as meaning having done at least some of ones own participant observation, depth interviews, main survey interviews, institutional or documentary primary data-collection, or coding of responses to postal questionnaires).

were treated as equals. Graham in that team continued to be ill at ease with the non-hierarchical ethos, but most juniors definitely liked it. Despite this, it was striking how often they perceived it as in some way dysfunctional for the research. Here are some examples:

J.P. "Was it run in an authoritarian sort of way?"
"No it wasn't, and this was why every now and then when I took unilateral action everybody was peeved . . . . I found this very nice, and this was the nice part about working on the project . . . . I was very lucky — too much for the good of the project, in that I don't think I should have been left or allowed to carve off a bit to my own devices. I think a critical line more often would have possibly ironed out some of the things that turned out to be difficult later. On the other hand, it made a much better experience for me."
J.P. "Well, can you tell me about your research meetings, how things were decided in them?"
"Well, of course, I've realized since that this is standard practice, it struck me as peculiar at the time, the ritual of consensus. It was impossible to take decisions by majority, though in fact with three people it was set up rather well for that. [Director], I think, could have exercised the power of veto or pushed the decisions as he wanted it to go but he accepted the ritual of consensus theory as well, so it made the procedure of decision-taking extraordinarily cumbersome. So if there were two alternatives, generally both were adopted, which is fatal, particularly in questionnaire construction . . . . I very strongly argued that we should study the [other group] for example, and I just wouldn't be stopped even though it was argued that there wasn't time and I was half convinced . . . At this point in time, I can justify it in terms of the research, but whether in terms of strict turn-round of effort, etc. . . . . . I know damn well I can't justify it, I should have been analysing the data and writing . . . . It's curious that in a structure where consensus is of such prime importance when it can't be reached the result is anarchy, because there is no clear basis for telling anybody not to do anything".

"Now really what I'm describing to you is a quite dreadful state of affairs which should never have become allowed to exist . . . . It's not finished now, and it doesn't seem likely that it ever will be finished . . . I think this happened for a number of reasons . . . . One was, I think, I made a number of wrong decisions . . . . the other, basically, is that I was allowed to make those decisions, this being the first thing I'd ever worked on since graduating. It

77

was my first experience of research on any scale, and while it was very pleasant and educative for me to have the freedom I had, and good for me, and I probably got my present job because of the experience I'd had, but for the project it was very bad . . . ."

"It may also be the case that democratically-run research units aren't a good idea."
J.P. "Why not?"
"It's my experience . . . that it does require someone to put a foot down, take a firm stand, give dates, demand decisions and so on. There were some issues where, if it was a particularly tedious or a particularly sunny day, we would avoid, and it would be a lot easier if one could have an arbitrator."

The word 'democratic' was often used by respondents, as here, though with varying connotations. The two main practices with which it was associated were decision-making by group discussion, with everyone's opinion in principle given equal weight and sometimes with the norm of consensus operating; and the allocation of research tasks, especially the more menial ones, in a way which did not regard rank. Sometimes in practice, as two of the quotations show above, the political model used was one of federation rather than of participatory democracy in a centralized state; this model could only operate when research tasks could be divided up and allocated as individual responsibilities.

Where there was a democratic ethos, it was not always applied with complete consistency, and junior researchers were very alert to these slips:

"We were then supposed to have a meeting and Howard didn't turn up, so we started without him and were making decisions, allocating tasks or whatever it was, and then Howard turned up . . . and then came out with his own ideas and insisted on them. Actually they were good ideas, but he did, to all intents and purposes, pull rank. I think there was a pretty good row. I may have said to his face that democracy all depended on his surrendering rank, it was a concession, and he could pull rank any time he wanted. That was an occasion where one could see ideology and reality in action."

". . . organisation was always fairly democratic in the research team, so there was an agreed system by which Jack and Keith between them would match what I did on coding, always aware what a mind-destroying job it is doing clerical work . . . .

A drawback it did have, although Keith and Jack wanted the research to be democratic, and took over some of the boring tasks themselves, the position on their priorities was rather different from mine, so it tended to get pushed to the back . . . ." (Keith and Jack both held lectureships).

This second quotation shows how consistency in principle can be hard to carry through in practice; in this instance the effective choice was between the research assistant doing more than her agreed share of the coding, and waiting for the directors to do their share and thus delaying the whole project. It is easier to be a 'democratic' director, in the sense of an egalitarian one, if one is employed full-time on the project. There was another instance where a director intended to be democratic, this time in the sense of shared decision-making, but sometimes failed because of his other commitments; here decisions had to be made in consultation with outside bodies, and the limited amount of time the director could spend on the research meant that he couldn't both attend other meetings and have discussions with his team. In this case a joint constraint was the expectation of outside bodies that the whole team would not attend meetings, and that the director would take authoritative decisions. There are many settings external to research teams which create this situation; it is administratively convenient to have to deal only with one or two people, and anyway most bodies take for granted a non-democratic model of organisational authority. A further factor which encourages directors to act autocratically is that it is common in the early stages of research for there to be no juniors involved yet, and so patterns are developed which can easily carry on, at least in relation to the tasks for which they have become established. Personally I find it rather surprising that no director expressed hostility, or even ambivalence, about the extent to which his own precious research idea had been taken over and twisted by junior team members; intellectual possessiveness was low, or at least remained unexpressed.

Where there was not a definite ethos of democracy there was commonly a devolution of authority, at least on matters of detail. This pattern tended to go with a director who construed his role as non-working or primarily advisory, since neither close supervision nor participation as an equal is easy unless the director is actually there most of the time. A pattern of relationships that could be construed as exploitation of a research assistant can also be seen as giving him a generous degree of autonomy, as this director's comment shows:

". . . the final literary presentation was mine in any case, though it was very much a joint effort of course; a lot of the ideas were Ian's, and he did deserve to be joint author. The actual analysis of the data, he used a good deal of his own initiative on that."
J.P. "How did it come about that he had so much scope to use his own initiative?"
"There was no point in appointing a research fellow unless they do a lot of work. I always expect research people to do the first draft of reports. Certainly you contribute a great deal in setting it up at the ideas stage, make a major contribution, and again at the final presentation stage, but hopefully one can appoint research fellows good enough to do most of what comes between."

The research fellow on this project had only just graduated, and was indeed surprised to find how much responsibility he carried and grateful to be given joint authorship, though he thought that only appropriate to the contribution that he had made. (The director's name came first on the publication.) Devolution of responsibility seemed to work well as long as understandings on what the director's role should be were shared; where they were not, trouble followed. In 3 cases there were radical discrepancies between what the director did and what his juniors expected. In the first one, the 2 junior re- search workers expected the director to tell them what to do, or at least to take the lead in joint decision-making; what they actually found, as they described it, is this:

"These research meetings recurred about every two months, which really wasn't enough, and Len Walsh would only devote two hours to it; he would almost certainly turn up late, and at least half an hour was taken up trying to decide when to hold the next research meeting. It was almost as if he was trying to escape any kind of involvement in the thing. This would have been fine if he'd given us very clear directives about what powers we had, about what we could do, we were very unsure about this — we didn't know how much money there was . . . ." [He went on to describe how the director agreed to give a conference paper on the research, then forgot about it until 2-3 weeks before, when the research assistants had to write it, and also forgot the deadline by which an application for a further grant had to be made.]

"He's a tremendous man, certainly the cleverest person I've ever worked with, a superb brain, and when he paid attention to

the research problem and turned his faculties on it full force . . . . Difficulties, of course, arose in this inconsistency of roles that we saw for each other. It was a learning experience for all of us. I was 23 when I came; I was in no position to assume responsibility for S.S.R.C. research. I naturally assumed that I would be told what to do for a large part of the time. . . .[Maybe Walsh didn't realize himself that he was changing his role. . . to a role where he was essentially an administrator.] . . . You can't do research if you have to make an appointment a week in advance; Maurice and I accommodated to this by doing it ourselves . . . ."
J.P. "Did Walsh say anything manifestly about what roles you were to play?"
"No, Walsh didn't operate like that, and he wasn't a man you could force to operate like that. You always came out feeling that you had been told all there was to know about this, and if you didn't understand it was your own fault . . . We couldn't inject an element of formality into the meeting or he laughed you out of court."

Of these two research workers both began with great respect for Walsh, but both gave essentially the same description of his behaviour, which was that in effect, and without saying so or giving them the necessary information to go ahead, he abdicated responsibility for his research. (In my interview with him, Walsh appeared quite unconscious of his research assistants' view of his role, though mentioning that he was very busy with other things at the time!) The consequence was not merely personal disillusion but a lot of wasted time as they waited for direction, increasing lack of commitment to the project, and eventually only partial completion of it.

The second case was one where the director behaved in ways that the research officers perceived as internally inconsistent: he expected them to do the detailed work, but without autonomy or the right to publish independently or share in the writing. The director was not an empirically minded man, and thought that it would be quite all right for him to go away for a sabbatical while his juniors drafted the questionnaires and got the interviewing done, and then he would come back and write up the results. He chose his juniors for their technical competence and prior research experience. When they showed signs of independence, and wanted to publish some of the work they had done which he was not very happy with, he became increasingly uneasy at his loss of control over the situation. From the juniors' point of view, they had been appointed as research officers – not assistants – on the lecturer pay scale, and took it that

that implied some autonomy. They worked very hard, and got a lot of data collected. They found the director's critical comments on what they did unhelpful, because his lack of experience with survey research (and perhaps also the narrowness of their training) made these seem impractical or purely negative. Their impression was that he proposed to come back after they had done all the detailed empirical work, ignore the theoretical framework on which they had based it and impose his own, and write a book with only his name on the spine and thanks to them in the preface. The accounts of events given by director and research officers differ considerably, and are somewhat confused, so it is impossible to work out exactly what heppened and in what order, but the eventual outcome is in no doubt: the research officers resigned with a strong sense of grievance, and the research has never been completed.

The third case of discrepant expectations about the director's role is less striking in the kinds of misunderstanding involved, since in this one he simply launched the research enthusiastically and then took very little further practical interest in it. Again, however, a junior commented that if he had realized what the director was going to do — and how little previous experience of empirical research he had had — he would have taken steps to organise things himself sooner. And, once again, the research has taken an inordinately long time to reach completion.

Whether the pattern followed was one of devolution or not, ambiguity of authority often led to misunderstandings, ructions, and lack of clear allocation of responsibility. An arrangement that seemed particularly prone to problems of authority was to have a team of 3 ranks with a research officer in the middle playing a supervisory role. There are not enough cases to draw general conclusions, but some examples will illustrate the type of problem that arose.

In the first example the research officer, who was only a year or two older than the research assistants, was in charge of the fieldwork, which was not in the local area. He assumed that he was meant to be in charge, but found that in practice the director played a larger role than he had expected:

"I can demonstrate empirically that Norman never left me alone, I can show you the number of letters he wrote to me. I received, on average, 2 letters a week, and spoke on the phone 3 times a week. . . it just wasn't possible for me to organise this and have any autonomy. . . . [Towards the end of the project] Norman used to annoy me fantastically. My role had been totally usurped. Karen, Liz and Mary would always go to him if they disagreed,

and the case was put in such a way that I sounded unreasonable
. . . With hindsight, I think it was to do with Norman wanting
to get back on the project . . . he wanted to do the work, but
there wasn't room for both of us to do the work. I wasn't prepared to do a research assistant's work and spend hours on the
counter-sorter, but he was, because that was how he could get
back in. I was accused of being incredibly idle on analysing the
data. . . ."

Despite this strong resentment, the research officer agreed with the
director that he had been too junior and inexperienced to be given a
position of such responsibility:

"I didn't have enough experience or authority, and I was mis-
appointed. I should have been a senior research assistant with
someone with 10 or 20 years' experience above in the field. . . .
Norman said 'you wanted it', but I say 'you shouldn't have let
me have it'."

The perceptions that Karen, Liz and Mary, the research assistants, had
of the situation were not of continual interference by Norman; for
them he was a distant figure who made occasional appearances to
find out what was going on, and who could be invoked as court of
appeal or arbitrator when there were disagreements. For them the
major factor undermining the legitimacy of the research officer's
authority was that he did not seem to be much clearer than they
were about what they were meant to be doing – and when he was,
they found his arguments for the operational validity of the concepts
he used unconvincing. Eventually, for these and other reasons, the
research officer played a smaller part than had originally been intended, and that certainly contributed to the delay in analysing and
writing up the results, though this was in the end done.

A second example was again a research officer in charge of a team
of research assistants, though here he was a little older and the director played a lesser role. Again, however, problems arose over the
legitimacy of his authority, as some quotations from his juniors will
show, and here this was the crucial issue:

"I think Oliver felt that we were a bit hostile towards him, not
being particularly cooperative. We felt that he hadn't given the
leadership or the authority that a person in his position ought to
have been able to give. It had shown up some of his inexperience.
If he had to find things out, we would have liked to all be on the
same level and would have liked a framework or guidelines and
he hadn't provided this. . . . If someone is going to be appointed

to conduct a piece of research. . . [one expects] that they would have been chosen for certain kinds of expertise, a reasonable knowledge of methods. I didn't, for example, think in terms of expertise being of a diffuse kind, that there may not be a 'right' way of doing things, that hadn't occurred to me, or that there might be a pluralistic way of doing it. Also, for certain personal qualities as well, an ability to stamp ones authority is going a bit strong, but to develop a situation in which you can have a hierarchy based on the acknowledgement of the possession of all these qualifications, and an expertise that didn't just rely on the power of being director to enforce decisions, but because of the argument deployed, it goes because of the ability to outgun you."

". . . there was a lot of tension because clearly Oliver was very new at his job. I had almost as much research experience as Oliver had. Well, no, I retract that statement; I had nearly as much knowledge, if not quite so much experience. Obviously Oliver was very insecure about his position, and I think it tended to make him over-react. I think that was for me probably why I wasn't very respectful. . . Oliver is a person who doesn't have a great deal of finesse; Lucy [other research assistant] was very conscious about this kind of. . . doing things properly. . . the best word for it, I would say, in Lucy's eyes Oliver lacked dignity."

Oliver, needless to say, had a somewhat different perspective on the situation:

J.P. "What sort of role did you plan for them [the research assistants] ?"
"We planned. . . we didn't, that's the trouble. . . we didn't think about the difficulty of dividing the work. . . . In the first few months I think we didn't talk enough. I used to leave them alone and hope they were reading around, me being engaged in finishing another project to be honest, so I didn't confront the issues early enough. It was left to the pilot survey last spring to really throw this up, the extent to which they resented that I drafted the questionnaire and pushed things through. They let me get away with it, then afterwards, when things went wrong, they blamed it all on me! There was very little joint responsibility. At the same time, I felt they were being unreasonable because they didn't appreciate how difficult things were."

On this project there were several personality clashes, and there was a considerable amount of overt conflict; at some points the director was invoked as referee, and succeeded in smoothing things to some extent, but the relative calm eventually produced seems to have reflected the resignation of despair, plus a shared interest in getting at least something written, as much as satisfaction. Obviously a number of factors interacted to produce the level of dissatisfaction that occurred, and no one of them can be identified as *the* cause. It is noticeable that the research assistants' complaints are sometimes internally inconsistent: Oliver is criticized both for taking the lead and for failing to be authoritative enough. A norm is evident that merely positional authority should be reinforced by the possession of superior expertise, but it is also felt that the mere holding of higher rank creates certain responsibilities irrespective of expertise. The situation in this particular project was complicated further, in ways which the quotations above do not bring out, by the research assistants' objections to being used for some routine tasks that they felt to be beneath their dignity.

In some other instances the research officers' problems were rather different. There were 2 cases where they found that their position was in effect one of responsibility without authority: they were formally in charge of situations where they had little actual control, either because there were no sanctions that they could invoke in case of disagreements or because the research design created insuperable practical difficulties of communication and co-ordination. In another one the directors felt that they had a problem, although the research officer may not have done — I was unable to interview him; he was in charge on a day-to-day basis, became very strongly identified with and possessive in relation to the project, knew about the whole of it in a way that no other team member could, and consequently the directors to some extent lost control.

The factor that all these cases have in common, despite their differences, is the ambiguity of the research officer's role for at least some team members. The norms of democracy and of legitimation by technical competence were, despite their areas of inconsistency, both available for invocation when differences of opinion arose. If the director was inactive, he could become the figurehead to whom one appealed over the head of the scapegoat who took the blame; if the director was very active, the rank of the research officer could appear pointless and his claims to superiority unjustified. These difficulties may only arise when the research contains intellectual problems to spark them off, or may have an autonomous life of their own; the data available cannot resolve this. There is no doubt that in the outcome the intellectual and the social issues become inextricably entangled, and that there are widely-shared norms about the relevance of hierarchy to intellectual issues that make the effective exercise of hierarchical control difficult, especially when the occupants of different ranks in the hierarchy are not far apart in general status.

Finally, there were 3 projects in the sample where there was no ambiguity about the authority structure: it was centralized and autocratic, with the director making the basic decisions. As one director, with charming frankness, remarked in response to a question, it was "Egalitarian, like Stalin was egalitarian!"; he went on to modify this by adding that" . . . there was quite a big age gap, and an experience gap; the experience gap was more important. So it was quite clear who had the last word." These projects were not university-based ones, but in relatively bureaucratized outside settings. Directors within universities who tried to operate in this way did not have much success, or at any rate provoked resentment and resistance; elsewhere it seemed to be accepted as normal, even if disliked.

As has been shown, research teams varied in the extent to which they operated on a hierarchical basis, and legitimation of hierarchical rank could by no means be counted on. The practical situation could be confused and ambiguous, and sometimes I have found myself compelled to take minor liberties with the data in order to bring out analytically relevant points; what may be true of one aspect of a project is not necessarily true of another, and one participant may see the situation differently from another. An amusing example of this is given by the joint directors of one project, talking about each other:

> "The responsibility in terms of exercising final judgment is Phil's, and that was probably true of most elements of the project. . . . I think he emerged inevitably, because he was (a) older, (b) more experienced, and (c) had a great deal to do with the wheeling and dealing in getting the money etc. It's written jointly, but I have been unable to pretend that it is not a senior and junior partner sort of set up."

> "I'm lucky in that there is no question of me being the guiding light of the thing, only in that I'd done a large project before and so could see some things coming, but if you leave that aside we never thought of it that way, it's a joint project."

Another director drew attention to a further very relevant point:

> ". . . above and beyond that they could do anything they liked. I

don't think I ever discouraged any of the above and beyond
things, but I certainly had to remind them from time to time
about [one aspect of the research design] ; whether this was
put as encouraging noises or authority I don't know! . . . it's
very difficult to draw the line between exercising authority
and encouraging [encouragement from high-status people can
be seen as an order] . . . in terms of discussions, interchange of
academic ideas and so on, one consciously attempted to apply
the principle of academic equals, you're as likely or more likely
to be right as I am, but again you never know how this will
come out [if you make strong statements in the heat of discussion they may be interpreted; as you get older, people will
not treat you as an equal.] "

It was evident that he was right, and that this was what was happening
in some cases; what may have been similar behaviour patterns did
not have the same meanings when they came from directors of varying academic statuses and personal characteristics. Some of the grievances of research assistants appeared to stem from this; for an
example, it will again be relevant to quote the points of view of
occupants of different ranks on the same issue. Two research assistants interviewed together speak first, then the director:

A "I think the whole situation of research assistants is so peculiar.
When you are a student you think being a post-graduate is really
quite a top dog. You all get to the situation, or go past past-
graduate to research assistant. It's like going from primary to
secondary school; you start at the bottom. . ."
B "The pay wasn't very much, just above the research grant; I
don't think that had much to do with it, but by the end of the
year we did come to feel 'if that's the way they regard the job,
that's the way I will do it' . . ."
A ". . .it was an uncomfortable meeting, I can remember that,
maybe because there were so many research assistants that we
became the silent majority!. . . We were never treated as
colleagues really, were we."
J.P. "Did you have an expectation of being treated as colleagues?
What did that rest on?"
A "General impression, I suppose, of what it was like. ..."

J.P. "Can you tell me something about the role of the research
assistants in relation to the results?"
Director: "[I hoped for more than we got. One always over-
estimates the extent to which people beginning in the field. . .

It's a question of assurance. They might have felt that we were wrong, but with all the friendly Christian-name relationship in the world, and trotting round to the pub afterwards, they wouldn't say. . . ."]

Both sides on this project agreed that what had happened was that the research assistants had made a negligible contribution to the making of key decisions, and had not developed specific interests of their own within the project; each side, however, saw this as being essentially the other's fault. It is probably particularly hard psychologically for junior people to participate and take the initiative when, as in this case, the mode of "democracy" made available to them was discussion in large meetings rather than devolution of responsibility for relatively autonomous task areas. This group of research assistants certainly felt very disillusioned with their experience, and thought they had a legitimate grievance. They probably had, not in the sense that there was literally no opportunity for them to affect decisions, but in the sense that the structure within which the decisions were made was such that, given their status and experience at the time, it was sociologically improbable that they would be able to be involved in the way that had been suggested when they were interviewed for the job, or that fitted their idealized conceptions of what research would be like. One cannot, however, take research assistants' complaints as giving a definitive diagnosis of a situation (any more than one can directors'), as the comments of the director of another project drawing on his general experience suggest:

"[One problem with a permissive set-up is that it can generate difficulties. If you said to someone a bit insecure 'you do this', they can go away and do it, and feel quite happy, even if they don't agree with it. If you say 'let's discuss it', and don't give them instructions, they feel insecure and say 'he's no good, he doesn't tell me what to do.'] I had one or two of those people. . . . Some people's personality can't stand research, they don't like to work in an exploratory way, open-ended, they're happier with some authoritative way of doing it. . . . [The system of defence about being thought incompetent in not knowing what to do is to say I'm incompetent for not telling them.]"

The substantive point that one can draw from these examples, apart from the fact that the experience of authority is subjective and perceptions vary, is that the bare existence of hierarchy has sociological consequences, and that to some extent these occur irrespective of the norms and intentions of those most immediately involved. It is normal for a junior to feel constrained to some manifest deference towards a superior when that superior can make the decision whether or not to be "democratic", has control over his present employment, and may affect his chances of future employment. It is also evident that at least some of those superiors who adopt a "democratic" policy expect this. The policy may be chosen because he likes to be nice to people and on friendly terms with them, because he thinks it expedient for the research since it encourages maximum commitment, or because it's the only practical possibility given the amount of time he has to devote to the research, rather than for any of the obvious normative reasons; it need not imply the intention to devolve basic decision-making. To the extent that it does not, there is a recipe for conflict. Even deferential juniors may not succeed in doing exactly what the director would have wished if he does not give them detailed instructions and supervision, and if they do not the director may see this as indicating incompetence on their part. Meanwhile juniors have a choice between attempting to conform to the director's wishes, which may be difficult when these have not been spelled out in any detail, and attempting to act autonomously, which may lead to objections from the director and is certainly likely to run up against constraints from the basic framework created by him. Where director and juniors are in perfect intellectual harmony, these problems are insignificant and easily soluble by discussion. Perfect intellectual harmony, however, is not simple to achieve. Several directors remarked that, if they were involved in a team project again, they would take more care to recruit only collaborators who were really compatible and thought the same way as they did. Given, however, the practical difficulties of finding workers with suitable basic qualifications, there might be little chance of using such refined criteria of compatibility, and such remarks commonly came up in the context of explaining why they did not want to undertake team research again.

But there are sociological reasons other than the initial composition of the team why different members should have different perspectives on the research. As in the larger society, holding any one position in the division of labour gives distinctive experiences and interests and so tends to create distinctive perspectives. It was very clear in the interviewing that directors and research assistants typically had different sorts of story to tell, as is reflected in the table showing who did which tasks; directors would spend most of their time explaining how the research came to be initiated and how the various political negotiations were conducted, and then skip to the problems of analysis and writing, while assistants would spend a large part of their time telling about what hell the fieldwork was and what the personal relationships in the team were like. One research assistant, though in a very egalitarian team, sums it up:

"I get the impression that it's very difficult with people doing full-time research and people doing part-time research and full-time teaching to talk about some things. Obviously, Ray and Ruth at all stages were interested in the subject matter. . . . The sorts of things that concerned them were not the sorts of things that concerned me. I was concerned with the trivia of the research process, that Mrs. B. had dropped out or had the flu. . . whereas they, not having been plugged in to the day-to-day running, though appreciative of the problems, didn't see it the way I did."

This emphasizes the social consequences, but intellectual consequences are deeply involved with the social ones. Division of labour implies division of knowledge, and eventually, in a team that was initially undifferentiated, becomes division of competence. Knowledge once divided can be hard to put together again. There were numbers of references to the ways in which directors become dependent on research assistants for their knowledge of the practical details of what has been done, and even equal team members can each have their specialism which the others do not understand. Once such a division has been established there is a danger that the project may in effect become a federation rather than a unified whole, and so the final book ends up as a collection of chapters by different authors. That, however, can be managed, and goes with a division of labour based on topic or area. Where, however, the division of labour is by skill worse problems can arise, because in a situation of sequential interdependence* one member cannot proceed without the other's contribution, and even when the contribution

* J.D. Thompson, *Organizations in Action*, McGraw Hill, New York, 1967. Thompson distinguishes three types of technological interdependence: (i) pooled interdependence, where all parts do not interact with each other but the performance of each is necessary to the whole; (ii) sequential interdependence, where B depends upon A being done first; (iii) reciprocal interdependence, where output from each part is input for the other. These types are in increasing order of complexity, and require increasingly elaborate organisational modes of coordination. Each type includes the previous pattern, so that organisations with reciprocal interdependence (which would include at least some aspects of most research teams) necessarily have sequential interdependence.

is made it may not be of the kind hoped for; if competences are too far differentiated the situation may be irremediable, while if remedies are attempted by users the initial economies of division of labour are wasted. One form of this type of division of labour that seemed particularly likely to develop in pathological ways was where one member of the team was given a special responsibility for computing. There were 3 cases in which a firm specialization of this kind developed, and in each one trouble followed, as the quotations indicate:

". . . we hit a swings and roundabouts problem. On the swings, Stuart became very good at handling the machine, very very competent, he had a real gift for it, and he developed from nowhere at scratch a real gift of programming. The roundabout was that, like all well-developed skills, he found himself happier practising it than doing something else, and we got the situation where sometimes it was a continuous battle: you get a problem that can be handled by hand in 10 hours, or by the machine in half an hour if only the program works. Stuart was always inclined to say that the program will work, and invest 2, 10 or 20 hours in getting it to work. . . I think there were cases where we found a sophisticated solution to problems we could have hit with a hammer. . . There was another roundabout, and I say this with as much blame to the so-called directors of the project and particularly me, it was also the case that as the computer became more and more fascinating sociology became less fascinating. . . the chap who was in control of the print-out had got absorbed by the problems of computing."

"Terry, bless his little cotton socks, did something that would have been extremely valuable where you have thousands of respondents. . . it went absolutely haywire. . . it made the output completely unreadable. You had to go through it, and then you were faced with the two places of decimals so it was impossible to add up. It was an over-kill of sophistication on the computer output side. . . Our computer print-out was literary, word for word, and it made analysis very difficult. . . The tragedy about it is that I'm sure in computer programming terms what Terry did was absolutely masterly, particularly with that kind of support in that kind of installation, but the simple fact was it just didn't suit our particular needs, and all his energies were tied up in that so often in other things we were one short. Also, for a year all the meetings were taken up with discussion of the computing, not with the analysis."

The irony of the situation is that in both these cases the computer specialists themselves saw that something had gone wrong, and explained that one of the reasons why they had developed such elaborate programs was precisely because of the division of labour. It seemed necessary to have very detailed labelling of the data because other members of the team were not going to have the same intimate familiarity with the program, and might not understand what was going on without it. In fact, in each of these cases when it came to the real analysis some of the programming had to be redone so that the output was effectively usable. The third case was not so extreme, but excessively elaborate programs that lost touch with the true needs of the project as sociology were still produced, and wasted a lot of time.

Programming seems to be an activity that encourages obsessive perfectionism, and the intellectual neatness of the means leads those most single-mindedly involved in it to lose sight of the end; the specialists' behaviour went beyond what could be explained by the desire to facilitate communication with their colleagues. (Probably temperamental factors also contributed to this.) In all these cases the research assistants in charge of computing had no previous experience with it, and had to teach themselves from scratch; this obviously took considerable effort, and partly accounted for the absorption in it that they showed and their lack of time for other aspects of the research. Perhaps if they had been defined as mere technicians the consequences for the project as a whole would have been less, for then other team members could have told them what was wanted and felt entitled to expect results. In many of the projects people outside the team were used as technicians; there were often difficulties in the relationship, and here the problems were typically ones of communicating what was wanted to a programmer with no sociological background, but they don't usually seem to have had such ramifying implications. Which pattern was adopted depended to a considerable extent on the facilities available. At one extreme, some universities provided a computer but no central programming service, while at the other extreme, some research units had a separate computing department staffed by programmers with accumulated expertise in the unit's field, and one would be made responsible for looking after the computing side of each of its projects. Presumably problems would have been less likely to arise if team specialists had had previous experience of the possible practical difficulties, and there are now some sadder and wiser men able to pass on the benefits of what they have learnt. Oddly enough, it did not seem to make much difference to the outcome whether or not colleagues had any previous experience with computers; what did seem to make some difference was the rigidity of the division of labour — where, for whatever reason, several team members took some continuing interest in the computing, it did not get out of hand. It may then also have been done less competently; that cannot be judged.

Some time has been spent on computing because that was the task that seemed most conspicuously to lead to pathological developments of the division of labour. It was not the only one, however, in which researchers could become absorbed at the cost of a broader perspective; in some cases, for instance, participant observation seemed to have the same effect.* Whether or not the division of labour took a pathological form, it frequently had dysfunctional consequences, which usually became evident at the writing stage when the threads had to be drawn together. It does not follow that to have no division of labour would be more efficient, but this does suggest that the form that it takes is of crucial importance.

There are two recurring themes in the data on large projects which are not overtly related to the division of labour, but I think must be interpreted as arising from it. These themes are the common, and connected, complaints of research assistants that the research had no hypotheses, and that they (therefore) did not know what they were doing. Sometimes, of course, it was simply true that the research had no hypotheses, but at other times the director would have said that it did have some; whichever was really the case, the interesting question is why it should have been felt as a cause for complaint. My interpretation is as follows. Hypotheses are most commonly the responsibility of the director, at least initially. In a completely democratic or egalitarian project, hypotheses would be worked out jointly by the whole team, and everyone would understand them and feel committed to use them. In a completely authoritarian project, at least if the research method is such that little initiative or creative understanding is required from the juniors, hypotheses can be handed down from on high, or tasks can be imposed without detailed specification of the hypotheses to which they relate. Most actual projects fall somewhere between these two types. They are

* Note that in this section I am forced to rely on participants' own judgments of what went wrong and what was successful. No doubt if I had full information my judgments would sometimes differ from theirs. When I have accepted their judgment, and built an argument on it, this usually reflects some consensus within the team that there was a mistake made or that things went smoothly. Where judgments differ about what was successful this too often reflects position in the division of labour.

neither completely democratic nor completely authoritarian, and their methods often require sympathetic understanding and commitment if they are to be put into practice properly; thus the research assistants have a strong practical need to grasp exactly what the project is meant to be about. (And they, in common with directors and lone researchers, are liable to find lack of structure and uncertainty disturbing.) But the means for them to do so may not be available. Directors usually want, with at least one part of their minds, not to impose a completely rigid framework on their juniors; they have some respect for the norm of intellectual autonomy, and moreover hope that the research will profit from the constructive initiatives of their juniors. Thus they do not give detailed directives or, where they do give detailed directives, these are at the level of theory rather than of the operational detail with which research assistants have to cope from day to day. Thus the juniors may still not feel that they are really being guided. (Where they are, moreover, they may still feel that it is inadequate, because there are difficulties obvious to them over the operational validity of theoretical concepts used by directors remote from the field.) When, as we have shown often happens, directors have many other commitments and cannot spend much time on the project, poor communications and the absence of the mutual socialization brought about by daily interaction intensify other difficulties. (On one project, where the director asked for questions to be submitted in writing and might take a week to reply, a sort of manifesto was eventually composed by the research assistants asking what the project was meant to be about and what the hypotheses were.) Where directors quite genuinely are leaving their assistants scope to introduce their own ideas, they may still be afraid to do so, and to some extent this is only natural. In a hierarchical situation they fear the consequences, and are not sure how far innovation is really acceptable. They may also really not be competent to do so, when they are young people with no previous experience of empirical research, and here egalitarian intellectual norms can be inappropriate. The intrinsic uncertainties and anxiety of research are compounded by lack of clear structure within the team.*

* I do not wish to imply that the balance of net advantage favours clear structure; the data are not adequate to indicate this. Not all projects with the same structure suffered from the same problems, and personality factors as well as sociological ones obviously had some relevance. On theoretical grounds it would seem plausible to suggest that clear structure would be more appropriate to some topics than others. On this, see Tom Burns & G.M. Stalker, *The Management of Innovation,* Tavistock Publications, 1961.

In broadly descriptive and exploratory projects, there is always likely to be too much data for the available hypotheses, and a certain vagueness of purpose. The methodological rationale for such projects has not been very clearly worked out; insofar as recent writers have dealt with the question, it tends to be in a context where participant observation is emphasized as the mode of data-collection and qualitative rather than quantitative strategies of analysis are preferred.* Basic textbooks in undergraduate courses, however, still usually favour a not specifically sociological hypothetico-deductive model of the research process. Young graduates coming to a research project thus tend to have expectations of very clear-cut initial hypotheses. These expectations are supported by the way in which most research results are written up, especially in journal articles, which gives little clue to the practical ways in which the results have been reached and the extent to which structure may only have been imposed retrospectively.** Few young graduates have had previous experience of professional social research, and so they lack other sources to draw on for an idea of how research is done. But the "reconstructed logic"*** of final publications and the abstract ideals of the textbooks are a poor guide to what typically happens, and so expectations are created that are doomed to disappointment:

> "We'll have to go back prior to the actual research when, in the process of leaving university and thinking what one was going to do, I had a vague interest or bias towards applied social research ... I suppose I carried with me into the situation, perhaps more immediately than the others [who were not coming straight from graduation — J.P.], a sense of how formally research was to be conducted: a set of hypotheses to be examined and tested in a systematic way, and some kind of statements made as a result about the truth or falsity of them, and I carried this very formal kind of approach with me as some kind of model against which I was going to measure how I did."

* See, for instance, Barney G. Glaser and Anselm L. Strauss, *The Discovery of Grounded Theory*, Weidenfeld and Nicolson, 1968.

** "The rhetoric of presentation in science is not 'to tell it as it is' but to disguise *ex post* what has been done and put it into an inhuman form of methodological orthodoxy and logical entailment." D. Macrae, Foreword to B. Bernstein, *Class, Codes and Control*, Routledge and Kegan Paul, 1971; vol. I.

*** Abraham Kaplan, *The Conduct of Inquiry*, Chandler Publishing Company, San Francisco, 1964, Chapter 1.

This research assistant was more self-conscious than most, but probably not unusual in other respects. These disappointments are probably less likely to occur when, as in the United States, empirical research is a routine activity going on all the time, and most students with an interest in it are likely to have had the opportunity of part-time employment before taking a full-time research job; I think there are very few sociology departments in Britain of which this would be true.

It is partly for the same sort of reason that another kind of disillusion occurs among research assistants, the themes of which may be exemplified in this quotation:

"I just wanted to do some research to see what went on from the point of view of the first year post-graduate being exposed to book-learning and the library aspect and only to a minimal extent to the actual research practice, so I was... it was very interesting to see what actually went on. [... it was a shattering and eye-opening experience when I came in contact with all those people whose names were familiar in books and they turned out to be no more intelligent than the rest of us. ...] It seemed to me at that time, I had the idea that doing research was an almost sacred activity, everybody fantastically committed and involved with the problems; but when I got into the situation we found a spontaneous bureaucracy developing, and it was a real nine-to-five or ten-to-four kind of occupation for the research assistants because they really were in a situation of exploitation, there was nothing in it for them and it was work of incredible tedium, you didn't need graduates to do it. ..."

This particular assistant found himself in an unusually trying situation, but the glorious expectations with which he started would have been to some extent disappointed in most projects; few men can be heroes to their research assistants, and most projects contain many routine tasks.

Not all expectations of research are general; some are specific to the one project, and created by the information that potential assistants are given when they apply for jobs on it. It was for this reason that I made a point of asking about the nature of formal contracts or letters of employment, and how far these were supplemented by more informal statements made at the time of interview. No formal contract was described which covered anything that bore on these problems; they all appeared to cover only matters such as salaries and holiday arrangements which could equally well apply to a non-academic employee. The nearest any came to specifying anything relevant was in giving the title of the job — research assistant, research officer, etc. These titles are generally taken to have a known and agreed meaning, though it was fairly clear in practice the only sure consensus was that "research officer" ranked higher. (On one of the most conflict-ridden projects, the appointments were advertised as "research officer" but always appeared in the university calendar as "research assistant".)

Formal contracts were often supplemented by informal understandings, though it was not always clear where these came from or whether they were fully shared. The points on which informal understandings were most commonly mentioned were authorship and division of labour. The understanding on authorship, when there was one, was that assistants would have joint authorship of publications, or could achieve it if they made an appropriate contribution; sometimes in addition it was made known that they could take aspects that were not central and write them up to publish themselves. Division of labour is a more complex problem, and the understandings reported were extremely vague, covering either such generalities as that everyone should muck in or broad allocations of tasks such as responsibility for one geographical area or one of the groups to be studied. It was also sometimes understood that assistants could, were expected to or must undertake research degrees. Even where understandings such as these held and were kept to, there was still plenty of scope for misunderstandings about their implications. And, of course, such understandings can turn out to be impractical in the light of the development of the research and the emergent role structure of the team. It would not seem practical to promise joint authorship to a fresh young graduate whose research capacity is as yet unknown, but some end up by making a contribution of which only senior authorship could give appropriate recognition.

One of the problems of assessing contribution arises out of the nature of the division of labour. A director whose main involvement has been in design and then in analysis and writing may perceive his research assistant's role as merely technical, and so not warranting the accolade of authorship. The research assistant in those circumstances is likely to regard himself as having done the real work, and to feel that he has suffered an injustice if his name is not on the publication. The director's hierarchical position ensures that it is he who makes the final decision. There were few real controversies over authorship in the sample, but the possibility was always there. When, as often happened, writing-up remained to be done after the grant had expired, this made it more likely that only the director would be in a situation to do the writing, and so strengthened his moral claim to recognition. How feasible it was for one person to do all the writing of course depended considerably upon the way in which tasks had been allocated at an earlier stage. Sequential inter- dependence could make all the information available to one person at the end; extensive participant observation more or less guarantees that the observers will be needed to take part in the writing.* People who have moved on to other jobs, however, may find it very difficult to make their agreed contribution to the actual writing, and there were cases where failure to do so delayed publication and/or meant that the writing was left to other people and so the legitimacy of their claim to authorship was undermined.

Some respondents, when I raised the subject of expectations and understandings, said that although they had not thought about it before it might be wise in future to be much more careful about con- tracts. It is by no means clear that this would solve the problem, since much of what may take place cannot be anticipated. However, perhaps the usual ambiguity of authority structure and total absence of provision on how to regulate disagreements could to some extent be dealt with contractually; in particular projects, there will be specific conditions of service (e.g. how long fieldworkers will need to live in the areas to be studied) that could be laid down in advance. Perhaps more to the point would be to spend more time in job inter- views on the mundane details of the work to be done and the way in which it is to be organised, and how the director sees his role. (For this to be done satisfactorily, at least one of the parties would need previous experience of empirical social research.) Some false expectations could, however, hardly be avoided unless the director and his potential juniors all already had some research experience and were also fairly familiar with each others' styles; such optimum conditions cannot often be met.

Other lines of approach to problems related to these were some- times suggested. Several people thought that the customary compo- sition of teams was inappropriate, and that it would be a good idea to have fewer graduates and more people at secretarial and clerical levels. This would presumably solve the problem of high expectations. Those who had had a full-time project secretary seem to have found her very valuable, and a few had used them for tasks such as coding and programming which fall well outside the usual range of office duties; no complaints were made that the work had been done

* In one very large project where some participant observation had been done by juniors it seemed probable that the results would never be used. The team had dispersed, and the juniors were so little in touch with what was going on that they tried to find out from me whether anything had been written.

inadequately for lack of social-scientific background. Research assistants tend to feel that they are wasted on tasks that could be done by someone less qualified – and perhaps they are; research directors seem implicitly to assume that non-graduates do not really exist except as typists or temporary employees. The temporary employees who are available have special characteristics: they are students, married women, or the educated unemployed. The educated unemployed are a mixed bag, ranging from resting actors to the drug addicts whom 3 people mentioned as among their coders! If more non-graduates were taken on as full-time employees it might be possible to appoint useful people from the pool available as temporary employees and do without the more marginally desirable of them. Another line was taken by those who said that more formalized procedures were necessary, and that their projects had suffered from insufficient bureaucratisation or inadequate supervision of juniors.

It is suggestive that those who put forward specific ideas on how to deal with problems intended to stay active in research, while others who had had similar bad experiences just wanted to give up empirical work, or do it again only when they could be sure of a team whose hearts beat as one. There seem to be two alternative strategies implied here, which could be identified with Durkheim's mechanical and organic solidarity.* The mechanical solidarity approach emphasizes initial factors in common, and assumes that the details will work out all right if hearts (or rather minds) are in the right place; it perhaps tends a little to the sentimentally unrealistic and the normative, though nonetheless practical in its emphasis on the improbability of all possible permutations of team members working equally well. The organic solidarity approach places less emphasis on recruitment of the right people in the first place, and stresses instead the development of organisational patterns to direct and control efforts so that they further the purposes of the research rather than of the individuals; it perhaps tends towards an unrealistic lack of concern with individual motivation and the strength of norms concerned with autonomy in universities. These strategies are of course ideal types, and most people would probably want to use some element of each; certainly they are not essentially incompatible with each other, and each has its merits.

We have shown that, although the boundaries of research teams were often not clearly defined, there are conventional patterns of allocation of tasks to different kinds of participants in projects of various types. The conventional allocation of tasks has the obvious

* E. Durkheim, *The Division of Labor in Society,* The Free Press of Glencoe, Illinois, 1933, Chapters 2 and 3.

advantages of any division of labour, plus the specific one of making it possible for directors to conduct research while also heavily engaged in other activities. It is not obvious, however, that the solutions reached are the most rational ones. It could be argued, for instance, that it would not be surprising if directors who have no direct contact with their own data interpreted them without much sensitivity to their nuances or departures from a pre-established theoretical framework, and if research assistants not fully involved in the design of the project collected the data in ways not sufficiently informed by theoretical understanding.* It cannot be demonstrated without more information than I have that these consequences actually occurred, but it can be shown that the division of labour created problems of communication and coordination among team members. The occupants of different roles inevitably experienced different problems and developed different perspectives on the research; the hierarchical structure of most teams could resolve persisting differences of opinion by the exercise of authority, but this was often regarded as illegitimate and hence created its own difficulties. "Democracy", though linked and regarded as legitimate, also had its own dysfunctions which contributed to delays in completing the work and the making of bad decisions. Division of knowledge could not just create intellectual gulfs that were hard to bridge, but also cause some people to lose sight of the overall purpose of the research; when this happened consequences, their precise form depending on the nature of the interdependencies that the division of labour had created, followed for the ways in which analysis and writing could be done and the amount of time it was likely to take.

In large research teams with many temporary employees a fixed and detailed division of labour is possible, but the number and changing nature of the tasks to be done in the course of a project means that it is hard to have a very precise division in the ordinary team. This is one factor that contributes to the frequent vagueness about who should do what, which in the cases studied was often encouraged by the lack of specificity in initial plans and understandings. To some extent this lack of specificity is unavoidable because of the inherent uncertainties of research, but these uncertainties were often

* Although no direct confessions were made to me of cheating practices such as those described by Julius Roth (*The American Sociologist*, vol. I, no. 4, Aug. '66, "Hired hand research"), the general logic of his analysis very much holds: the nature of the commitment of team members, and the manner in which they perform their tasks, depends upon the structure of the employment situation in which they find themselves.

100

increased by the lack of relevant experience of both directors and assistants. Conflicting norms were available to be invoked in situations of stress and to legitimate felt grievances, whether or not these grievances could be regarded as objectively well founded. Perhaps the outside sociologist may simply suggest that the character of the whole research situation in universities is likely to create felt grievances among junior team members.

A division of labour that is successful and appropriate in one respect is not necessarily so in another: specialisation improves expertise but increases the scope for intellectual divergences; "democracy" improves morale and commitment, but makes lengthy discussions necessary and can prevent decisions getting made at all. We do not have a measure of the overall success of projects, and it is hard to see what such a measure could be. One practical criterion, however, that has some relationship to the idea of "success" is whether or not the project was finished on time.* When the projects studied are classified in this way, a very clear pattern emerges: the largest projects and those at universities were the least likely to be finished on time. It is impossible to distinguish the effects of the two variables because in the sample studied almost all the largest projects (those classified as types G and H) were university ones, and only one of the projects with no connection with a university was not finished on time. However, it seems likely that each contributed something, since within the pure university ones the numbers finishing on time were 4 of the ABD types, 2 of the 5 CEF, and none of the 7 GH. Any number of hypotheses could be devised to explain why this should be so. It seems plausible that the largeness of university projects could be attributed in part to the fact that each project has to be set up from scratch and recruit the workers it needs, and so incorporates within the team (as defined) people to perform tasks that in research institutions are done by permanent staff specialists who do not count as part of the team. Both university habit

* It was not always obvious whether or not a project had finished on time, since original deadlines were sometimes extended and the criterion of completion can vary; in ambiguous cases respondents' own definitions of the situation were taken, and in the last resort I relied on my own judgment of the available information. Ten projects could still not be classified; for 5 there had been no definite deadline, in 3 the research had been broken off prematurely, and in 2 the interviews referred to a programme rather than a single project. Those that broke off prematurely should perhaps be counted in above. They would confirm the general pattern; all were university projects, and in two the breaking off was plainly related to the nature of the division of labour.

or convention and the absence of concurrent other projects to enable economies of scale in the use of staff specialists encourage directors to recruit generalists rather than specialists. Thus the apparent size effect might be in part due to the differences between more and less bureaucratized modes of research organisation. Obviously there are many other characteristics of university research that might help to make it less likely to finish on time, but most have nothing particular to do with team organisation. One that does is whether or not the director(s) had other commitments, and so limited time to spend on the research; only a third of the projects where the directors had teaching commitments were finished on time, while two-thirds or more of those where they had other kinds of commitments or none were. Similarly, projects were less often completed where research assistants were doing higher degrees. (It is of some interest that, although the directors of university projects were much more likely to have no previous experience of empirical research, this certainly did not account for their failure to complete on time: those with no experience more often did so!) Once a large and complex research team has been set up, it presumably creates problems of coordination and communication that do not exist for smaller teams, especially when these can draw on external administrative resources.

Despite the limitations of this study, and the inherent methodological problems of the subject, it seems evident that team organisation, and in particular the nature of the division of labour, has consequences for the outcome of social research. It is to be hoped that further investigation may clarify the relationship and elaborate these points in a more systematic way.

CHAPTER 6

Research Careers and Career Structure

The typical piece of academic empirical sociological research is funded by a grant from some outside body, made to the director, which pays for the employment of one or more junior researchers. Grants are almost invariably for a period of two or three years, though they can often be extended if a fresh application is favourably received. The director usually has a permanent teaching post which does not depend on grants. Thus for the director his basic career structure has no special connection with any one research project, although to complete research successfully will in a general sense further his career; for the research officer or assistant, the two are intimately linked. These junior researchers have to find new jobs when their contracts expire, and cannot afford to wait for the right one to turn up unless they are prepared to fact a period of unemployment; the new job will frequently entail moving house.

Of the 30 research assistants in my sample, 9 had previously been undergraduates and 10 graduate students. None of the graduate students had completed Ph.D.s; some interrupted degree work to take the job, others had completed lower qualifications, not always in sociology (e.g. Dip.Ed., social work course.) Of the remainder, 4 came from previous jobs as research assistant, 2 had held academic jobs outside universities, 3 had held jobs related to the topic of the research (e.g. teachers going on to do educational research) and 2 had other jobs which they regarded as temporary. Typically the research assistant was a young person within 2 or 3 years of graduation.

Of the research officers* in my sample, only 2 had just graduated and 6 had been graduate students. One of the new graduates was doing a Ph.D., and is classified as a research officer only because he succeeded in finding an external sponsor for it who was interested in the results. One of the graduate students was in the same position, and again none of them had completed Ph.D.s. Seven of the research officers had come from previous jobs as research assistant (3) or officer (4), 3 from jobs related to the topic of the research, and 2 from other permanent jobs. There were also 9 whose previous or continuing job was as a lecturer in a university (8) or college of education (1); 6 of these were seconded full-time for short periods,

---

* Here people with the title senior research officer are included.

or were allowed time for formal commitment to someone else's research, and 3 had actually made the career transition to a research post. Thus the research officers were on the whole more senior and experienced than the research assistants, but still a young group; most of those who had not been mature students (of whom there were four) were only in their twenties at the time.

There are two popular beliefs about research careers: that opportunities for a career in research are negligible, and that teaching has higher status than research and so a research career is undesirable. The first suggests that people want to stay in research but cannot do so, at least not without making unreasonable financial sacrifices; the second suggests that people choose not to stay in research, and look for teaching jobs wherever possible. My data can throw some light on the perceptions and conscious motives of the sample in these respects. Firstly, people who wanted to stay in a particular field of research sometimes found it impossible to do so because the funds could not be obtained, or not in time to provide continuity of employment:

"I left [independent research unit] because there was no future in. . .research of the kind I was in. . . I was waiting for an S.S.R.C. grant, but could not let my career depend on that. They got funds after I left. What I really wanted to do was develop a [research topic] unit which had started. We had done four or five projects, and I would have liked to go on binding that up."

This speaker was not a humble research assistant but a senior research worker, and his case was said to be by no means unusual in that unit, which depended almost entirely on specific contracts from outside bodies. Numbers of people who were not to the same extent forced out nonetheless found the insecurity caused by lack of tenure hard to bear:

". . .the present project is for two years, and that's all I can solidly expect. . .but the unit sort of hopes to go on and do other research after this which I could stay for if necessary." J.P.: "Would you prefer to move on to better things?"
"No, I don't think so, not better things, not things I would consider to be better. I have sometimes wondered if I couldn't find something more secure as research goes on in these 2 or 3 year jobs, as I don't want to lecture, but I don't know if there's anything I'd rather do than research, except for the security angle."

104

"I still hanker after a research life. . . I was actually living and learning most then. But the more you learn about sociology the more impossible this research seemed to become. . . I've got a family now and so I can't live dangerously."

The problems hinted at by the latter speaker were made explicit by others:

"One of the reasons in the end why I stopped doing research was that I had three research jobs and every time [one had to move house and lose friends. By the third time I began to feel was the disruption worth it. . .] "

"I had two very short-term contracts, one of 21 and one of 9 months. That interfered considerably with my personal life. With a 21 month contract it wasn't worth buying a house. [If I'd known there'd be a further 9 months it would have been.] ."

As a consequence of this, some of those respondents who were in senior positions, with responsibility within research organisations for hiring junior employees, felt that it was difficult to get appropriate people:

". . .it's aggravating in terms of being able to recruit people, and get good people; in terms of being able to attract men it is probably much more important. Both Angela and Bridget [current research assistants] are waiting to start families. . . There have been people who've stayed on and done more than one project, but at any one point all that one can offer them is work on the particular project."

"For a start, we can't recruit the best on a two year contract without a promise beyond that."
J.P.: "Are they in practice expected to leave at the end?"
"No, the problem is that because you can't guarantee it it restricts the appeal of the post tremendously — you get very few people from university coming to us, though we're on university scales."

"The only way to keep check is to get somebody good to run it, but he may leave because there is no proper career structure . . . There's a shortage of good research workers; people who are good presumably go to universities and lecture and become professors."

All these speakers were from non-university research units; the same problems did not seem to be felt in universities, presumably because they have direct access to the labour supply of new graduates, and can also hold out the inducement of the possibility of career continuation in posts that do not depend on *ad hoc* grants. Two of these speakers also pointed out that in their units, which were quite large and bureaucratized ones, there were limited promotion opportunities at higher levels because there were simply very few senior posts, and no possibility of creating more in recognition of individual merit. One of them left a governmental unit because, having attained the rank of senior research officer in his early thirties, there were only one or two higher posts left to which it was possible for him to aspire. It was also felt to be difficult to move back into the university sector. This was partly because the style of research and publication elsewhere was such that university people tended not to know about it, and these other researchers tended not to belong to university-based invisible colleges. There is also another problem:

> "If you're tied to university scales and are reasonably competent at research you can end up, say, as R.O.2, which is senior lecturer's salary. . . . If you leave, where do you go to? [Other colleges] don't want to know at £3-4000; universities don't want to know if you have been eight years in a purely research institute, because what do you teach — survey methods?"

Thus he suggests, plausibly, that what at one level is a qualification can at another be a disqualifying professional deformation. Why are more senior research posts not available at universities? Presumably because it is customary for much research to be directed by teaching faculty whose time is free to grant-giving bodies, so that these bodies have an obvious interest in encouraging the continuance of the system. One distinguished researcher reported that when he applied to the S.S.R.C. for a grant for a project they refused to pay for him to do it himself, despite the fact that he did not hold a teaching post, and insisted that a research assistant be employed under his supervision instead.*

Researchers who specialise in one particular area are especially vulnerable to shortages of funds. Researchers in general units, who are prepared to turn their hands to anything, can stay in employment

* My suspicion, grounded solely on subjective impressions, is that the attitudes of academics contribute to this. They are reluctant to see established full-time research posts because they are jealous of the occupants, who can do research all the time and so can get more publications and improve their chances of promotion relative to those who also have to spend time on teaching.

but may find that they have to do projects in which they have little
personal interest:

> "I'm paid to do research on contract, and I do a lot of other
> research and have to disguise this. I'm extremely alienated;
> I just want to do research I like rather than what I'm paid to
> do. It's really an impossible position. I think the only answer
> is to have an academic job and manipulate it."

This person, with a very prolific publication record, has now moved
to a senior academic post; there are probably others less competent
and less lucky.

As far as these limited data go, they do suggest that there are
difficulties in establishing a satisfactory career in research outside
universities, or rather that the opportunities are considerably fewer
than the total number of people currently involved in such research
at any one time. The system of short-term grants creates great insecurity, and moves to other kinds of job can be hard. Criteria of
what constitutes a satisfactory career are subjective, although there
are certainly some accepted norms. It seems probable that researchers
in the non-university sector use the university career system as their
reference standard; in comparison to the near-total security and long
automatic salary progression of the lecturer, many other job situations are likely to look inferior. But holders of research posts in
universities have just the same insecurities, and may be even more
likely to have to move house to get a new job than people who work
in units with a programme of research in one area. Do they, however,
actually have difficulty in continuing an academic career?

An analysis of career destinations shows something about the
chances of establishing a research career, and the extent to which
there is a trend to move to teaching posts or out of academic life
altogether. The table below summarizes the immediate occupational
destinations of those who held jobs dependent on university-based
projects.** (It includes the people on projects in the sample whom
I did not interview when those I did interview had given me the
relevant information about them, but excludes anyone who was only
seconded to a project or whose contract, even if a short one, did
not die with that project.)

** There are problems of definition here, which at the margin have
to be resolved arbitrarily. Projects have been classified as university-
based if they were financed by a grant held by someone at a university, or if the researchers were based at a university even if the
research was commissioned by outside sponsors.

Next jobs (of those employed on university-based projects.)

	University teaching	Other teaching*	University research	Other research	Other	N
Research assistants	14	2	17	2	2	37
Research officers	10	4	7	1	1	23

* This was always in other institutions of higher education.

Firstly, the number who did not stay in academic life or research of some kind is negligible; the three people coded "other" consist of one young man who became a graduate student and 2 young women who retired at least temporarily when they had babies. Secondly, a considerable majority remained within the university sector. Of those who did not, 4 did not express any dissatisfaction with this outcome. The comments of one on his disillusion with university are quoted elsewhere; another was making a career in social work and held a post in that field probably regarded as equivalent to a university one; a third person was a married woman whose husband moved to another university and she took a Polytechnic lectureship, but I think would really have preferred a university post. The last person made no comments. The 4 other people whom I interviewed made this sort of comment:

J.P. "What is this job you've got?"

"It's at [college of technology], lecturer in sociology. . . ."

J.P. "Are you really pleased with that, or is that just the job you happened to get?"

"I applied for quite a lot of university jobs, but I didn't even get interviewed; this was the only non-university job advertised which fitted my special interests. So in one sense I'm very pleased; on the other hand it's not very high status. . .but the important thing is, if one's got one's own course and its fairly successful, that's fairly strong grounds to apply elsewhere."

In subsequent job changes two of those who did not express dissatisfaction and one of those who did has moved to a university job, two in teaching and one (the married woman) in part-time research. No job changes were mentioned in the other direction. It may have some significance that 90% of the men stayed in universities, but only 50% of the women (with those who left the labour market omitted); moreover half the men, but only 3 of these 16 women,

got university teaching posts.* The scanty evidence on sex discrimination is discussed in Chapter 7; these figures do suggest
that some sex-related social process is relevant, though the numbers
are very small. (There is no difference in the proportions going on
to teaching and to research.)

Was there any indication that people were being forced out of
research against their wills by the state of the labour market? The
short answer is: no. Inspection of the interviews with all those who
moved on to university teaching jobs reveals only one person who
said that he would have preferred to stay in research. He, moreover,
was not expressing a general preference for research as such;
he held a departmental research assistantship with a fixed term,
and would have liked to retain it longer in order to remain full time
on the project so that he could give it all instead of only part of his
attention. Two people said that they had always intended the research
job to be a preliminary to a teaching career, and most of the others
treated the move as an obvious one to make and not requiring any
special explanation. In some cases, anyway, the transition entailed
a shift of emphasis rather than a complete change, because they
moved from a research job where they had done some teaching to a
teaching job where they continued voluntarily with the research.

There was also very little indication that holding research jobs
weakened career chances in that it was difficult to move from research into teaching. Inspection of the interviews with all those who
moved on to research jobs revealed only 3 who might have preferred a teaching job: one said that he would have preferred to be in
a university, without specifying whether he meant teaching or research; another said there were only a limited number of jobs available when he needed one, and has subsequently moved to a university
lectureship; the third implied indirectly that he needed more research experience, given that his first degree was not in sociology,
before he could apply for a teaching job – and he too has now got
a lectureship. Several others specifically said that they preferred
research or didn't want to be lecturers; two were undecided whether
they really wanted to research or teach, but when faced with a
choice of jobs had, at least this time, chosen another one in research.

But perhaps there were career problems in the sense that those

* This effect is not due to there being a higher proportion of women
among the lower-ranking research assistants; as the table shows, a
higher proportion of research assistants stayed in university life, and
moreover the sex differential holds among research assistants alone.

people who moved to further research jobs were not bettering themselves, or did not have the same promotion opportunities? Of the 19
people interviewed in this category, the next jobs of 11 appeared to
be a clear step up: i.e. the job was research officer if they had been a
research assistant, senior research officer if they had been a research
officer. Of the remaining 8, 5 remained as research officers or assistants and one became a research fellow; for 5 this next post seemed
in content to represent a reasonable career progression, and for the
sixth, who was a bit older, it was the expected pattern at that stage.
This leaves 2 about whose careers there is some doubt. One was a
married woman who took the only job she could get in the area
where her husband was based, and felt that her position was being
exploited. She has subsequently got a lectureship. The other was a
single woman who did not want to lecture; she has experienced
difficulty in finding research jobs, and the ones she has found do
not seem to constitute a career progression. She did not appear very
career-oriented, though very much committed to research, and complained only about the lack of security.

The general pattern, therefore, did not seem to be one in which
there was an objective lack of career opportunities of the kind that
people wanted; most people found broadly what they wanted, and
for those who did not the reasons often lay in their personal circumstances rather than the state of the labour market. Thus it seems
probable that the sense of lack of career structure is due to the un-
predictability of the particular opportunities that will be available
to an individual when his contract expires, and the general insecurity
caused by lack of tenure. But most of the people I interviewed were
young; what will happen to them later on? The structural framework
of social research in this country is such that there are relatively few
senior positions available in full-time research either on a permanent
basis in a unit or on *ad hoc* grants. Perhaps some of them will
experience difficulties in staying in research; of the 19 researchers
mentioned above, 6 had got teaching posts by the time I interviewed
them. To the extent that an eventual teaching career is seen as normal,
people are less likely to form expectations in the light of which an
absence of research opportunities is experienced as deprivation.

It seems of some interest, against the background of this discussion, to summarise the total pattern of job changes on which
there is information.

Directions of job changes

A.

From university* to university	90
From non-university to university:	18
From non-university to non-university:	14
From university to non-university:	10

* This includes being a student, jobs on university-based projects, and university teaching posts.

B.**

From research to teaching:	33
From research to research:	35
From teaching to research:	10

** Here changes from or to being a student, or holding a job in neither teaching nor research, are omitted.

The figures in this table are the sum of all those cases on which I had enough information for classification, whether or not the person concerned was interviewed. It excludes those who returned to jobs from which they had been seconded. The changes counted are only those to and from the job on the project with which the interview was concerned.

Changes to, or within, universities very much outnumber those out of the university sector. Moreover, of the 10 people who moved out of the universities 4 also appear higher up the table because they moved back again, and another has moved back subsequently; as was reported earlier in the chapter, of those who moved out of universities, about half were dissatisfied with the move. Of the 18 who moved into the universities, 3 moved out again; 2 of these in subsequent job changes have come back, and the third is one of the dissatisfied ones. Thus there seem to be a few marginal people who have some difficulty in establishing a university career, a few who choose not to do so, and a large majority who want to and have succeeded so far. The people who experienced difficulties all come from relatively unorthodox backgrounds: they were mature students, had first jobs in other fields, or first jobs abroad. (Others, however, with the same characteristics were among those successful.)

The table also shows that moves to teaching from research are far more common than moves in the opposite direction; this trend is even more marked if subsequent job changes are also taken into account, for of the 11 known subsequent changes 7 were of people shown in the table as moving from research to research moving from that research job into a university teaching post. (Only one of them was a move in the other direction, and that was a married woman moving from non-university teaching to part-time university research.) Of the 10 people shown as moving from teaching to research 5 have moved back again, and one has not yet found his next job. (Another one originally intended to do so, but found he liked it and had a permanent position and so stayed.) Apart from this, none of those who moved from research to teaching are known to have moved back again. The nature of the system is such that one cannot know quite what meaning to attach to this flow. It cannot be taken to reveal a deep love of teaching as such, which few people expressed; nor can it be taken to show dislike of research, since most people were moving to posts where they could be expected to do some research, though not necessarily empirical. (A number did express disillusion with their empirical research experience.) However, in the great majority of cases the move from research to teaching was a move from short-term contracts to virtually permanent tenure, and this probably contributes to the common perception of a move from research to teaching as a promotion. Once again, at any rate, there appears to have been no lack of opportunities.

It would be rash to generalise from these figures. Most of the job moves to which they refer took place in the late 1960s, when sociology was expanding fast but the new cohorts of graduates produced by this expansion were only beginning to come onto the labour market. It is very possible that the experiences of the generation interviewed will turn out to have been atypical. Nonetheless, these experiences as recorded do indicate that at that period it was not very difficult to make career progress within research to teaching. They also show that, in the sample interviewed, major flows were into and within the university sector and from research into teaching. But this career progress for the individuals could only be achieved at the cost, in most cases, of geographical moves likely to disrupt their research, and the flow into teaching makes it probable that continuity of experience in research would be hard to maintain.

CHAPTER 7

Private Lives and Projects

The individuals who take part in research projects have lives of which the research is only one part, though often an important one. In order to understand what happens in the research context, the ways in which the research experience is related to other aspects of their lives must be taken into account. This chapter, therefore, is concerned with the consequences of participants' private lives for the research process. The next chapter, by a somewhat artificial separation, is concerned with the consequences of the research process for private lives; in reality the influences are reciprocal. The distinction between 'private life' and research is also artificial, but analytically convenient; everything other than the formal organisation and intellectual content of the research is covered by the term 'private life', which is a sort of shorthand for factors that textbooks on research methods do not usually mention.

The first aspects of private lives to be considered are those that led researchers to become involved in that particular project in the first place. The researchers either initiated the project themselves, or were recruited to it or commissioned to undertake it by someone else. The public and official reasons for research involvement are normally expected to be to do with intellectual interest in the topic, but these were by no means the only reasons actually mentioned.

Those people who had initiated their own research, and who were not employed on it as a job, most commonly saw the topic chosen as one that fitted into their intellectual career, and had chosen it for that reason; the same held for Ph.D.s, and to a lesser extent for those whose "own" research it was although they had not themselves initiated it. (These were all academics in teaching posts who had been invited, or taken the opportunity, to attach themselves to a research project started by a colleague.) Among those, however, for whom the research constituted a job, or who had been commissioned to undertake it, only 27% had chosen the topic because it arose from their intellectual careers; nearly half (44%) had an *ad hoc* interest in the topic, while nearly a third (29%) worked on that topic primarily because they wanted the job, had chosen arbitrarily, or had had no choice because the project was one that their permanent jobs required them to undertake. If those for whom the research formed part of an intellectual career are combined with those for whom its interest was *ad hoc*, to make up a group of all those for whom

113

interest in the topic was a dominant reason for choosing it, we see that people are increasingly likely to fall into this group as the research is more their own. This is hardly a surprising finding; the interesting aspect to explore is how it came about that some people got involved in research without interest in the topic being the most important factor.

First, however, we can say a little more about the nature of the interest that initiators had in their topics, since it was not always exclusively academic. The topics were classified in terms of the extent to which they were autobiographical or arose from the researchers' own experience. For 71% of the researchers I saw there was nothing personal about the topic; this proportion was reduced to 50% among those who had initiated their own research and were not Ph.D. students. In a very small number of cases the research was truly autobiographical in spirit; more commonly the interest was less personal, although it still arose from initially non-academic interests. In this category were a number of university researchers who had been inspired by the events of the late sixties to investigate student unrest and its causes. Others had initially become involved in an occupational group because a close relative belonged to it. In a few cases I had assumed that a topic must have had a deep autobiographical meaning for the researcher but it turned out that I was wrong, at least on their account of the matter — for example:

"I decided I really ought to work for the Ph.D. and I looked for an area of sociology . . . where there was a significant sociological issue or area, and where because of my privileged access to data I could make a major contribution and, wrongly, I assumed that I had greater access to [institution] than other sociologists . . . ."

J.P. "From what you have said, it sounds as though it wasn't very autobiographical the way you started on the research, as one might have expected that it would be."

"There was very little personal development in it. People were registering their Ph.D.s and I had dropped my M.A. research . . . . I was perhaps trying to rid myself of an aspect of my past by studying it . . . . But had [somebody] come down with a scheme on [other topic] large enough, I could well have registered that."

Even where the topic could not be classified as relating to the researcher's own life experience, people quite often mentioned that they had been drawn to it (and to sociology in general) by their political interests as much as by purely academic ones. For instance

". . . socialists in particular were concerned about [economic situation of deprived group], so it was because of my political interests that I first decided to look at [them]."

"I was influenced by the then current New Left muck-raking tradition of C. Wright Mills, *Power Elite* stuff, and suppose all that I wanted to do was a sort of revelation of the power structure of our society."

J.P. "Was it influenced by the political climate?"

"Of course it was. . . . I was a socialist at school, a member of the L.P.Y.S. [Labour Party Young Socialists] and that is one good reason why I might be interested in work, since I had some nebulous idea of work's importance in Marxist circles . . . . I was off and on a member of I.S. [International Socialists], that was a positive political commitment when an occasional idea about the self activity of the working class could be transferred into an idea about workers. . . . As far as I was aware, a conscious idea of looking at the work place [I thought it was important so I should look at it.]"

These quotations demonstrate the ways in which political attitudes and interests, sometimes of a very vague nature, could lead people into particular research areas. Sometimes the interests arose independently, but there were a few cases where charismatic teachers of sociology with strong political views had influenced their students to perceive sociology in terms of its political implications and to select their research topics accordingly. It will surprise nobody that all the political views mentioned were left wing; the reasons for this have been discussed by various writers and will not be pursued here.

Another kind of personal factor influencing the choice of research topic was perceived career needs, particularly among those in teaching jobs who undertook commissioned research or were drawn into projects started by senior colleagues. The quotation on page 114 illustrates the way in which felt pressure to do research on *something* could in practice lead to one particular topic, though which one it was could be almost accidental. There were sometimes, however, much more specific pressures:

"I was an untenured member of staff, needing to do some research relevant to the needs of the department. . . . I'd been asked to do several other things in this department and refused."

J.P. "Did you not think of doing some research of your own?"

"No, the research of my own was being done primarily about [other field], but this was regarded by the department

as nothing to do with their interests . . . it was necessary to be
seen doing something relevant to the department's interests."

"Thinking back on the interview, something almost
happened without us noticing. We were both new members of
staff in the department and in no sense were pressures put on
us to do this research, but the latent structure of the situation
was such that there was indirect and in an unexpected way a
very strong pressure to be keen. . . . [The Professor] obviously
wanted to get people involved in a piece of research. The
department and [university] would be judged by the quality
of their research — I guess this was in his mind. . . . He has this
tremendous charisma, and if you respond to that. . . . And
also I think at the time one rather got the impression that he
would take some part in it himself."

I did not interview senior members of the departments concerned to
ask about their perceptions of the situations of these junior members,
but even if their accounts had been different it is still relevant that
their juniors perceived it in this way and consequently took on these
research projects, both of which were commissioned by outside
bodies. (Both projects ran into considerable difficulties: in one case
they were anticipated and part of the reason why the researcher
would have preferred not to do it; in the other they were not foreseen, but he felt that he would have foreseen them had he not been
carried away by the situation, and to some extent the difficulties
arose from taking on research in which he did not have a strong
personal interest at an inappropriate career stage.) These two cases
were not typical, and where there were departmental pressures
they could be much milder, or at any rate less successful, as in this
next case, where the pressure to do some research was effective but
hints on topics were not taken:

"our revered leader had been making noises about the de-
sirability of getting research going. . . . There was a certain
amount of gentle professorial pressure being put on. . . .
Neither Bert nor I felt in the least inclined to collaborate with
[Professor], so when we started thinking about [research
topic] over the next few weeks one of the things at the back
of our minds was that neither of us had sizeable research
commitments at the time. . . ."

In another project on which there is data the research topic appears
to have been chosen by a departmental research committee, and
members of the department who did not wish to take part had to

opt out. A junior lecturer who came to play a key role, though rather vague about how he got involved, obviously experienced at least some pressure to take part in a project to which his existing interests were relevant. In another case an established academic moving to head a different department took with him a research student protégé to become an assistant lecturer, and the assistant lecturer became involved in the department head's research project, and here the two parties concerned report different perceptions of how this came about. The assistant lecturer speaks first:

> "My official title was assistant lecturer . . . and it was simply expected that I would contribute assistance in the research. It was not part of my contract of employment . . . ."
> J.P. "It was not part of your contract, but was it part of the informal understandings?"
> "It emerged . . . Things emerged, developed. indeed it only emerged in the course of the year that I was going to be involved at all."

The head of department's version is this:

> ". . . I invited Colin to go to [university] and I think the job — was he appointed lecturer in the first instance? Yes, he was. . . ."
> J.P. "Was this on the understanding that he would take part in the research?"
> "No, certainly not. I would certainly not have brought any pressure to bear on him. . . . Almost certainly in the context of the desirability of him getting a Ph.D, and I think he must have expressed interest in doing something in this area. I'm pretty certain that the desire to join it derived from the research interest established while at [previous university]."

This was another case where the junior person was strongly influenced by the charisma of the senior, although here he didn't have any particular objection to the research and so there was no feeling of having been brought into it against his will; the general impression he conveyed was of a malleable young man who was prepared to do whatever seemed to be expected of him. (Once again, however, problems arose later connected with the manner in which he became involved; the lack of formal definition of roles made responsibilities unclear, and difficulties followed.)

Pressures from seniors were not the only way in which career needs could influence the choice of research topics. The following quotation shows how a relatively senior academic could take up a

117

commission partly because it provided career opportunities:

> "I saw in this the opportunity to make what I felt might
> be a distinct sociological contribution to the work of [unit
> based on another discipline] . . . . The mere fact that this was
> a very important stage in my personal career and that close
> association with them gave me independence from the [other
> discipline] that I had not previously had led me to attach
> more importance to it than I might otherwise have done [we
> built up virtually independent teams] ."

Each of the cases cited has its idiosyncracies; cumulatively they indicate that even where a topic is chosen quite freely the reasons for
the choice may be not entirely academic ones, and that it is by no
means unknown for there to be general or *ad hoc* pressures on academics to do research into particular topics or fields, or reasons why
they should decide to do so, which relate to their personal rather
than intellectual lives.

We now return to the group for whom the research was not their
own, but who had jobs working on projects initiated by other people;
how did they come to be working on those particular topics? Numbers of people have some commitment to the idea of a career in
sociology and find that a research job is the only, or the most appropriate, opening available; for them it would be lucky if it turned
out that the research jobs open when they started looking for one
included even one that fitted well into their intellectual career, let
alone a choice. Two married women chose jobs within the constraints of their husbands' career needs; they looked for something
suitable in the geographical area to which his new job was taking
them, and found research jobs which were reasonably appropriate.
Married men too experienced constraints, though of a different kind:

> "I'd done my first degree and the problem then was I
> couldn't do an ordinary M.A. or Ph.D. because my wife was
> pregnant and I had to get a bit of money and this job seemed
> quite an interesting one and gave quite a reasonable salary."

> "[. . . I wanted an academic job but I was just married and
> I wanted money and therefore the idea of doing a doctorate
> wasn't particularly attractive. . . .] So I was looking for a job
> which would permit me to do research but pay me more than
> a grant and [project] did attract me because it paid more."

(However, my data do *not* show that those who were married and had
children had in general more often joined the research simply because

118

they wanted the job; marital status is probably confused with age, but numbers are not sufficient to hold age constant.)

Obviously some people needed jobs badly irrespective of their marital situations:

"I only got a 2.2 – I couldn't do an M.A. or a Ph.D. which I wanted to do. My only chance of a job in academic life was a research project . . . . I joined the project because I wanted a job, not because I was interested in the sociology of [topic] . . . ."

"I'd been three years there and decided at a quite late date in the year I came here that the time had come to move, and I wanted to get out pretty quick because [it] was a rather unstable institution and I didn't like the things that were going on internally . . . and then it was a question of looking round for a job . . . . I suppose I arrived because I was offered the possibility of employment rather than having a burning desire . . . ."

In these two cases, and this was fairly typical, the people concerned needed a job and wanted it to be in academic research, but the particular topics they ended up working on were more or less accidental; they became to some extent interested in them by the fact of working on them, but it was in no sense a personal intellectual commitment. Some research assistants seem to have fallen into jobs in research at all, let alone on that particular project, in a more or less accidental way, with very little sense of where they were going:

"I wanted to do research, but I wasn't strongly committed to the idea, it was about the only thing I felt I wanted to do. I didn't want to go into industry, I didn't want to teach, so I felt it was probably the best thing I could do . . . ."

J.P. "How was it that you were recruited to the project? Did you reply to an advertisement, or what?"
"I don't know, actually. It was a surprise to me, actually. I wasn't a very committed sociologist or student. They must have thought I had something – I didn't even get a good degree! . . . They knew I was looking for a job . . .   they simply offered it to me . . . . I didn't even know how long the job was going to last, but I hadn't got another and beggars can't be choosers so I took it. I had a feeling at the time that I was just going to interview in accordance with instructions."

(In fact this man had the role of a responsible research officer with considerable independence, and performed it very satisfactorily).
Here is another case, where he starts by referring to a previous job:

"I don't know how honest to be with you about my own . . .
I was . . . I never looked on myself as a sociologist; I suppose
I do to some extent now, I suppose I have a certain amount
of commitment to sociology now, but certainly when I joined
the [previous] study and went to [second university] I didn't
think that I would remain as any kind of professional in sociology.
   . . . When I left university I didn't know what I was going to
do, except that I'd decided on the one thing I wasn't going to,
and that was work in any kind of commercial organisation if I
could avoid it . . . . I suppose I looked on the [previous] thing
as quite good fun and a way of making some bread while I
sorted myself out. I did become quite interested . . . .
[Director] was determined that I should become a sociologist
and kept on saying 'why don't you get yourself a teaching job?'
or 'do a master's' — then he suggested I try and find some kind
of research job [and write to director of subsequent project] ."

(This researcher too appeared to do both jobs very satisfactorily).
   In cases like those of the juniors quoted; the seniors who appointed
them sometimes mentioned reasons to do with their interests and
special qualifications for choosing them for the jobs, but these
tended to be that they could make a distinctive contribution to a
planned division of labour because they had a back-ground in another
discipline, or competence in an area of sociology that would provide
another perspective on the topic; thus their interests, even when
used as a criterion of choice, were not necessarily defined as closely
related to the central core of the project. One might speculate that
both parties were taking risks of future trouble when they entered
into an employment relationship on this basis; more about that later.
   However, the situation was not always so dark; there were some
cases where people had been strongly attracted by the particular
subject of the research, and the fact that they had not themselves
initiated it was relatively unimportant. This was, of course, particularly likely to be true where individuals had been personally invited to join a project by someone who knew of their interests, and
was more likely to occur at the director or research officer than at
the research assistant level; for 44% of them, but only 19% of the
research assistants, did interest in the topic appear to be the prime
reason for taking the job. (Research assistants were particularly likely
to have been interested in something other than the topic — usually

120

the opportunity of getting into sociology or research irrespective of the topic, or working with that director or in that department.) This impression is confirmed if we look at the ways in which people were recruited to the jobs. Of the 82 relevant people, 37% were recruited by personal contact, 21% through a referral from some third person, and 43% by advertisement*; the topic fitted into an intellectual career for nearly twice as many of those recruited by personal contact or referral, and had been "chosen" primarily because a job was wanted by twice as many of those recruited by advertisement. (But it must be noted that there are still quite high proportions with some interest in the topic in all groups.)

We have seen that there are a variety of ways in which private lives, broadly defined, can affect the research topics that people end up working on: they can choose topics that arise out of their personal experience, or spring primarily from extra-academic political interests; particular topics can be taken up because of career pressures, in combination with other accidental circumstances, or because they provided the only available job of the type wanted. To say this is partly to explain why people were interested in certain topics, and partly to explain why they worked on them without being especially interested in them. (I have not attempted to discuss how it was that people for whom the topic fitted into an intellectual career had come to have that kind of intellectual career; some of them told me about this, and again non-academic factors had played some role). The structure of the academic labour market is such that it is predictable that a significant proportion of those employed in research jobs at junior levels will not have a personal intellectual commitment to the topic on which they are working, and this probably contributes to some of the common problems of sociological research teams.

Purely personal and domestic factors are also relevant to other phases of the research; here we are concerned with private lives primarily in the sense of family roles.** Most junior research workers are in their twenties, and thus at a stage in their life cycle when the typical pattern is one of courtship, marriage and the birth of first children; it is these junior researchers who, in the conventional

* There were 3 or 4 cases where employer or employee got directly in touch with the other without there having been any prior contact or an advertisement. These have been counted in the "advertisement" category, since there was no personal relationship.

** Initially I attempted to classify all references to private lives in this sense (the meaning of which will be clarified by the examples cited below) into four categories: private life helped the research, private division of labour, are most likely to be required to take part in intensive fieldwork, and therefore to be exposed to conflicts between rival demands on their time. Married women, especially with children, are more likely than men to experience these conflicts. Among those I interviewed, 44% of the women but only 12% of the men were known to be single, which suggests one of the consequences of this. Items codable under the heading of "private lives" occurred less often for the single. Another variable related to the frequency of such items is the mode of data collection used in the research: depth interviews, observation and participant observation go with many references to private lives, documentary, institutional and survey research with fewer.

As the earlier part of this chapter showed, research topics and useful contacts could come from people's private lives, which also sometimes provided motives for taking particular jobs. A related theme is that of the spouse whose influence or encouragement helped the work's completion:

> "I started writing it up because Jane had got a job as a research assistant and it just affected me personally. . . . I got the Redbrick job without having finished it when the Redbrick work situation was very favourable, and Jane pushed me. I probably wouldn't have done it if I wasn't married."

A number of spouses, however, gave more concrete help; they actually did some of the work themselves. In community participant observation this could hardly be avoided, since simply by living there both spouses were participating; help, however, could go well beyond this, as when a very attractive wife smoothed relationships with key

life hindered the research, private life was helped by the research, private life was hindered by the research. I made some cross-tabulations on this basis; however, I am extremely doubtful whether the nature of the data is such that the results are meaningful. Some respondents mentioned these matters very much in passing, and made it clear that they were minor; it is probably accidental that other comparable respondents happened not to think similar things worth mentioning at all. The technique of questioning was not uniform: I probed any such reference that sounded significant, since this was one of the areas that I was interested in, but I only normally introduced the subject myself when the respondent was involved in fieldwork or meetings that entailed being away from home outside normal working hours, or the research (as in participant observation) was inherently likely to involve other members of the family in some way. Another problem was that potential items under these headings were quite often mentioned by colleagues rather than by the person concerned, and it was not clear what status could legitimately be given to these mentions. Most of the analysis, therefore, continues to be qualitative.

informants, or another wife acquired relevant information through her job. One teacher wife provided useful background data for her husband's research by setting appropriate essay topics for the children she taught to write on. A girlfriend of appropriate background proved useful in another project as a deliberately planted observer on the local organisation of a political party to which the researchers were known not to be sympathetic. Several wives were also brought in at later stages to help with typing, routine statistical tests, or hand counting of data when a computer was not available. In only two cases were husbands reported to have helped with wives' research. In the first case his position in another academic field proved useful in fending off a threat of plagiarism of research results by a member of a client group. In the second case he went with his wife on a few occasions to meetings of predominantly male groups which she was attending as a participant observer. (She remarked that they then talked only to him.) It goes without saying that almost all these instances of help were unpaid. Presumably husbands were not so much unhelpful by temperament as normally fully occupied with their own careers — and anyway there were fewer of them in the sample.

Social research is perhaps only typical of a wider range of occupations in that it often in effect makes use of a married couple as a team when only one spouse (normally the husband) is being paid for participation. Whatever their norms may be, it seems evident that conjugal roles among sociologists are such that wives follow and support their husbands' careers in the conventional way. My information on spouses was often incomplete and sometimes non-existent, but from what there is a pattern emerges. Only 21% of the married men had wives with definite careers, although as many again had jobs of some sort, and none of those in employment was reported also to have young children. There were only 3 cases where wives really had careers on the same basis as their husbands. The men were thus fairly free to pursue their careers, and numbers of references were made to wives' preparedness to move anywhere, capacity to find a job wherever their husbands' careers took them, and so on. Among the married women in my sample 54% were known to have no children. More significant is that of the 9 married women for whom I had information on husband's occupation 8 had husbands in academic life. This says something about the conditions under which it is normally practical for married women to work in research; an academic occupation provides both flexibility of timetable to fit the demands of research, and an understanding of research needs — as well as simply ensuring that one lives somewhere where research

123

is likely to be going on. It is interesting that the only husband not in an academic occupation caused difficulties for the research, and was divorced shortly afterwards.

Although a systematic comparison of men and women with similar characteristics cannot be made, it seems worth saying a little here about the special career problems of the women. Three of them thought or knew that they had experienced some sort of sexist discrimination:

"... I had great difficulty in getting a job [on leaving project] ... I still have a letter on file saying 'you're the best qualified candidate, but I don't think it's your cup of tea because all the students are men!' I went [there] in the end on a temporary lectureship which was reviewed at the end of the year [and made permanent.]"

"I fairly enjoyed teaching and would have liked to go on teaching, but I'm not of the calibre, or because I'm not young and male."
J.P. "Is that how you think about yourself, or how other people do?"
"Probably the way I think of me. . . . But I think people tend to forget about you because you are different from other people. I'm just not the same sort of. . . ."

"[on previous project] my consciousness was not raised. I think they treated me very badly . . . because I was a woman . . . I was given incredible dogsbody tasks to do . . . I did millions of chi squareds . . . ."
J.P. "Were you like that on [this] project?"
"No, because I was very aggressive . . . I didn't want another bum project on my credentials so I fought for statistical analyses etc. I knew more statistics than Alec and I could converse with Barry and also with Charles because I had a degree in sociology. I think I combined the qualities that Barry and Charles did not feel that secure about. I think at [previous project] the bosses felt professionally more secure. Barry and Charles were given a project at a ridiculously early age."

Despite their difficulties, and in the case of the first two speakers there were severe domestic constraints on the range of jobs they were prepared to consider, all these women had established quite respectable sociological careers. Not all the women interviewed wanted definite careers, or had originally planned anything of the sort even if they ended up with one. This woman took an extreme position, that probably owed more to youth culture or personality than to social norms about woman's place:

> "I don't see my life in career terms; I don't see myself as eligible for university even if I get the M.Sc. . . . I don't somehow see myself wafted into the higher levels of university life, and I don't think that's where I want to be anyway . . . I think I probably want to stay at home and breed Dalmatians and grow roses. We're looking for a small farm, and if we find one we might start a smallholding . . . [on the understanding with husband that she can do something now that may fail and he may want to do the same later]."

More typical were some married women who had followed their husband's career, taking the most interesting jobs they could find where his career took them, giving up work when they had a baby, and planning to take on at least part-time work when the baby was a bit older. Women of this type, however, by definition tended not to come up often in my sample. It was surprising to me to find that there were some older women with very distinguished careers, which I had always assumed to be planned, who did not themselves perceive them in that light:

> "I had always had the idea that one should be able to work and have a family, but in my hierarchy of values it was probably more important to marry and have the family than the career bit . . . So I've done a variety of jobs that don't perhaps make a career, there wasn't a plan in my mind . . . Always, given the choice between family and job, family came first; I don't think they thought so, but it did really."

> "I didn't ever envisage myself having a career. . . . I was married and I had a husband in [university town] and I saw myself as eventually having a family and being a good housewife, and for a long time everything that happened was just an odd happening . . . so it was not until I came to [other university town, when husband moved] that I really faced up to the fact that, whether I wanted it or not, now I really had a career . . . ."
> J.P. "It's fascinating, isn't it, how things look purposive retrospectively."
> "It didn't feel purposive at all at the time. An academic career —I didn't think I was good enough for an academic career . . .

125

My standards of an academic were [world-famous female academic] who had supervised me . . ."

The first woman quoted did have children, and the second did not; perhaps if the second *had*, she would just have been a housewife. Those younger women who had young children must have had practical problems, but when they held lectureships these do not seem to have been salient enough to get mentioned. The one female research assistant with small children had considerable difficulties, especially as her husband was earning very little at the time, as did a divorced research officer with somewhat older children. It is not surprising that few women at that stage in the family cycle were among the fieldworkers. My broad impression of the situation of the women is that, insofar as it differed from that of the men, this was due more to conventional conjugal roles and the practical problems of running a dual career family than to active discrimination against them. The lack of deliberate career planning was by no means exclusive to women, though a higher proportion of them than of the men claimed or appeared to have had no plan at all; single women alone were more like the men.

Returning now to the problems for both sexes raised by the conflict over uses of time, one respondent commented:

"One of the problems there – we lived so far apart, and we both had young families. We were all driven into home-centredness very early. It was quite an important element in the project that we were all young family men and quite hard up, having very, very little time, and not having a strong enough personal thing to overcome all those constraints."

Several women had problems arising from their domestic roles, for example:

". . . I had trouble with girls looking after the children; the one I had at the time got pregnant and decided to get married and leave . . . . I didn't turn up at the office until 9.30 or 10.00 in the morning because my baby-sitter didn't come until about 9.00, and I left to pick up my child from nursery school around 4.00 . . . ."

This woman found that her male colleague complained she was doing less work than him, although she could claim to make it up in other ways, and this led to bad relationships within the team. However, such difficulties were by no means exclusive to women. A man with three children, engaged in a project with an element of participant observation of a work situation, said:

> "What I didn't do but would have attempted to do if I'd
> been single . . . if I'd had a different status myself, I'd have
> investigated [another aspect of subjects' situation], but
> since I had the wrong sort of status, and didn't have the right
> sort of time either, being married with children, so I didn't
> do that either. . . so that meant I didn't spend a lot of
> time at their homes."

Another factor that in a few cases took time from the research was
illness, physical or mental. In one of these cases colleagues suspected
a man of suffering psychosomatically when the research situation
was stressful or made it convenient, and there were two cases of
"breakdowns" which appear to have been precipitated by research
events. Other illnesses had no such relation, but caused very similar
inconveniences and delays.

There were several ways in which roles from private life could get
mixed up with research roles, and this could cause problems for the
research;

> "I became very involved with, and identified with, the
> [institution] staff, and I got some sort of social work kick
> out of interviewing them, because I used to interview them,
> some of them, in very open-ended cathartic interviews. . . .
> I used to go back and see people when I was going about.
> When I was in Birmingham I used to spend time drinking
> with one set of institution staff, which gave me some
> support. It made me a bit inhibited about interviewing the
> [inmates]. I felt somehow that having become friendly
> with the staff to interview a whole lot of inmates about
> what the staff did, which was frequently very terrible, was
> difficult, so what is lacking is much interview material from
> the inmates."

This researcher eventually married one of the staff met in this way.
Although mixing socially with the staff obviously was in some ways
useful to the research, the account above makes it clear that this was
at the expense of doing other things that might have been equally or
more useful to its substantive conclusions, though probably not so
functional for the researcher's psychological survival in a fairly stressful situation. Another instance, of a rather different kind of role
conflict, was one where the same man was involved almost as a non-
working director in the initiation of a research project, and then subsequently found himself involved as one of the clients for whom the

127

research was being done. His position need not inherently have been difficult, but it became so when acute conflict arose between the researcher and the client group, and one strand in the conflict was the issue of whether the study should be treated as an ordinary academic one or as one done strictly for the clients' internal use, as these comments show:

> J.P. "Have you experienced any tension between your roles. . .?"
> "Yes, I have throughout, because as [an academic] I was prepared for John Bates to do exactly what his research dictated, that seemed the only way to do it. But, on the other hand, as [member of client group] I had to try and discuss it with [other members] who thought he was muckraking, and had to try and undo some of his personal gaffes with people, and I was continually saying that to publish the research report would not harm anyone when I was beginning to have considerable doubts myself."

This was a fairly unusual situation; a commoner one, to be expected in mixed teams of young people, arose when there were love affairs within research teams. Some of these resulted in marriage. Affairs were not necessarily disruptive, but they certainly could be, whether or not they were happy and smooth running. It may not be co-incidental that the two which were reported to have caused difficulties were ones between couples whom the team's organisation did not define as equals. In one case the problems seemed to arise more from the breaking up of the affair than from its inconsistency with research roles, though there are hints elsewhere that it might have exacerbated other problems:

> "Sally and I went out together for quite a long time, six months after the research began, and that more or less broke up during 1970 and was one of my reasons for going to [other town], and this did cause terrific ructions, but not for long I suppose. . . It's not that it has been different ever since, we are extremely close friends now, but for doing research to-gether we now know each other too well, we know each other's weaknesses and one has to have an extraordinary amount of self-control not to exploit this now and then. . . . Things became very good after I was in [other town] and she took up with someone else."

Both these research projects had dragged on long after the original deadlines, and although each had had many other sources of difficulty the affairs and their consequences contributed their bit to the delays.

These examples lead into another general area, that of social relationships within research teams. When I was interviewing team members I always asked what social relations beyond those necessary for working together were like, because I felt that there was reason to believe that these personal relationships have consequences for the manner in which research roles are played; the data bear out this belief. For the moment I am concerned only with the occasions when respondents reported that personal relations had in some way affected the progress of the research; this to some extent entails making an artificial separation, since in reality no clear line can be drawn between the "social" and the "work" relationships. Even where it perhaps can the influence is reciprocal, as some of the examples will show. For instance:

"When we did have contact with Henry it tended to reflect the phase of the research relationship. If the relationship was good, and we were speaking to each other, which we didn't do all the time, we could have trivial social relationships; if the research was not going well, he would sit in a corner and say nothing, well he wouldn't get invited."
Wife: "I wouldn't say that socially the research project was a great success!"

Another member of the same team commented on this and the general atmosphere of which it was part:

"At that time Henry fell out with Jim because they quarrelled about who should do this piece of work, and they didn't speak to each other for a long time, which made a pretty awful atmosphere, and Henry had to personally work with Tom, [a senior team member] on occasions, which he absolutely hated, and gather sorts of information which he thought useless anyway. . . . it involved a lot of really boring work in coding stuff and there were a lot of arguments between Henry and Tom over how this work should be actually carried out, and he thought a lot of it was below his dignity and there was some most godawful rows he had with him. . . in the end Tom thought he'd better get this sort of thing sorted out and he did in fact tell Henry that he thought he ought to resign, at which point we closed ranks. . . ."

In this team every member felt some personal incompatibility with at least one other member, and what might in another setting have been minor irritations were fed by and reinforced dissatisfactions with the conduct of the research. All of them regarded it as a bad experience, and it seems surprising that publication was reached more or less at the time planned; however, not all members of the team participated equally in the writing, and some at least regarded what they had produced as unsatisfactory.

In another project on which there were at least sometimes bad relationships this seemed mainly attributable to aspects of the work situation:

> "We used to have these extremely unpleasant research meetings. You can't know why they were so unpleasant, the people concerned basically liked each other; if any dislike finally grew up, I think it was as a product of the unpleasantness of the research, not independent. . . there were awful slack periods, you do the bloody questionnaire then you wait for the replies to come in, it was like World War I waiting for the enemy to come and the tension would build up."

Another respondent explained difficulties with a colleague like this:

> ". . . Tony was trained in anthropology and he, in a sense, wanted to do a piece of anthropological research. . . . The way it panned out was me doing the anthropology, not him, me beginning to change my style of life and dress. My alcoholic consumption trebled in about six weeks; from being somebody who didn't like pubs and hardly ever was in them I was hardly ever out of them. . . . I think he was a bit jealous that I was doing the anthropological stuff. . . ."

Thus an accidental development of the division of labour gave a basis for bad feelings. Tony himself also reported on another way in which this happened with a third member of the team when he himself was heavily involved in the fieldwork.

> "With Kevin we had a tremendous strain . . . . He came to live near us. . . and Kevin was doing a desk job most of the time, working at home a lot and also working on his house. . . .
> As we lived near him, my wife was very sensitive to what was happening to me [I was on a 12-hour day and he was working on his house in the afternoon.] I found it a very great strain not to lose my temper with him over little things in meetings, to try not to introduce neighbour knowledge into the research situation. . . ."

The reciprocity of the influence of work and personal relationships was not always so clear, but a final example of this sort of pattern comes from a project where a group of research assistants working very closely together became deeply disillusioned:

> "As. . .people we were quite friendly, like we would meet after,
> sometimes for a drink perhaps, or go to the jazz club in the
> evening. . . so there was a social thing between us as well. . . .
> So perhaps we were more solid in our alienation as a result."

Some further examples show fairly straightforward instances of personal causes having research effects:

> "There were certain interpersonal differences amongst us,
> namely that I didn't get on all that well with Martin, and
> Mary didn't get on all that well with Martin. . . . Those
> particular pairs couldn't work well together, and partly as
> a result of that we decided to split into two groups and do
> two projects. . . . The decision was based on personal needs
> as much as on intellectual strategy, though it was always
> agreed that both studies needed to be done."

In this case the incompatibilities were intellectual as much as social, so it is only marginally relevant to the point, but seems worth mentioning because of the very clearcut consequences that followed. In another case one team member plausibly suggested that the director's inability to exercise adequate control over a research officer (on which other parties agreed) was due to their social equality, since they were much the same age, had been students at the same university and were both "trendy bejeaned guys". The research officer was a disorganised person with strong ideas of his own and difficulty in finishing anything, and so this lack of control was one factor contributing to the inordinate delays in completing the project. Another instance gives almost a mirror image of this one; here, an excessively deferential junior took a long time to learn to question the plans (or lack of them) of a charismatic senior whose protégé he had been:

> "Another thing it's taught me is not to be as deferential to
> authority as I was at the outset. Whether it was hierarchical
> authority or sapiential position [he] had, I don't know. But
> I certainly was deferential, so I deferentially sat around for
> eighteen months doing nothing."

In another study there were very bad feelings among fieldworkers, which at least one of them attributed in part to the personal strain of the fieldwork situation as well as to the organisation of the research. Whatever the causes, things reached the stage where, as she described it, communication on important aspects of the research was seriously reduced:

131

"We were sitting chatting there over coffee, but very often we just didn't know what the others were up to, and at times social relationships were such that one didn't dare to ask in case it was seen as suspicious or trying to check up on people."

In another project, where all parties agreed that relationships had been extremely friendly socially, there had nonetheless been considerable intellectual disagreement. I asked one person directly about the issue, and got a rather ambiguous answer:

J.P. "Did your social relationships have any consequences for the decisions you made or anything, do you think?"
"No. I don't think I know the answer to that. One could start and speculate. . . I mean, we sort of didn't. . . but somehow we were able to avoid things because we had the social relationships, or didn't speak out because we were all so friendly. At particular moments this may have happened."

He also remarked at another point:

". . . Dave and I have probably had a certain amount of friction over our work, and I find the personal relationship we have, like we go and stay for weekends. . . is maintained by not talking about work or the project as far as possible. . . ."

Theirs was an exceptionally strong friendship; probably in many other cases if work matters had been kept out of social occasions there would not have been an adequate basis for any real relationship left.

Sometimes the allocation of physical space was such that it created friction that might otherwise have been avoided:

"We occasionally had coffee or lunch together and that was about all. Absolutely nothing apart from that, we are both such different people. I should mention this, we were sharing a room for most of the research project so I found it better to do most of my work at home."

"I think from my point of view having to share a room, especially with two other people, is fairly inappropriate in research, because you've got to work together far more close-ly in any case. All the time you are trying to achieve compromise . . .(etc.) and the process can be exacerbated if you have to sit in each other's pockets all the time."

It may be more than coincidental that both those two speakers were women sharing rooms with men; I did not ask systematically about

132

room allocation, so can throw no light on this from other data. In the first of these two projects there had been intellectual conflict of a fairly painful kind, but on balance it was seen by all parties as having been fruitful; in the second, there was also conflict but of a more disruptive kind.

Another way in which social relationships could affect research outcomes was through the consideration towards colleagues that it created. The case of the director who let his research assistant take an M.A. and thus lost a significant part of his time is quoted below (p. 144), and there are others:

". . . we're reporting the research in two stages. . . . [partly because] this helped me solve my guilty conscience about not getting the research assistants properly involved in the writing up. . ."

These next comments are from different members of one team, all talking about the same man:

"Once having appointed the chap as research officer. . .he was more a principal than we were (etc.) and this is the way we did operate – he ran it. Whenever he objected to a plan (etc.) the data processing proved too difficult for him and we took his word. . . ."

"There were probably times when each of us took each position. Before 1970 it was the research officer who determined the outcome because he had tenure. I don't suppose we'd have been prepared to sack him anyway. . . we had a relationship with him."

[Director might have given the project up.] "The other thing about hiring the research officer, even when it was 18 months one had a sense one had really got to finish the project, something had got to come out of it, because this man's career depends on it."

"I think Alan in retrospect has often said that they should have fired him or threatened him or done more regular evaluations of his work. It was at one point a question of whether Don or I should have six months' more contract; I couldn't do that because I would have felt incredibly guilty at taking Don's job."

Here is another case where consideration for a junior prevented the research coming to an end, although here he was not felt to be doing unsatisfactory work:

133

"... there are fearful problems which arise from the need to keep people's jobs going — when the logic of the research says stop *now*. I certainly kept the project going for at least one year because of Tim Bailey's financial/career needs. This was a mistake... Now while this is partly clearer in the light of hindsight — it *was* very clear to me *at* the time. I felt I could not "ditch" Tim like an unwanted tabulation. My own "security" made this undoable."
(This quotation is from a letter sent to me with afterthoughts after the interview.)

Lastly, a senior director talks of his junior director:

"...I have got...personal involvement in that it is very important careerwise for my co-director, and that puts a heavy investment on... If I sometimes say to myself why doesn't it just go away and jump down a well, it mustn't, or it will have severe consequences for William, and since we're not just colleagues but close friends. ..."

These sorts of consideration sometimes seemed beneficial to the research, in that they increased the chances that it would ever get finished, and sometimes positively harmful when they led to the continued employment of unsuitable people, or the continuation of research commissioned by clients who turned out to have ulterior motives. The comments quoted indicate that, in addition to personal friendships there were norms operating which prescribed that the instrumental needs of the research should not be the only criterion to be taken into account. Sometimes, no doubt, a simple dislike of unpleasantness also contributed. Some people mentioned their deliberate avoidance of stating intellectual disagreements in research meetings because of the personal unpleasantness that this could involve, especially when the disagreements were fundamental and persisting ones. Several respondents suggested that the avoidance of conflict, or excessively pleasant personal relations, had been positively disadvantageous to their projects:

J.P. "What were personal relationships like within the team?"
"Well, they were rather jolly actually...we all had coffee together. .... The trouble was, while we were busy meeting over cups of coffee Mike and I might be discussing the best make of chisel, or how to make a bookshelf. It was very nice, but not what we should have been discussing."

That project was one which had suffered considerably from Mike's difficulty in finding enough time from his teaching commitments to keep in real touch with what was going on in his research. Here is another case:

> ". . .my definition of the totality of the research was that the relationships within the team were harmonious for almost the whole time. That was partly due to Joe in terms of his temperament, which had good and bad effects. If you want hardness, hard decisions taken, you don't get it; on the other hand, it's a situation in which potential conflict is minimised."

> "Joe's much more quiet, and not. . .it is difficult to say he is. . .either he didn't want to or didn't think it was his task to act as sort of master coordinator, partly because of the way the project had developed. Everyone had very much carved off slices that were their own responsibility [and there were certain stages where we needed someone to act as umpire]."

Joe was a director much respected and liked by his juniors, but they nonetheless felt that research problems could have been solved, and sooner, if he had not laid so much emphasis on consensus and been so nice to everybody. Here is another similar example:

> "We never had a row. I think this was awful — if only one of us had been able to say (etc.) It would have cleared the air wonderfully; we were all too mealy-mouthed — we really wanted, at heart, I wanted to on many occasions. I always found myself leaning over backwards to see their point of view, and came away accepting a set of rationalisations that I thought were pretty poor. . . ."
> Wife "I was always saying why don't you go and have a row."
> "And I never could. . . [about one issue] we never could face him on that because it was so threatening to him."

Not everybody longed for a row, but that speaker was not the only one to think that the absence of overt conflict could be dysfunctional. The next speaker is not suggesting that in the case of the research he took part in this desire existed even in a covert or repressed form:

> "If you were to look at those papers, I think you would notice a lack of coherent style and argument — this reflects joint authorship. I think at no time in that period was there any overt or covert animosity among those people, and maybe this was a fault! Maybe we weren't sufficiently committed to

our ideas to object if someone else seemed to be sticking
irrelevancies in, or going against the line that you were
taking. We were all very tied together outside the work
situation too. We did a lot of things together, all our
families were very close, and this did militate against any
one person trying to force a coherent line. We weren't
proud of them, but we weren't worried about being
proud of them."

These instances suggest that one's natural initial assumption that
overt conflict within a team must be bad can be questioned, and
that in particular personal pleasantness and the maintenance of
smooth personal relations were sometimes dysfunctional for the
overall goals of the research, even if they made life much nicer in
the meantime.

Friction or social distance could arise purely from the internal
dynamics of the progress of the research, but there were also strictly
personal characteristics that could set team members apart from
each other and perhaps provide a basis for other cleavages. Age, sex
and marital status were quite often mentioned:

"They did the normal things that academics do — they invited
me round for meals and so on, but obviously there were
situations when it was embarrassing. I think it was apparent
to them, as it was to me, that dinner parties with academics
weren't at that stage my cup of tea."

There was a smaller age gap than usual between this research assistant
and the research directors of whom she is speaking, but she was single
and a new graduate while they were married. In this case relationships later became informal and excellent, but the quotation brings
out one source of distance. In two other cases, when asked about
social relations in the team, respondents mentioned the importance
of the age gap in limiting them; in both the gap was about fifteen
years, and in one this was between hierarchical equals. Here are some
references to sex and marital status:

"I don't know if three men alienated the rest; anyway,
that's sort of how it split up in the end — and there was
some agony... To go back to the sociable relationships
part, I have a feeling on reflection that Jenny may have
felt the three of us were a bit clannish, or that she was
slightly outside, since we have families and met each other's
families and all lived relatively closely, whereas she dashed
off to London every night. Her living problems were

different — she was always having problems with landladies etc."

J.P. "What sort of social relationships have there been within the research team?"
"We've all tried with Ellen. I know both Martin and Howard have tried in various ways; it's a bit difficult, 4 married men and a single woman. . . . The men in the end, I think, have got fairly close. This worried me no end early on, how we'd cope with this, so that it didn't seem to shut one or more people out."

Ellen herself said, in response to a general probe from me about the relevance of her sex to the events of the project, this:

". . . I may be being very unfair here, but I think probably. . . and again it's difficult to say whether it's because I'm a woman or the person one is, but my feeling about one or two people here is they're pretty hard line and you haven't got to show any weakness in argument, not lack of logic but tentativeness in expression, and it also depends to a certain extent on background and interests, and always here it has been the boys out of school.
J.P. "What do you mean by that?"
"It's been a bit rowdy, a joint activity like football matches. They could be. . . they appear on certain occasions to be cohesive for reasons other than social reasons, if you know what I mean."

It is probably not accidental that both these cases were of single women in teams where the other members were married men, given the general composition of the population of research workers. It is to be expected, given the way the system works, that the major demographic sources of cleavage will be age gaps between director and assistants (in a context where an age gap is often also a significant cultural one), and sex and marital status gaps (with the women more often being single) among hierarchical equals. In other contexts no one would find it particularly surprising or interesting that such mixed groups did not have a lot in common socially, or spontaneously form friendships outside the work setting. There seems, however, to be a latent but widely prevalent norm that involvement and unity should be total, so that people feel uneasy when things are less than *gemeinschaftlich*. One respondent articulated this norm when talking about a colleague who did not stay when an extension of their original grant had to be applied for:

"Although he said he would come back to us, you know what research is like; you immediately get involved with a new set of excitements and colleagues etc. You know the social demands of sociological research, you don't just work together, you go to dinner together etc., so it's difficult to be involved in two groups at the same time. We used to think the bugger left us out in the cold, but having since become involved in other projects I can see why, with his project just starting and his colleagues would have felt he was betraying them. Since sociological fieldwork is highly uncertain. . . it is necessary to build up *esprit de corps* so that everybody can cope with the daily problems."

In a few cases research directors had conscious policies on social matters; the extreme case I came across was this one, where the director speaks first:

"It was a small group, very close, and our families were close too. We were stuck away in our ivory tower in the basement all in the same room. I have always insisted that the research group should be in the same room. When we were able to be lavish we also had side rooms where you could retire, but there always had to be a decision to leave the group, not to come into it. . . . It was very much a total system. One had to ask the group about doing anything, had to be totally involved in the group."

"We all lived very close to each other, except Brian; [director] put deliberate pressure on members to live on the south side of [town] if possible, and we saw quite a lot of each other. Jim was not married, although he got married within a year with Eric as his best man. . . It was all very groupy. We carried this a long way, probably further than most people."
J.P. "Did you take personal compatibility into account as well as academic competence when you were recruiting people?"
"Yes, compatibility was borne in mind when we were recruiting. . . We used to read each other's desks every night and tell everyone all the news; everyone read everyone else's letters. . . We had a lot of meetings at evenings and weekends."
J.P. "What about your relationship with the rest of the department?"
"We didn't have coffee with them very much. Out of the money that we made on expenses, by claiming for train fares when we all went to conferences in the same car and so on, we bought

coffee equipment for ourselves and made our own coffee."

By no means every member of this group had been completely converted to this ethos, and some left partly for that reason, or found that their personal habits forced them to develop work patterns that were not consistent with it. On the whole, however, the group did seem to show remarkable cohesion, despite the usual intellectual stresses and differences, and they were fertile in publications. A vague benevolence, a few invitations at the beginning of the project and a diffuse sense of grievance when any member of the team showed less than total commitment were commoner than this. The emphasis on sociability seemed to go with a strong version of the democratic ethos, which is discussed in Chapter 5. Some people, however, either in general or on particular issues felt that it was more appropriate to keep work and private lives separate:

> "I tend to separate off employment relations from social relations and regard the two as quite distinct. I expect a certain kind of contact from employment, which can be extended but not necessarily."

> "[Director], I think I saw his house once, and it was very much a work relationship, but I felt that was good. He spoke as if he had very little social distance with juniors, but this was my own version of it. He preserved social distance very well. Margot was the one I had most contact with. . . . We were quite friendly. It was a difficult relationship — a combination of her needing help [etc. — she had family problems] and not trying to let friendship too much take over the work relationship."

Both these speakers had difficulties of various kinds in their teams, but that is probably fortuitous.

Not all cohesion was developed on the basis of internal relations; there were a number of references to the importance of enemies outside the team, or at least on its margins, in promoting solidarity — e.g.

> ". . .there was never any overt row, though from time to time I think we all exasperated each other and voices got a bit acid. . . But then Delia [a clerical worker] came later on and fulfilled a tremendous function, the focus of hostility and aggression, and we all loved each other very much and hated Delia."

Such solidarity was certainly experienced as valuable by those concerned, since it was usually mentioned in the context of discussion of the internal friction which it enabled them to transcend, but one could question whether it was objectively valuable to the ends of the research when the perceived enemy was a client or unit director (seen as making unreasonable demands). Conflict of ends or tactics was not uncommon, and it cannot be assumed that the members of the immediate team were necessarily "right". Solidarity no doubt increased their chances of winning battles, so this is another respect in which social relations have consequences for the outcome of the research. One might speculate that socially introverted teams would tend to go with a "grounded"* research style, but another variable that would also be relevant is the methodological beliefs of the team. The particularly cohesive and "total" team described above did work very much in the conventional hypothetico-deductive style.

Another aspect of private life which has very direct implications for the progress of research is the individual's career pattern and aspirations. Any one project represents a stage in the individual's career, and a team project is the point of intersection of several career lines. (The general career structure is discussed in Chapter 6). Most full-time research jobs are on short contracts, and few of those who hold them plan to stay in research indefinitely; the typical research worker, therefore, must have his next job in mind, and that will commonly be in teaching. It contributes to this that the norms of the academic community specify (I assert on the basis of informal particpant observation) that the ideal academic career is to hold a full-time university teaching post in a department of one's own discipline, and to move up that hierarchy; this is to be preceded by apprenticeship in research as either a Ph.D. student or a research assistant. There is a paradox here: research is a high-status activity, but research jobs are not high-status jobs. The full-time teacher is expected to conduct research, and this contributes importantly to his academic standing and promotion prospects; this may go some way to explain some of the patterns of participation by research directors discussed elsewhere in the book. Here we are concerned primarily with juniors employed full-time on research, for whom the career structure and associated status system encourage three behaviour patterns in particular: they tend to become involved in teaching as well as research, they often attempt research degrees, and the

* Barney G. Glaser and Anselm L. Strauss, *The Discovery of Grounded Theory* Weidenfeld and Nicolson, 1968.

demands of prior and subsequent jobs mean that quite often they join projects late or leave them early.

There are often opportunities for research workers to do some teaching, and they are often eager to take them, for two main reasons: firstly, this provides experience and training for those who have not taught before which will increase their chances of getting a teaching job next; secondly, research workers are often a marginal group within the department, or located outside the departmental structure altogether, and doing some teaching helps to integrate them into its social and intellectual life.

Here are some examples to illustrate these points; the first one comes from a research worker whose first degree was not in sociology.

> "Over the last two years I had made decisions . . . one of which was that I'd do quite a bit of teaching to learn a bit of sociology . . . [then a teaching job was advertised] I was torn between research and teaching, and decided to teach."

> "All through this period I've been doing 2 hours teaching, which means 6 or 7 hours a week. . . . This has taken up perhaps more time than is justified, given that this is a full-time appointment."
> J.P. "But everybody knew about that."
> "Yes. I never quite had the courage to say no; (a) I didn't want to, and (b) if there was any chance of having an established post in the department, clearly if one had made a contribution. . . And it forces you to read things."

Both those quotations came up in the context of explaining why the research took an excessively long time to reach completion, which raises an important theme. Other researchers, however, did not get the teaching opportunities for which they had hoped:

> "I came here hoping either or both to be able to turn my part of the research project into a Ph.D. thesis and also to have some very small amount of teaching experience so that I might be able to go on to a proper academic job. Neither of these things turned out for me."

> ". . . having had a research job for 3 years and done very little teaching does to some extent count against you. I've done a little bit of teaching, but that is only stuff that's filtered down through [director]. Something I was quite annoyed about in the second year is that [director] got quite a lot of teaching and I didn't get any, though I'd done quite a lot in India and then I wasn't treated as

141

suitable for teaching."

Those two speakers (who as it happens were on the same project) felt that part of their problem was that they were administratively and geographically located on their own with no departmental connections. Researchers who did manage to get more teaching were likely to feel happier about it; the first one I quote was at the same university as the two above.

". . . teaching was non-existent for my first year, which was a very bad thing, because it made me feel that I didn't have a proper foothold in the university. . . . My teaching commitment was supposedly 6 hours a week, but during the final 18 months it was approximately 11. This has represented interest and commitment on my part — and a shortage of tutors in [field]."

"We all help out with a few tutorials, so we are involved a bit in the teaching side of the department. In a sense we are a little body attached to the department rather than fully integrated members . . . . [The research director is responsible for the teaching of one side of the course] and he very much involves Fred and I but our research can benefit the students, I think he sees it that way, that's nice."

Finally, an example of lack of social integration with no overt reference to teaching, to indicate what the problem can be — and another kind of solution to it:

"I was at [university] 9 months before I set foot in anyone else's house. I was very bitter about the role of research assistant and how they were neither faculty nor graduate student. I used to go around with the M.A. students, but I wasn't really one of them. When I produced this paper, that was the breakthrough. I circulated it to communicate with them since they wouldn't talk to me. Then they congratulated me on it and started being all friendly with me. . . ."

Almost identical comments were made by another research assistant from the same large department; she couldn't solve the problem in the same way and became quite seriously depressed, eventually going to live in another town and commuting a few days a week to escape the university atmosphere, and this itself created some problems for the research.

It is for the same sorts of reason that many research assistants are anxious to do graduate degrees, normally on topics that arise from the project, and that directors may offer the possibility as an inducement. The advantage of taking a degree, apart from the obvious one that it constitutes a formal qualification, is that it provides some independence for the research assistant. It is a form of career insurance against the possibility that the project as a whole is unsuccessful and, perhaps more importantly, it enables him to have something that is his own, which he can control and for which he can claim the credit. Given the possibility of disputes about authorship of the eventual publications, and the probability that whatever the arrangement the director will in practice be given most of the credit and the work cited as by Smith *et al.*, these matters have some potential career significance, though by no means all research assistants are initially conscious of them. Academic and personal norms of intellectual autonomy, and simple preference for being able to follow ones own ideas, are also very relevant. One may suspect that some directors regarded the provision of such opportunities as a *quid pro quo* helping to legitimate a division of labour on the main project that gave research assistants mundane tasks and little autonomy, although no one said so explicitly.

Some departments or individual directors did have definite policies on the issue. One independent research institute gave very strong encouragement to its research workers to take higher degrees, allowing them to use the data from the projects they were employed on and to take a day off a week to work on it and paying up to 50% of their expenses. This was done in response to the severe career problems research workers found when they left the institute. Only short contracts could normally be offered, and there were opportunities for renewal at the end only if there was external finance available for a suitable further project; this meant that even with formal qualifications it could be hard to find an appropriate new job at the right time. Apparently about half took the opportunity offered. A director said that some "reject the whole idea as being forced upon them", but there could also be other reasons why it was not done, as suggested by the comments of a junior research worker who ended up taking an M.Sc. course:

> ". . . because of the nature of the work I was then involved in . . . I was spending weeks and weeks, Sunday to Friday, away doing the field work. So any course involving evenings was out, and the Redbrick course was Saturdays, so it seemed to be the only one I could do."

He did complete the course, despite the heavy workload that it entailed.

Another case of an institutional policy of encouragement was in a university department, where the Professor expected all research staff to register for higher degrees unless they could put up a specific case against it; my respondent, another member of faculty who directed a project, did not mention the rationale of this. He, however, had found from experience that it could have significant disadvantages:

"This means that our projects tend to be of three year duration, which is a ghastly constraint . . . These sort of career considerations mitigate [sic] against proper team research because if your lords and masters say 'you've got to collect your own data [etc. — academic boards require originality for Ph.D.s] it's going to make chaps cagey about sharing ideas in the team situation."

An assistant on another project made a comment to similar effect when he was describing arguments within the research team:

"There was also the sense in which one saw these alliances in relation to the possibility of pursuing ones own individual area of interest for a higher degree or publication, so an element that one was thinking of in arguments was what would fit, what would personally suit you; it wasn't necessarily very altruistic."

At a personal rather than an institutional level some research directors follow a policy of favouring degree opportunities, at least under some circumstances:

" . . . one of the things that has dogged the work is that I am too tenderhearted about exploitation, so I decided that Anne — the research assistant — obviously wanted to escape from her previous university 2·2, so I agreed that she would do an . . . M.A. part-time; she is just finishing it now. So this meant that a good half of her time was not spent on the project. If one doesn't exploit, then perhaps one gets better stuff out of them; anyway, one shouldn't. That created problems with the coding, finding coders. . . ."

The research assistant herself said:

"I spent too much time on the M.A. but insufficient time, and similarly with the research. One would go through very frustrating periods when things had to be done, but I couldn't let the M.A. drop. . ."

and she added, bringing in a rather different theme,

"I got ideas from doing the M.A. . . . . At that time I'd never
heard of Cicourel and at that time I was engaged on coding
. . . . For a short period I got sold on Cicourel and worried
about the viability of the interviews."

This last comment suggests potentially beneficial cross-fertilisation,
although in the short run the effect may have been inconvenient.
The director clearly did not regard the net effects of his policy as
beneficial to the project, even though he thought he had behaved in
a proper way. Such policies were not always perceived by those on
the receiving end as altruistically motivated:

". . . one of the understood conditions of the appointment was that I should do a D. Phil. . . . . They obviously
wanted someone doing a D. Phil. to keep someone there
for 3 years!"
J.P. "So it was them pressing for you to do this rather than
vice versa?"
"Oh yes: when I was appointed as research assistant I didn't
want to stay anyway."

But he did stay, and the end of the thesis seemed in sight when I interviewed him. The director of the project said he thought that in this
case doing the thesis had been beneficial to the project, though the
project had not been beneficial to the thesis. The other research
assistant on this project had been very eager to get a qualification; he
was determined to do a D. Phil. rather than the initially planned M.Sc.,
and did it on a topic unrelated to the project. The consequence was
that the strain of riding both horses at once proved too great, and he
had a sort of breakdown which prevented him playing the role
originally planned in the analysis and writing up. The director saw
this as a drawback of his own generally non-authoritarian approach,
because he had foreseen difficulties — though not as great as those
which actually arose — yet did not forbid it.
   One fairly large university research unit had a policy which
avoided some of these problems:

"The principle was that you could not get a Ph.D. out of the
project, but if you had made sufficient contribution over
some years the group might agree to support you for a time
to do your own Ph.D. . . . ."
J.P. "Did anyone feel that this was a grievance that they
couldn't get a higher degree out of it?"
"Now and again some people wondered and worried. They

were told 'don't worry, you'll publish anyway.' "

Only one member of the group actually got a Ph.D. on this basis —
but there were many publications, with junior contributors acknow-
ledged as authors. With hindsight, I wish that I had thought of asking what the financial arrangements were, since the unit was
supported by grants earmarked for specific research; there was
probably some diversion of resources that would have surprised the
grant-giving bodies, and could hardly have evaded detection if done
on any scale.

The occasional individual got a Ph.D. out of a research project
where it was no one's policy but his own that he should be able to
do so. An enterprising research officer in a governmental unit, the
only worker on his project, was one of these:

> J.P. "How did you organise getting permission from DoX?"
> "I didn't organise it; I simply wrote to [Ph.D. supervisor]
> who happened to know someone I knew, and told DoX after
> I got it!"
> J.P. "Was there any distinction between the doctorate and
> the report?"
> "No. The only bow I made was to put in the introduction that
> it was going to be submitted."

Presumably this did the department no harm; what the official reaction was I did not ask, and my respondent reported none. A less
unusual case is that of the occupant of a research post not tied to any
particular project who took the opportunity of a large data-collection
exercise initiated by others to add to it a component of his own
which he used for his thesis; in return he made a substantial technical
contribution of his own which was much appreciated.

One research director in principle favoured providing the opportunity for assistants to do degrees, but he was new to the university
on which he was based and it turned out that he could not live up to
his promises:

> J.P. "Have any of them got degrees out of it?"
> "No. I was totally new to [university] and so must pro-
> fess my innocence; we did say at the interviews that they
> would be given every help and encouragement to do a
> higher degree. [One research assistant developed a proposal,
> but it turned out that he would have had to pay all his own
> fees, and he had a wife and baby to support.] So he was put
> off by this and the red tape. He would have had to have a
> supervisor; I couldn't, and [other director] wasn't qualified,

so it would have had to be in with someone else outside the project. . . . It would have been hard slog and difficult to fit in in the time and he needed 6 terms, so how would he have survived the remaining 2 terms [after the main project ended]?"

This was a source of grievance to the research assistants concerned, particularly since for them it was part of a more general pattern of disappointment of expectations of the project. It indicates again the timetabling problems that can arise, which are discussed further below.

For a last comment on issues of general policy we turn to an experienced director of a unit discussing the matter in general terms:

"Take Bob, on the one hand we wanted Bob's work to feed directly into the main drive of the study . . . On the other hand I was conscious that here was a young man that had got to make his way in the sociological world, who therefore needed to define his problems very closely in sociological terms and also needed a Ph.D. — and these things together applying over a whole field of people meant that the core got lost while each individual went out into the periphery, either because he was that kind of person or because the Ph.D. makes it necessary [to separate something out in order to say 'that's my contribution']. So the fundamental career needs of young staff tended to be inimical to the research needs of a tightly organised programme . . ."

This last point, as well as several made in earlier quotations, indicates that the fact that research assistants are doing Ph.D.s can influence the main project. In this case, as in one mentioned above, the influence took the form of affecting the topics covered, or emphasized, within the broad research area; obviously this could only happen when the degree topic formed part of the project. Whatever the topic, the fact that separate degree work was being done could cause problems for the main project, especially in its final stages; the quotations above cover a number of cases where assistants found it very hard to be involved in two pieces of work simultaneously, especially at the writing-up stage when deadlines for both were approaching. Individual self-interest and moral obligation to an employment contract and a team of colleagues could be in conflict when the degree work was not a central component of the main project. One director faced with this situation took steps that the assistant perceived as illegitimate:

147

> "He told me [that] . . . since neither the book nor the thesis were finished, I ought to put the book before the thesis, because other people were affected by it. In fact it was blackmail: he was my supervisor and if I didn't do the book he could block it."

It was not uncommon, as in this case, for both book and thesis to be unfinished when the research grant expired and the notional original deadline for each was reached. Of the 10 projects which had junior members doing theses, only one appears definitely to have been completed on time; 2 more had no clear end and so were unclassifiable, and the remaining 7 were not completed on time. This contrasts with the 15 university-based projects where juniors were not doing theses; here 7 were completed on time — perhaps an unimpressive proportion, but certainly a higher one. Of course it does not follow that delays were caused by the theses, but it seems possible that they contributed to them, although other factors were also involved. On the other hand, it was not simply a matter of theses being completed at the expense of the main project; of the 15 theses undertaken by junior research workers, 13 were definitely not completed when the main project's original deadline arrived. (In some cases it had never been expected that they would be, and so this was not a departure from plan.) How the time taken compares with that for theses done by full-time students I do not know, but at any rate to get a thesis from someone else's research project does not seem to have been a soft option.

Those doing theses experienced a number of problems specific to their situation in addition to mere lack of time. First of all, and this is why some people who had hoped to do so ended up not doing theses at all, it could prove difficult to find an appropriate topic. Here a director and an assistant from the same project disagree about how far this could have been done:

> Director ". . . it wasn't impossible; it would be possible to chop off part of the data and do something with it, and certainly anybody who was interested, for instance, in developing more complex forms of multivariate analysis could do something . . ."

> Assistant "It was also suggested that we might like to take bits and write articles beforehand, but there weren't any discernible bits in that sense, so these things were floated but there wasn't really any possibility of doing them."

What from the assistant's perspective is the impossibility of finding an appropriate distinct topic may from the director's perspective be the assistant's incompetence or lack of experience; one cannot judge who in general is more likely to be right, though probably both viewpoints have important elements of truth in them. However, this cannot be considered only in terms of the subject matter of the research. The director quoted above went on to say " . . . but that would be an activity that couldn't even start until the end of this summer . . .", i.e. after the first stages of analysis had been completed and when the assistants' contracts were coming to an end, so that they would have had either to take the data away with them or to finance themselves to stay on in the area to work on it. Another aspect of the constraints of the research timetable is commented on by the assistant on a large project who said:

". . . the initial attraction was supposed to be the opportunity to pursue ones own interests, but the routine work effectively precluded that and not a single one of the lot has produced any academic work except for one dissertation on anything related to the project . . ."

(And the one dissertation was actually written after the contract ended.)

Where an assistant perceived a potential topic, there could still be problems in disengaging it from the main research, whether as thesis material or as an ordinary publication:

"The rest of the project is the history of me trying to carve something out, which I did do to a large extent . . . I had at least half time to do my own thing. I felt I could do it, she [Director] felt she should tell me what to do, and it was very awkward. She'd ask what I'd found out, and the next thing I knew it was one of "our" main findings . . . It made it a bit difficult afterwards. I couldn't publish things separately because in a way it was all there in the book. I did publish some things eventually; it took the move to Redbrick and being my own master before I could do it."

"It became clear that there was a lot of information that couldn't be used. . .I'd just extracted various things from him [Director] by going through diplomatic bargaining. . . Quite what claims he could make I don't know, so in the course of negotiation on attribution I've asked [Research Unit] to get him to specify that now the book is done the remainder of the material is mine, and he has agreed to it."

The project from which the latter quotation comes is one on which there was serious overt conflict about the eventual attribution of authorship, which is not a typical situation. Both cases, however, show the difficulties of sorting out whose contribution is which when the division of labour has not initially been organised in such a way as to make this clear; this can be necessary either to meet universities' originality requirements for theses, or to provide legitimation for claiming areas of data or interpretation as one's own in other contexts. These problems relate to the general ones of contracts and division of labour which are discussed in Chapter 5.

Another area in which complications can occur is that of thesis supervision. An earlier instance in this chapter showed that there can be difficulties when research director and supervisor are one and the same person — though presumably in this case the director, if conscious of the pressure the assistant felt him to be exercising, regarded the opportunity as a convenience rather than a difficulty. This situation certainly decreases the potential advantage for the assistant of having some basis of his own independent of the main project. When, as can happen, the supervisor is someone else, different issues may arise.

J.P. "Who's your supervisor?"
"Joe Brown; I haven't seen him very much though. I'm in the odd position that my actual research and data collection and so on is as a part of the team, so Joe, as a supervisor, has had a very marginal role. As far as the data collection is concerned Joe has had nothing to do with it. I have had conflicting advice — what [director] says on the thesis takes second place, and Joe has no say on the research report. They are very different; Joe wants the thesis to be very narrow and tightly-packed, [director] would go more for getting all the information down. . ."

"David Higgins was given to me as my supervisor, and David Higgins was not getting on then well with [director] and co. and David tried really from the start to divide the team. He was helpful to me, but anti — [other team members] and trying to get me to go it alone all the time, saying 'they'll never publish' . . . [I was in the awkward position of trying not to alienate David but also not to alienate [other team members] .]"

This second case is extreme, but the first one makes clear that it is hardly surprising that differences of opinion should arise between supervisor and director, however good relationships among all concerned may be, and that this can create an embarrassing position for the assistant. The reconciliation of differences of opinion within a team can involve a delicate balancing act; when a further person is involved who is not a party to the discussions, but whose views are seen by one member of the team as likely to have important personal consequences for him, it could be disruptive.

In sum, my data suggest that the fact that assistants were doing research degrees could have definite consequences for the projects on which they were employed; some of these may have been good ones for the project as a whole, but others sound as though they were at the least inconvenient, and may have contributed to delays and dispersal of energies and interests. Some project directors had definite policies about degree work, but it was usually not explicit what was their rationale, beyond a vague altruistic consideration for the assistants' presumed career needs. Assistants were often keen to do theses, perhaps especially when a research assistantship was planned to be the first stage in an academic career, but they did not find the soft option they might have anticipated; some could not even get started, while few seem to have finished as soon as they might have hoped.

Another way in which career needs could affect research progress was through the pattern of moves from one job to another. The grant and contract system ensures a fair amount of movement among those working in research in any case, but there were unscheduled moves which took place over and above this. Research workers sometimes joined projects later than planned, and sometimes left early, and these moves had a variety of consequences, some of which we shall illustrate.

There were a few cases where research workers joined a team later than planned because they could not get away from the previous job any sooner. One of these was a full-time working director who arrived back in England from a job abroad to a situation where his junior colleagues had already been appointed by the non-working director, so that he had had so say in the appointments; this may have influenced the smoothness of their subsequent co-operation. Another was a research assistant who arrived a month or two after the others had taken up their posts and found that they had already pre-empted certain roles and made some contacts for participant observation. On his own account:

> "The division between Alan and myself, for example, the fact that he branched off and did so much of participant observation, I think largely came about because he was there 6 weeks before I arrived at the stage when access to [factory] was problematic and he went in when they only had 1 pass

151

and having made the contacts the process became self-fulfilling."

His colleague Alan independently said:

> "It was most unfortunate, because the first time he arrived
> was the day of [important event in the factory] and he met
> us in [factory] after we had done all these interviews . . .
> We were beginning to know people and, of course, he
> arrived not at the office but actually in [factory] without
> knowing people already, and you can see the psycholo-
> gical result of that. From the very beginning he felt kind of
> disadvantaged. He felt somehow behind everyone else —
> and this had two results for him personally. First, he was
> always trying to catch up, and second, he had to capture
> some area of his own, to establish a research territory which
> he could call his own, where he could have privileged power
> and understanding and knowledge and so on to hold against
> us. . . ."

All parties to the project agreed that the division of labour that consequently arose was one which had had severe disadvantages for the
research. Another problem mentioned by participants in two projects
was that when someone joined a team after some preliminary work
had been done they could not have the background knowledge of
how thinking had developed, or the experience of participating in the
earlier planning stages, and that this could have longer-run consequences:

> "I would say the four of us had a much stronger investment
> and commitment to it than Vic ever had. It's understandable
> —he came in at the stage when there was not much he could
> have done in the way of shaping the project, the decisions
> had been made . . . I think both Martin and I, Martin more
> strongly than I, would feel that it would have been nice if
> Vic's commitment to the project had been stronger . . . if
> you phoned Vic at ten past five, you couldn't get him; his
> commitment to the project was reflected in temporal re-
> strictions on when he would work."

> "[. . . it was difficult [training late arrival in research proce-
> dures] because we knew the rationale, but she had to take it
> all pat and didn't have the same understanding of why —
> though it was easier for her when we made changes. . .] "

Of course such difficulties could occur just as much when the late
arrival of one member had been planned all along as when it came

152

about because of the contingencies of their private lives; general problems of research timetabling that relate to this are discussed in Chapter 2. However, the point may be taken as established that late arrival on the scene could occur although not part of the original plans, and could have unanticipated effects ramifying throughout the project as well as causing the obvious short-run difficulties.

Some "late arrivals" were replacements for original members of the team who had left, and these normally came on the scene at a later stage than the cases mentioned above. Curiously enough, the same kind of problems do not seem to be mentioned in connection with them, perhaps because the same initial expectations were not aroused; the newcomers seem either to have initiated a new phase of the project, or to have been used for relatively menial tasks clearing up at the end. The problems that then arose were fairly obviously a consequence of the departure of their predecessor rather than of their own late arrival. This brings us on to the quantitatively more important theme of team members who left early. "Early" in this context means before the departure had been planned, usually before the grant expired; the research was often unfinished by this point, but people who left then out of financial necessity are not classified as having left early. "Leaving" does not necessarily imply abandoning the research; indeed, most maintained at least some nominal contact. It implies stopping work altogether, or taking up another job, usually in another part of the country. We shall consider here only those cases where people left for personal reasons; discussion of the consequences of early leaving in general is included in the section on timetables.

Eight of the 55 projects in my sample were affected by 10 researchers leaving significantly early*; a further 6 researchers left 6 projects a bit early, but when they were nearly at an end in any case. Of this latter group, 3 were full-time research workers whose next jobs required them to start before the formal expiration of their contracts on the project, and who were therefore released. Another had elements of this, but disillusion with the research was believed to have helped to precipitate her departure. Of the remainder, one took a lectureship in the same department, instead of an extension of his research fellowship, at a point when the continued availability of research funds was not clear and there were considerable difficulties within the team; the other found it virtually impossible to

* In this section I have not counted as leaving early any participants in large research programmes, since individual projects within them did not seem to have clearcut beginnings and ends.

153

combine writing a thesis with work on the main project, and so a very much reduced commitment of time to the project was arranged.

The 10 who left significantly early were somewhat different. One is an odd case : he had a one-year contract, but it was understood that it would be renewed at the end of the year — which it was not. His colleagues perceived him as having been sacked by the steering committee, and were not pleased with this; his own account of the matter was that he had freely chosen to leave to take up a place on an M.A. course! At any rate, he left, and another research assistant had to be found to replace him. One woman left a project because she became pregnant, and another because she had a baby and various personal problems as well, and although it was vaguely expected that they would write up those parts of the research for which they had been responsible they do not appear to have done so. The other 7 cases were all people who left for better jobs : one Professor and one Reader took up posts abroad, two lecturers were promoted to Professorships at other universities, a lecturer moved to Oxbridge, one research officer got a lectureship elsewhere and one did in the same university. In one of these instances the move seems to have been precipitated by discontents in the research situation, but in all the others it was a normal career move. One project was completed more or less in accordance with plan; the research director continued to be actively involved in supervising field-work and interviewing informants, though not to the extent he had originally intended, and the writing up was facilitated by his success in finding a post for his assistant at his new university when the grant expired. The assistant did, however, have more autonomy than had been planned. Another project, whose extension had been envisaged, more or less collapsed when the director went abroad; it had already been showing signs of ill-health before then, and might have collapsed in any case through loss of motivation. The other 5 fall somewhere in between these two in terms of their degree of success. Three projects (accounting for 4 leavers) had not reached the stage of main publication at the time of my interviewing, though in every case it was several years beyond the deadline originally planned. There seemed to be no reasonable doubt that the problems of communication at a distance had contributed significantly to this in 2 of them; in the third, the director had been very much a marginal participant in any case and so his physical move probably made little difference. The final project did reach publication, but not without tremendous ructions. The director went abroad, in effect leaving a research assistant in charge; the assistant found himself playing a key role of responsibility, and when it came to the writing up there were bitter disputes about acknowledgement and authorship that could only be resolved by the mediation of third parties. Thus the general effect of members leaving projects early was not a happy one, and it was not uncommon for moves in pursuit of career goals to take place. The numbers involved are so small that it would be rash to draw any conclusions from them, but nonetheless it seems suggestive that a higher proportion (14%) of directors whose job did not depend on that particular project left it significantly early than of full-time research employees whose job was linked to the project (4%). It would not be reasonable to suggest that the cash nexus is more powerful than intellectual commitment; but for one group career needs are more narrowly constraining than for the other.

Then there were a few people for whom career contingencies had a benign effect on the research, at least in the sense that they encouraged its completion:

> "When I left as a research student I was in a complete mess,
> I didn't know what I was researching into, what I was going
> to do with it when I got it, I was thoroughly disillusioned and
> confused. If it hadn't been that I'd got a job that I loathed,
> and was very fearful that I'd never be able to get a decent
> university job unless I had completed it. . . ."

> ". . . I'm only now coming back to the data, and that's because
> unless I get more publications I won't get a tenured post!"

No doubt there were more people than these, although they did not mention it, who would not have had the impetus to carry a project through to completion if they had not felt a career need for publications in order to get tenure or promotion. The effects are benign in the sense that the projects are written up, or written up sooner than they would otherwise have been. Perhaps sometimes such projects might better have been left incomplete; their authors could be fairly cynical about their merits, or have lost interest or changed their ideas by the time they got around to writing.

Thus, this chapter has shown that the career structure and the status system of universities motivate people to behave within a project in specific ways that promote their private ends, and that these private ends are not always wholly consistent with the original plans or the eventual success of the projects on which they are employed. The sophisticated research director attempts to construct his plans in a way that anticipates these contingencies, but he does not always have the necessary information to act upon. Family situations affect the motives and commitments that individuals bring to their work, and may be responsible for variations in their capacities to perform research tasks. Once in the research situation, purely personal characteristics also have some bearing on what happens.

It is not to be expected that in social research, any more than in any other work setting, relationships among colleagues will typically be of an entirely impersonal and bureaucratic kind. Nor, on the other hand, is it sociologically reasonable to expect that, in a team recruited by advertisement from people with diverse backgrounds, personalities and domestic situations, everything will automatically be sweetness, light and total commitment — though some people did appear to expect this. Quite apart from the social characteristics of those concerned, the research often gives rise to a variety of stressful situations, in which those involved may have divergent interests; a certain amount of intellectual conflict is normal and likely to spill over at least temporarily into interpersonal relations.* Smooth relationships do not necessarily make for better research, and conflict can be functional; unfortunately for the search for easy generalisations, it can also be dysfunctional. It might be possible to specify which types of conflict are fruitful and which harmful, but my data cannot be more than suggestive on this. They can be taken, however, to establish that work and social relations within research teams are intimately connected, and that the social relations are not just marginal but can significantly affect the progress of the research.

* Martin Bulmer has suggested in a letter that teams of 4 or 5 might be especially prone to interpersonal conflict; in larger teams there is more room to maneouvre and form coalitions and alliances. This is an interesting suggestion, and sounds quite plausible.

CHAPTER 8

Projects and Private Lives

This chapter is concerned with the consequences of the research process for private lives. The most obvious aspect of private life for which research participation is likely to have consequences is the individual's career. Sometimes these consequences were hoped for and planned, sometimes they were fortunate by-products, and in a few cases they were both unintended and undesired. Among those who became involved in research with planned career consequences in mind were some established academics who took research posts with very clearcut motives:

"... I think at the time my sort of reasoning was, well, I've been in [university] about 8 years ... one's teaching commitments were fairly heavy so, right, I said, I saw this as getting a quick pay-off, a bunch of publications, a bit of research experience, whereon I would be in a better position in a few years to see what senior lectureships are going."

"I felt that for career purposes I needed to get more research done and publication, and was finding it very difficult to make any headway really."

Neither of these two was really successful in the way he had originally envisaged; quick publications did not come. They were atypical in that they moved from teaching to research posts, and it was probably this atypicality which made it seem necessary to them to explain their career strategies. Others were seldom so explicit once past the initial stage of getting an academic job at all, though no doubt they frequently had similar considerations in mind. Numbers of people described their own careers as haphazard and unplanned — for instance, here is someone talking of his Ph.D. thesis:

"I had very little vision of what I would do after, or what an academic career line is like ... It wasn't published for a long time ... In the meantime there had been 3 or 4 papers. I can remember saying to [distinguished and prolific colleague] and I know he was shocked, though he didn't say anything, I've never thought of myself as publishing papers. He was quite shocked — it was a very unprofessional thing to say ..."

"You could argue that I was supposed to be finishing my Ph.D., which I didn't finish until last year. It dragged on. If I were really career-minded I would have done that [instead of *ad hoc* project] but I am not basically oriented to an academic career in the sense that I want to end up with a Chair, so I don't look at it in terms of career strategy."

Readers will be relieved to learn that the second speaker has subsequently got a Chair anyway, and that the subsequent career of the first has also been distinguished. I do not wish to imply that either was not giving an accurate account of his motives and feelings; there does not seem to be any reason to assume that deliberate careerism is the only route to success. I think that there are signs of conflicting norms in this area: on the one hand, the public norm of modesty, and interest in the intellectual life for itself rather than for its career prospects; on the other hand, the more covert but taken-for-granted norm of striving for prestige and personal advancement and admiring its achievement. However, until relatively recently there was little scope for career planning in British sociology, since there were so few jobs altogether that it could be largely a matter of luck whether appropriate opportunities came up; more recently the vicissitudes of government policy have had similar effects, at least at the lower end of the ladder. Thus an emphasis on the importance of luck and accident may be quite realistic. Definite career plans were more commonly mentioned by those just starting out, and by those who did not plan to stay in sociological research or academic life:

". . . one of the things one can do as a clinical psychologist is to do research . . . I did look for research jobs because I thought I needed research experience . . . I thought it would not do me any harm in any career in psychology."

"I only got a 2:2; I couldn't do an M.A. or a Ph.D. which I wanted to do. My only chance of a job in academic life was a research project . . . I joined the project because I wanted a job . . . In terms of career, it's obviously absolutely fundamental. It was my way into academia. Hopefully it will provide me with the sources of self-advancement one requires in academic life, and it lies slap bang in the middle of my application form for any jobs."

Some of those who started by not intending to become academic sociologists changed their minds as a result of their research experience, while others successfully pursued careers which were relatively unorthodox by academic standards:

158

"... the important thing was I changed in the year away [on sabbatical] ... I wanted something different. I was always interested in policy research; it was time to get into policy ... I definitely saw it as a movement away from the university, not merely as a teaching place, but the university style of research." J.P. "Where would you see your position in relation to sociology?" "I am in a very marginal position — partly because I have always been marginal to sociology as such, and secondly, I don't think people in these research contexts want sociologists or psychologists as such, they want someone with some experience both theoretical and practical in the social sciences and forget the discipline. . . . Those concepts are meaningless in administrative situations . . . . What I want to do is to get the reputation of doing a good job wherever I am."

J.P. "What sort of consequences has this had for your career?" "It's turned me off university for a start! But I began to be turned off that some years ago. . . . I wouldn't really want to do research as a career pattern . . . it equipped me to do better the kind of work I am doing now, which is more development work in the social services . . . I prefer to actually influence events, and so tend to reject university because one can only do that at a fairly high level."

These quotations give a perhaps salutary reminder of the existence of other norms and criteria than university ones, which regard only "pure" sociology as intellectually valid and only a sociology department as providing an employment situation of unambiguously respectable status. One consequence of this for the non-university researcher was pointed out by someone who worked in a government department:

"... one had to say that one was going to find out what way of running these institutions is best, and this tends to make it atheoretical, at least at the beginning, because you really can't afford to buy any particular sort of approach, and it's multidisciplinary in that it would be difficult to say that the thing was sociological or psychological or social-psychological. This in turn means that nobody much is going to read it, and it also affects the contacts you are likely to have with the universities and other people . . . the people doing this sort of research tend to define themselves as researchers, and they base such claims to expertise as they've got on their ability to do chi squared and their interest in validity. . . . That is important because it determines very much what sort of thing is produced."

159

A further consequence of the situation she describes is that those who have once had jobs outside universities or pure sociology may find it difficult to get back again if they want to. Because they were conscious of this possibility, a number of my respondents reported that it had affected their career decisions:

J.P. "Why did you make the move to Redbrick?"
"I think the main thing was this disciplinary problem, feeling that both in intellectual and career terms one needed to have a subject base . . . So I started to apply for jobs in sociology, thinking it was my only chance, as perhaps it was . . . I tried to present myself as a person who had just accidentally got involved in [topic], and I was trying to define the educational research in ways which would emphasize or provide me with a sociological interest . . ."

"It's most depressing in terms of the career aspect of this research that social and working-class historians are very interested in it but sociologists aren't really, so I don't really know what to do next. To do further research on [topic] would further confirm myself as away from the main current of interest, so I'm considering replicating some American work because that would be a survey and would win more respect and interest . . ."

"I nursed the illusion that one could be truly interdisciplinary, and there was a positive advantage to be gained in trying to be equal between the two, but I found that in terms of university politics and social contacts this was a mistake." [This was at a university which in principle emphasized the interdisciplinary approach] ;
J.P. "Do you now regard yourself as a sociologist, then?"
"Yes, except insofar as I nurture a feeling of inferiority as far as bred-in-the-bone sociologists are concerned. I worry that perhaps my conversion came when I was a little long in the tooth."

Others made similar remarks of a less detailed kind. To the extent that they really identified themselves as sociologists and took other sociologists as their reference group they were likely to feel these pressures. It would be interesting to investigate what affected the formation of a self-conception as sociologist. One obvious hypothesis would be that it follows from early socialisation; my data, however, do not show disciplinary anxieties being felt only by those who had first degrees in single honours sociology, or first posts in university settings, and they do show some people with such backgrounds moving out of the magic circle.

The respondent quoted above was one of several who underwent some sort of change of academic identity as a result of his experience in the one project. Two had become computer and statistical specialists as a consequence of their projects' division of labour; each started with a sociology degree which had had no particular bias in that direction, became a research assistant soon after graduation, took on the role within the team of having the primary responsibility for data processing, became fascinated by computing, and developed a permanent commitment to it which is reflected in their current jobs. A third person started as an anthropologist, and to some extent influenced the team to which he belonged to use an anthropological style of work, but was himself influenced by them and by the departmental setting so that he now defines himself as a sociologist. There were other instances where people coming from adjacent disciplines such as social psychology, and sometimes deliberately chosen as such, worked within sociological teams without losing their original academic identity; none of these commented on any career consequences of this.

One of the questions I always tried to ask was how, if at all, taking part in the project had affected the respondent's career, in the sense either of intellectual career or of worldly advancement. Nine people said that it had made, or would make, very little difference to them because it was just another project, which they sometimes saw as part of a long-term programme of work in a field; most added that they were at a career plateau where one more publication had no special significance, or that there was no higher post to which they could be promoted. All of these people were directors of the projects we were talking about, and eight of them already had the rank of Reader, Professor or its equivalent. (The ninth was an established lecturer with some publications already who had accepted a commission from a governmental body to do research into a topic with policy implications. The research had been dogged by practical difficulties, the eventual publication was under governmental auspices, and she had not succeeded in making it as sociological as she had originally hoped. Shortly after my interview she moved to a better job at another university, and I note a more recent academic publication which has some connection with the research; perhaps when she spoke to me she was too depressed by the difficulties experienced?)

A number of people said that they thought, or feared, that the lack of success of their research would actively harm their careers:

161

"the only consequences are negative, in that it's been very much slower than I would have regarded as morally ideal. There was an implicit snide comment . . . in a recent review in which he hinted that certain large pieces of research and nothing had come of it, so the time taken to get much out of it, it will be if anything a negative factor in my career and my reputation . . ."

["We said to the sponsors that we would do certain things, and we haven't completed it, and as a research entrepreneur myself I am worried about the possibility that the failure to deliver the goods in one area might lead to failure to get funds in another"].

" . . . I think it has corked me up quite a lot — I know it has, over quite a considerable period. I was interviewed as far back as 1968 for 2 quite separate jobs as head of department. I believe, and again this is boasting, the kind of experience I've had and my, I think, competence and ability justify that . . . I was told on both occasions [that I would have got the job had I published]."

" . . . in the early years I obviously considered myself quite fortunate to be on this project, because it seemed to be quite a big, important project which was going to produce something quite significant. Now, in terms of getting other jobs and so on, because it has been such a long time in coming to fruition I don't find it all that helpful careerwise, except in the general sense that I have got a certain amount of research experience. Another thing is, that I sort of feel that it has rather typecast me . . . I made quite an attempt to break off into [other field of sociology] at one point, but because I've spent all these years in [medical sociology] it was difficult to get out of it, so I seem to be stuck as a medical sociologist whether I like it or not."

The first two speakers held senior posts with tenure, and so for them the relevant consequences were for their general reputations and for chances of getting future grants; the latter two were more junior, and for them delays in publication directly affected the rank and character of the further jobs that they could get. None of the projects here referred to could yet be classified as total disasters; either it was too soon after the planned date of completion for the eventual outcome to be obvious, or there had been at least one publication but this had taken a long time and did not represent the full range of data collected. There were other similar cases, and such consequences seem fairly typical. No-one who had held a rank as lowly as research assistant mentioned negative career consequences, unless one were to put failure to find a dissertation topic in that category.* At that level it seems probable that experience gained is the important thing; publications are not expected, and assistants are not held responsible for shortcomings and delays. (But if they do get their name on publications, that of course helps). A somewhat different case is that of several people who had been involved in research into student unrest within their own universities, and had found that this placed them in politically delicate relations with the authorities or colleagues; the ill feeling which often followed was personally unpleasant, but on the whole they did not seem to think that positive career damage had been done, though they could not be sure of it. Most of them, however, were either too senior or too junior for promotion prospects to have much immediate relevance, so perhaps general conclusions can not be drawn from this.

It was much more common for positive consequences to be seen to follow. Several people made personal contacts through their research jobs that led to subsequent teaching jobs in the same or a related department, or working elsewhere with someone who had been a colleague on the project. More often it was a matter of acquiring qualifications that led by impersonal routes to further jobs. For example:

"In career terms it made my career . . . The book had got me into the publications racket straight away. From the moment it was published I was never short of invitations to publish . . . So, obviously, it had a tremendous effect on my career − straight from student to lecturer in [very short time]."

"When I applied for jobs I didn't think I had a chance of getting the job at Essex and was very surprised and relieved. To have got the job, one would have had to do a book or some research. I don't think it was the specific research, it could have been any comparable research."

"The effect of that project hasn't benefited my career − well, I suppose it has, when I got the job here. The [department] has a philosophy of being associated with industry, and the fact that I'd been on that . . . I think helped a lot."

The meteoric rise described in the first quotation was rare; that

---

* Perhaps an exception is those people who felt that experience in educational research was sometimes regarded with suspicion when they applied for jobs in school teaching or colleges of education; they also felt that it was sometimes an advantage. In any case, this was independent of the degree of success of the research.

163

research assistant was very lucky, as well as competent. The other two indicate the more usual pattern, in which experience of research qualified people for more independent or for supervisory roles in other projects, demonstrated competence helped them to establish an academic teaching career, or the knowledge gained of a particular field or technique made them well qualified for specific jobs in either teaching or research. Almost all the people who mentioned this sort of career consequence had been employed at the assistant level, and the jobs they moved on to were normally of the kind that one would expect to come next if they were going to make a career at all in academic sociology. There were also a small number of cases where more senior people said that their research experience had been directly instrumental in getting them promotion, or that without it they would not have shown the breadth of interest considered necessary for a senior post. (The qualifications acquired were not always unequivocal advantages; one person found that, although he had become highly qualified in a particular field, the market in this field was so narrow that he was lucky to find a suitable next job when his research contract ended). A few people mentioned career advantages of a less job-linked kind, in that their research publications had attracted general publicity because of their policy relevance; one person said that he thought he had become quite well-known in part because his work had been on an esoteric and mildly exotic topic:

"This field is somewhat esoteric in sociology, and it's a great advantage to be involved in an esoteric field, providing that it catches the imagination sufficiently. Most sociologists know very little about it, and they imagine it's much more abstruse. . . . If it had been in a field more widely covered, it wouldn't have commanded the same attention. It's also true, I think, that if I'd written about [topic] and been quite wrong, it's quite unlikely that any sociologist would know, so I think it is the case that it wasn't a bad thing to have done, in the sense that it was a field in which it was quite easy to make some sort of mark. . . ."

Those who had not necessarily used their research experience for career advancement could nonetheless draw on it for their routine teaching when they held teaching posts, and several mentioned its importance to them:

"It had a good effect on teaching, a good effect on my syllabus creativity, that's one side of it. . . . Also it's just been research experience . . . A large part of my work is helping M.Sc. candidates with their dissertations, and I feel much happier talking about their problems having done it myself."

"It made teaching first-year classes here far easier than for most people having had to be a jack-of-all trades on the community; power, class, delinquency, religion etc. etc. — you have to read the lot . . . [Town] is far more my Trobriand island than [locale of prior research] ; it's my measure, my sample of Britain, I know the place."

"It has been an enormous benefit in teaching industrial sociology during the last few years to be able to refer directly to [industry] in illustrating all sorts of points — in fact I have done so so frequently that it has become something of a joke for the students, this week's [industry] reference."

Presumably this is the sort of effect that research is meant to have according to the conventional account of its importance for university teachers; in the light of that it is perhaps surprising that there were not more references to such effects.

I asked about intellectual careers as well as worldly ones, and in reply heard many fascinating accounts of how interests had developed and how people saw the particular projects we were discussing as fitting into their long-term research plans. This will not be reported on here, both because of the great difficulty of describing such detail without violating anonymity and because there is nothing conventionally surprising in it. What will be reported briefly are some of the ways in which a particular piece of research could fail to constitute part of a coherent intellectual career.

Research that had been commissioned by sponsors was likely not to fit smoothly into an intellectual career, although senior people with permanent research jobs, or who had done a fair amount of contract research, seemed more likely to be commissioned to do research in which they were really interested in any case. Presumably this was because they had established reputations for competence in particular areas, and so work of that kind was likely to come their way. University lecturers, or more junior people, were less likely to have an established reputation or an effective choice in the matter. One small group of people, not commissioned by outsiders, who did *ad hoc* research on subjects of marginal general interest to them were those inspired by student unrest to do research into their own universities.

It was perfectly possible for people to find a project interesting in itself even though it was not central to their continuing interests, and for several people that was how it had been; it was quite

165

enjoyable while they did it, the experience and knowledge they had gained would be useful, and they had now moved on to something of more personal interest. It was just as common, however, if not more common, for people who had initially felt much the same about their projects to become keenly interested in the general field as a result of working in it, and to build their subsequent intellectual careers on that foundation. This, naturally, was only likely to happen with people at the beginning of their careers. This comment indicates one way in which this can happen:

> J.P. "You've stayed pretty much in the [topic] field since then; was that a consequence of this?"
> "I don't think I had the intention to do that particularly, it's partly simply grown; having done one thing people ask you to do a paper, or one's curiosity is aroused and one follows it up. . . . My interest in this field is so much part of my life by now that I would find it very hard to abandon."

This speaker chose his Ph.D. topic in an accidental way initially, but has continued to work in related areas ever since. Sometimes the effect could be more diffuse, as in this case:

> "Intellectually, it's obviously very central to my intellectual development. I had the rare opportunity of working with [distinguished sociologist] . . . and I don't think there are many sociologists who've been lucky enough to get involved in that way. So I learned about Weber and Durkheim; well I really got a feel for them, in the context of ongoing research . . . People who have been involved in research talk about theory differently, so my intellectual and sociological and political development have been very heavily indebted to that period. . . ."

Not everyone drew such positive lessons from their research experience; there were numbers for whom the main conclusion that they drew was that the methods used in their project were inherently unsuitable or inappropriate.

With respect to non-career aspects of private lives, the research was again seen as having both favourable and unfavourable effects; here, however, most people mentioned unfavourable effects, with only a few favourable ones to counterbalance them. Six people met spouses through the research, usually other members of the research team. One researcher believed that it, and the associated publicity, had helped him to acquire other members of his family:

166

"I have an adopted child, and I was first accepted as a prospective adoptive parent when I was in [previous job] and I was fairly low on the local authority waiting list. Within a fortnight of my photo appearing in various . . . journals the adoption officer came round with a quite different approach and a most beautiful child. Perhaps it's very very naughty to say that our [Simon] owes his existence to the [research job], but I can only say that the smoothness of adoption underwent dramatic changes. . . ."

In addition to these there was the odd favourable comment about the value of the research experience for personal development and maturity, and on the relative convenience of research jobs as opposed to others for respondents' domestic situations.

The unfavourable comments are of more interest, both because there are more of them and because there is more indication that the effects to which they refer arose from the nature of the research experience rather than idiosyncratic personal situations. Ten respondents said that their research took time from their families or general social life; sometimes it was just the occasional late meeting, sometimes much more extensive encroachment on normal leisure hours. Here are some typical comments, showing varying degrees of felt deprivation:

J.P. "Did you find that you couldn't have any private life?"
"That was very much in the background. Meetings would start at 7.30 or so and go on to 9.30, and on Sundays it was morning and afternoon for an hour and a half . . . Sundays were completely dominated by it, and many a week night."
J.P. "Did you feel that this was a depressing deprivation of your social life?"
"I don't think so, not that I recall. I was very interested in it, it was not just another piece of work that one had picked up, it was exciting, almost an adventure. . ."
(That was a single graduate student.)

". . . I think that I'd done my fieldwork away before we were married. . . . So that I don't think I was away for long periods. I was preoccupied with it all the time. It's very funny, I just remembered about it. . .we had this journalist friend, he used to come and sit and just chat with [Anna]. I knew Anna liked that; there was a need there that I never properly met. I was always reading or worrying about how I was going to organise it."

J.P. "Did all this . . . working on the research and so on

167

affect your family life at all?"
"Yes, but it's inseparable from my general. . .absolutely un-
relenting, remorseless interest in work. My family has always
suffered from that, I've always had a tendency to overwork. . .
I think my family regard me as a very nice appendage."

Wife. "The thing that really struck me as being obviously
absurd is, that you are expected to do research and teach. It
was obviously an absolutely massive thing to take on. . . ."
"I always feel in our department that you're not meant to
be married, you're meant to be a celibate."
Wife. "Yes, that's obviously true."

As these quotations show, it was sometimes the sheer quantity and
timing of the work that needed to be done that affected social life,
and sometimes more the psychological involvement in it. The respondents quoted so far are those who only said that the work took
time from ordinary social life; there are six more who said that for
them it had more serious consequences. For some it caused notably
strained relationships with their spouses:

J.P. "Did the research give you any domestic problems?"
"We don't have any children, and. . .we've got the most flexible
marriage I know. . . . The biggest personal problem was tiredness.
It's causing problems at the moment in that [Ted] is getting fed
up with me working [on the writing up] ; come 8.00 p.m. he
thinks it's time to stop, and because I'm in a panic about it I
keep on and I get very bad tempered and I snap. . . If I.d had to
do the routine housewife thing of cooking in the evening, and
being back at certain times, it would have been very different."

J.P. "How did [Nora] feel about it?"
"I think this. . .certainly in that respect the strain of research
told on our relationship. . . .I was using Nora, and she knew that
she was being used, for research purposes. On top of that [he had
to do observation in the evening, sometimes involving heavy
drinking] ; I felt I knew Nora was going up the wall, but I must
grab as much as I can. . .certainly Nora and myself felt very
annoyed about the research because it did so constrain the time
we had together. It meant that she couldn't blow her top in
public either. . . We had rows about the research, some of them
fairly serious. We never got to the point of Nora threatening to
leave, but she would complain of the research coming first."

J.P. "How did your wife feel about all this with you going off
and on?"

"It was very difficult for her; we had a very young baby at the time, at one point, and she was leading a physically isolated kind of existence, so that certainly for at least a year was a tremendous strain on her."

J.P. "Did this affect you in the research at all?"

"I think it did, I think it caused almost a breakdown at one point, at least I defined it that way. It affected ones marital relations very much because ultimately I felt I was a [factory worker] rather than a sociologist, which didn't mean one beats ones wife. . . There was the physical exhaustion at being in [factory], and the reaction to that tended to be to drop in front of the telly oblivious of the world (etc.) and spending the day making efforts making conversation with people meant that the last thing one wanted to do coming home was make conversation to people! So this is bound to create strains."

Two further men said that the pressures of their research had at least helped to precipitate their divorces. (And there was one more who said that the disruptions of frequent moves forced on him by a series of short research jobs contributed to his divorce.)

Contrary to my expectations, the people who found that the research encroached on their private lives were *not* drawn mainly from those who were involved in heavy fieldwork, especially participant observation, or had to work unusual hours or travel long distances to find their subjects. Method of data collection probably did make some difference: 32% (7 out of 22) of those who did participant observation reported personal difficulties, but only 16% (14 out of 87) of those who did surveys, and this shrinks to 9% when those who did participant observation as well are excluded.* Thus these factors contributed, but there was also a fair contingent who simply found research such an involving intellectual activity that their absorption in it left less time for other activities than they, or their families would have liked. However, the whole group were overwhelmingly (15 out of 16) drawn from those who, whatever their rank or the method of data-collection, had been actively involved in the day-to-day business of the research in more than an administrative or analytical capacity, and they constituted 1 in 5 of these.

My impression is that most researchers tend to think of the demands of social research on their time and emotional energies as unusual, and in some respects no doubt it is. However, it might

* When those who did surveys as well are excluded from the participant observation figure it too shrinks to 9%, but this does not mean much as it represents only two cases.

put this in perspective to make a comparison with some of Young and Willmott's recent data.* In their sample 36% of the professional and managerial group, and 18% of the clerical, reported that their work interfered with home and family because they had to spend time on work instead of with their families, and 9% and 4% that it interfered by causing strain, worry or overtiredness. This suggests that there are a fair number of other middle-class occupations that create similar problems. If my impression of the way researchers perceive their situation is right, it seems likely that this perception might be a reference group effect; the practical standard of comparison likely to be salient would be what it was like being a student or what it is like doing routine teaching, and there is also a normative reference to the ideal of intellectual concord and democratic team harmony.

However, the demands made by research can be considerable, especially for fieldworkers, who are commonly at those stages in the life cycle where these demands are most likely to conflict with domestic commitments. There is a conflict of norms here: one norm prescribes total commitment to the research, another prescribes that at least an ordinary amount of time should be spent with one's family and in social and leisure activities. When wives were unhappy about the time taken by the research it created pressures on the husband to trim his research commitments to fit his family life rather than vice versa, and these pressures were sometimes successful. It was probably commoner for men to resolve the conflict the other way and sacrifice family to the research. There are hints in the data that those who resolved it in favour of the family were those for whom there was something unsatisfactory about the research topic or organisation, or who were for some reason socially not fully involved with other members of their team and therefore not so sensitive to its social controls.

Thus, although this chapter takes various aspects of research workers' private lives as its dependent variable, and in this way explores the nature of the research experience for its own sake, in the end it nonetheless brings us back again to the project. If the work situation affects people's private lives, that in turn affects their attitude to the work situation. Sometimes the effect is a short-run one, and sometimes it is a longer-run one expressed in the pattern of a career. To the extent that research work demands a particularly high level of normative involvement it is likely to create unusual tensions

* Michael Young and Peter Willmott, *The Summetrical Family,* Routledge and Kegan Paul, 1973; p. 165.

between work and domestic commitments; perhaps this contributes to the propensity to leave full-time research as one gets older. These comments are speculative; they suggest, however, that in research as in other types of work the inter-relationships among conjugal roles, orientations to work and involvement in work would be worth further exploration.

CHAPTER 9

Conclusion

This book started with an ethnographic, a theoretical and a normative purpose. In this conclusion the data collected are reviewed and related to these purposes, though without attempting a complete summary of what has been said in earlier chapters. The purely ethnographic data stand as description, and as such have fulfilled their purpose. Here the primary concern is to draw out their implications for the other purposes, and to avoid excessive detail a broad ideal-typical approach will be used.

The characteristic way in which sociological research in Britain has been organised is for the director(s) who develop a proposal to receive a limited grant over a fixed period of time from a funding agency, and to use this to pay other full-time or part-time workers who will, with varying degrees of autonomy, work under his direction. The director is normally someone who has other commitments; in higher education these will be in teaching and administration, in research units in other projects. Thus there is typically a division of labour in which the person who initiated the research is not involved in it full-time, while at least some of the day-to-day work is done by other people who are recruited *ad hoc*. These other people come to the project with their own interests, expectations and motives, and for them it is a work situation as well as one of intellectual activity for its own sake. The group thus formed develops its own social structure, and pursues the research topic in a context where there are external constraints from the immediate institutional setting and from sponsors, clients and respondents. It has been shown in earlier chapters how all these factors interact in a variety of ways to affect the events of the research process. Some particularly significant chains of connections are sketched in below.

Faculty members at universities are expected to undertake research, and research is a high-status activity; it does not, however, confer high status to have a full-time research post or to spend much time on the more mundane and mechanical empirical research tasks. Funding agencies normally only make grants to people with established posts; there are few established research posts, since most depend on grants to specific projects. University teachers, especially at a time when their subject is expanding rapidly as sociology has over the past decade or so, have quite heavy teaching commitments and, if relatively senior, administrative commitments too, they are

172

unlikely to get leave for more than one or two terms of a project. A large number of projects, therefore, are under the direction of someone who works on them considerably less than full-time. Sometimes this direction may be a more or less nominal sponsorship to get the project funded and staffed, sometimes it implies quite full participation. Where the sponsorship is nominal, there is always the possibility of exploitation of research workers and of disillusion among them when it is found that the great man himself is seldom seen. Where it is more than nominal, the director's other commitments usually create serious problems for him in keeping in touch intellectually and practically with what is going on, and for the project as a whole in keeping to its timetable and reaching completion. The typical division of labour is one in which the director takes an active part in initial politics and research design, most of the fieldwork and coding is done and/or supervised by his research workers, and the director then returns to activity at the stage of analysis and is heavily involved in the writing up of the material. This division of labour creates a division of knowledge and experience in which the director is primarily involved in the more theoretical aspects of the research, while his research workers are primarily involved in its practical and operational aspects. Given the high status of theory, and academic norms of intellectual autonomy, this division tends to create low morale among research workers; it also, in combination with the director's lack of time, makes detailed communication between them difficult and so creates an anomic situation for the juniors. Research assistants tend to feel that the director's theorizing is inadequately grounded, while directors deplore their assistants' inability to make an appropriate theoretical contribution; when the legitimacy of authority is in doubt, conflicts can arise. Overt conflict, differences of perspective, and lack of time all make it hard for the project to keep to its original timetable, and over-running is common. When the grant expires, the team normally disperses, and this makes analysis and writing difficult, both because there are physical barriers to communication and because now no one is working on it full-time. As time goes on and the writing-up is still not completed, it becomes disproportionately harder to do; the data are increasingly out of date and so lose relevance, the team's ideas develop and change so that the data no longer seem what they would now wish to have collected, and they all become involved in other projects and interests.

Another line of connections may be followed through by looking at aspects of the grant system. Grants can only be made on the basis of fairly specific research proposals, and they provide fixed amounts

173

of money over predetermined periods of time. Research workers can only be appointed when a grant has been made, and so cannot normally be involved in the formulation of the proposal and the thinking that lies behind it. The directors who make the proposals quite often have little experience themselves of empirical research, and lack of time and of funds usually prevent them from doing anything like a pilot study before putting the proposal forward; this makes it difficult for them to be realistically specific. Unpredictable outside events can affect the course of research, and at the level of ideas and of data new themes are always likely to emerge. Thus it is easy for the original proposals to show both poor planning, which does not take into account the practical implications of the strategies to be followed, and too much planning, in that insufficient provision has been made for flexibility and adaptation to changing circumstances and the interests of research workers. Either is likely to mean that is is difficult to keep to the original timetable, and so the grant runs out and the team disperses or an extension is applied for; as the money comes to an end, or appears likely to, research workers who depend on it for their salary need to start applying for other jobs, and these may eventually force them to leave early even if it turns out that an extension is given. Once they have got other jobs they not only have less time for the original research but also less personal motive to put effort into completing it, since it is likely to seem less essential for their immediate career than doing well in the new job. Because most research jobs are tied to particular projects the occupation is an insecure one, and so there is an incentive to look for tenure (and status) in teaching jobs; for the duration of any one project this means that juniors are anxious to do Ph.D.s and take on teaching which will help to qualify them for that, and so spend less time on the main research. A long-run consequence for British sociology as a whole is that few of those working full-time in research have much practical experience to draw on. This means that they frequently come to it with unrealistic expectations which are doomed to disillusion, and this disillusion may seem attributable to the particular methods employed, or the style of the direction, rather than to the inherent nature of research. Interpretations vary, but whatever the interpretation mistakes are made and morale suffers. The director faces a dilemma: if he plays a more directive role it takes more time, and may risk lower commitment to a project which juniors cannot feel is really their own; if he takes a less active part the research is likely to suffer technically, and he may be accused by his juniors of laziness or exploitation.

It seems evident that there are strong relations of interdependence among these networks of variables, although the nature of the data (and perhaps also the inherent character of the subject matter) is such that it is not always easy to impute causal directions. If funding agencies made grants that covered the time of principal investigators, directors would be more likely to take part full-time in all stages of their own research (and would presumably need fewer juniors); if teaching posts were not of higher status within universities, lecturers might be more willing to do full-time research. If more senior people commonly occupied research posts, they might have higher status; if they were not felt to be of lower status, more people might be interested in staying in them as they became more senior. If people in research posts were more senior, divisions of labour which allocated the routinized tasks to them might be less common; if research posts entailed less routinized work, they would be of more interest to more senior people. If teams were less hierarchical in their division of labour, fewer surveys might be done; if fewer surveys were planned, there would be fewer low-status routinized tasks to be performed. If directors were not so busy teaching, they could devote more time to their research; if they had more time to devote to their research, its completion would not be so protracted. And so on. Rather than looking for clear starting-points of chains of causation it might make more sense to think in terms of there being a social system, of which sociological research forms a part, whose parts are functionally interdependent. If the system in some ways seems to constitute a vicious circle, another aspect of such patterns must be borne in mind: to the extent that it does form a system, change in any one part will have consequences for the others. Some further comments are made below about the likelihood of change.

Many of the propositions made above do not look very surprising in the abstract, but it is clear that their implications are often not recognized in practice. One reason for the sense of familiarity they give is that they bring out the similarities between work in sociological research and work of other kinds; it is curious how little, as Julius Roth* points out, sociologists have thought of applying the theories and insights of the sociology of work and of formal organisations to their own research activities. In social research jobs as in others there is a hierarchy of authority whose legitimation is problematic, and the compliance of lower participants can not be taken for granted; qualitiative division of labour creates tasks with varying scope for interest, autonomy, status and identification; the structure of sanctions

* Julius A. Roth, "Hired hand research", *The American Sociologist*, vol. 1, no. 4, August 1966.

to reward conformity and punish deviation may be more or less successfully designed to elicit the desired behaviour; employees come to the job with varying prior orientations to their work, and varying opportunities for self-selection into jobs congruent with their orientations; different technologies impose constraints that make some organisational forms more effective than others. It is likely that social research is at an extreme of the continuum on a number of relevant variables, but that does not mean that these variables are irrelevant or that comparisons are not illuminating. The nature of the task in most sociological research is a mixture of creative imagination and highly-routinized and repetitive work, so it is inevitable that research as a work situation should have elements both of flexibility and of standardisation. The degree of open-endedness and lack of structure is probably greater than in most other work tasks, and this is increased by the fact that it is normal for key participants to spend only an unspecified part of their time on it. This, together with the fact that all those involved have usually been socialized into the ethos of the pursuit of knowledge for its own sake, makes it unclear how far the activity should normatively be regarded as *work* rather than freely-undertaken intellectual exploration; hence some of the ambiguities of the situation. It is possible that this flexibility, plus the likelihood that any one research team is only formed *d hoc* for a particular project, may leave more scope for variation related to the characteristics that individuals bring to the situation than does the typical occupational setting. This does not, however, imply that research events are to be explained in purely psychological terms, for the relevant characteristics are themselves socially patterned ones such as group norms, career stages and domestic and personal circumstances.

The aspect of research to which least attention has, inevitably, been paid in this book is its substantive intellectual content. It might be felt that it has not been shown that practical arrangements have strictly intellectual effects, and that unless this is done the data are of limited concern to anyone without a specialized interest in the sociology of work and organisations. To some extent the comment is justified, because no systematic attempt has been made to look at the character of the publications from the projects studied. I think there are a number of points on which it is nonetheless fairly obvious that intellectually relevant consequences are likely to follow from the patterns of social organisation. This statement may be buttressed by adding here some direct comments made in the interviews about ways in which the participants themselves saw important research decisions being affected. For instance, several people said that a survey was used not because it seemed the method most appropriate

176

to their problem but because it was the only method that could be used with the time and resources available; several others reported that they had collected qualitative data which was never actually used because they did not have time to analyse it. Similarly, the nature of the division of labour, and the consequent lack of commitment and understanding of some of the more marginal participants, was noted to have had effects in these cases on the quality of data: (i) market research interviewers (brought in to speed things up) did interviews on a difficult topic which were qualitatively unsatisfactory because of their lack of specific training; (ii) coding was done sloppily because the coders were paid by quantitative results; (iii) coders were recruited by a research assistant from among his unemployed acquaintances, and he supervised them only loosely. The task was coding test results, and a sample check revealed that their errors tended to be of under-estimation. Thus the crucial research 'finding' that test scores were lower than on a previous occasion might have been an artefact of the style of supervision. Subtler points in the tradition of the sociology of knowledge would require other kinds of data; I would be surprised if such an analysis did not reveal some significant influences.

Returning now to the main theme, the propositions outlined above give a sort of ideal-typical account of the university team project in British sociology in the recent past. The picture drawn is not an encouraging one; all lines seem to converge on an outcome in which the project takes an excessive amount of time or remains unfinished. Such outcomes are indeed common, although of course there are projects that are successfully completed. Looking at the projects in the sample, and dividing them impressionistically into those that have been more or less successful, a pattern emerges. Successful projects tend to have been those that were outside the universities, that were directed by full-time researchers, and that had only a small number of people directly involved; unsuccessful ones tended to be within the universities, to have part-time directors and to involve large numbers of people. They may also have had other factors in common, but it seems likely that these factors are more than accidentally related to success; by now one can see why some should hinder and other promote a successful conclusion. Can any suggestions be made that would help a higher proportion of future research projects to success?

The ethnographic purpose of this book has been relatively easy to carry out. At first I naively thought that its normative methodological purpose would be equally easy, and envisaged writing a concluding chapter giving colleagues the benefit of my recommendations for the future conduct of social research. This no longer seems realistic, although there are certainly points in the data reported that might provide some useful hints. The reason it no longer seems realistic, although there are certainly points in the data re- ported that might provide some useful hints. The reason it no longer seems realistic is that the theoretical conclusions reached suggest that crucial features of the social organisation of sociological research in Britain are beyond the control of the individual research director. He cannot, as an individual and in the short run, control the state of the labour market for sociology graduates, the grant policies of universities and funding agencies, the norms of the university system or the extent to which research careers are available; all he can do is adapt to these external constraints.

Thus, although I think it has been quite convincingly shown that there are many factors in the conduct of sociological research which the textbooks do not take into account, it does not follow that al- ternative contents for that kind of textbook can now be suggested. The shortcoming of the textbooks is not that they do not give ade- quate recipes for producing the desired results, but that they do not specify the circumstances under which it is likely to be possible to use those recipes in practice. They are both philosophical rather than sociological and individualistic rather than social in their orientation, and there are excellent reasons why *recommendations* to *individual researchers* should take that form. What can be drawn from my data is not so much recipes as some light on which social patterns are con- gruent with what kinds of intellectual decision. Thus one may say that bureaucratisation goes well with survey methods, while partici- pant observation and unstructured interviewing go with a relatively egalitarian division of labour.

There is also, however, a whole area of research planning and management where intellectual decisions are not involved but where the practical decisions made affect the success of a project, and this is the area on which the data in this book are most suggestive of recommendations. Some of the conclusions from which recommen- dations might be drawn are these:

(i) If team members are not chosen with an eye to intellectual and personal compatibility, there are potential sources of friction.

(ii) If the career needs of participants do not coincide with the needs of the project, the project is likely to suffer.

(iii) If the intellectual interests of participants are at the periphery of the project, it is likely to get diverted and become fragmented into distinct sub-projects.

(iv) If inducements are held out to research workers that may not be able to be given, they are likely to become disillusioned and lose commitment to the project.

(v) If the interests of sponsors and researchers in a project do not coincide, or cannot be pursued jointly, trouble is likely to ensue.

(vi) If sponsors have contractual control over the form to be taken by data-collection or publication they are likely to exercise it in ways that do not serve the interests of sociology.

(vii) Junior research workers quite often take jobs on projects for reasons other than deep intellectual interest in its topic, so identification and commitment cannot be taken for granted.

(viii) Division of labour creates division of experience and perspective, and this can become conflict of interests; it is often hard to put back together again intellectually what was thus divided, and a research proletariat can be alienated and become class-conscious.

(ix) Inadequate supervision of semi-skilled labour permits errors to occur.

(x) Too much democratic discussion in a research team can lead to procrastination and unhappy compromises.

This book as a whole, and this chapter in particular, may seem to lay too much emphasis on the things that can go wrong in research. It is possible that the data lay an unduly heavy stress on mistakes and disasters because of the way in which the sample was chosen. I have attempted not to make the implicit claim that the sample is representative, but whether it is or not it seems to me that in the current state of the field it is legitimate and appropriate to pay more attention to the things that go wrong than to the things that go right. By doing this one makes it clearer that the social context and organisation of research have consequences that researchers cannot afford to ignore, and that prescriptions for the right logical structure of research are incomplete without consideration of the social structures through which decisions are reached and implemented.

However, beyond these points, it does seem likely that a particularly large number of things were going wrong in British sociological research in the late sixties, for a variety of historical reasons. That was the period of the boom in academic sociology, when the number of sociology students in universities expanded enormously in a very short time. It was therefore necessary for the number of academics teaching sociology to expand too, and it did; this expansion, however, had to draw on a labour market which, inevitably, contained relatively few sociology graduates. Thus many young people joined university faculties before completing their Ph.D.s, and quite a number became sociologists whose first degrees were in other subjects; both old and new recruits found that expansion, and in many cases the founding of sociology departments from scratch, gave them a very heavy load of teaching and administration. This expansion coincided with two other factors: the relative cutback in university funds in the U.S.A., which meant decreased opportunities for foreign graduate students to study there, and the powerful intellectual fashion for non-empiricist European traditions of social thought, in particular Marxism. The age structure of academic sociology became heavily skewed towards the younger end, and there was a lot of movement between universities in pursuit of career advancement. All these factors meant that for new entrants to the profession there was little time or opportunity — or indeed often inclination — to be socialized into a tradition of empirical sociological research.* There was also little incentive to devote oneself to acquiring its laborious practical and technical expertise when it was not needed for career advancement and when fashion was against one. Publishers responded to the expansion of the student market by commissioning a whole range of texts, and it was very easy to publish reviews of the field or theoretical studies resting only on library work; a large superstructure of secondary works was produced without much growth in their primary base. Those people who did persist in empirical work often felt threatened by the powerful critique of empiricism and positivism, which made it much easier to pick holes in other people's research than to do one's own. This probably helped to delay publication, both because the criticism is internalized and because it makes it necessary for the writing to be mulled over longer.**

Against this background it seems less surprising that many of the projects studied here suffered from the lack of experience of their directors; this lack of experience in itself contributed to mistakes which helped disillusion their research assistants, who found ready to hand an idealistic set of expectations with which to compare the reality, and an ideology which interpreted any falling short of these expectations as due to the inherent nature of positivistic social science rather than to lack of expertise in it. (Sometimes, of course,

* These tendencies are encouraged by the fact that some undergraduate sociology courses contain no training in research methods; in those where it is taught the content may be so abstract and philosophical as to give no practical guidance, or so concentrated on techniques that the relationship to theoretical ideas is not evident. The tendency for it to be a separate course taught by a specialist encourages the idea that the normal sociologist is not expected to know about these things.

** I am indebted to Martin Bulmer for this last point.

they were right.) I find it very worrying to note how many of those interviewed, spontaneously said that the moral they drew from their experiences was that they would not wish to do that kind of research again. Eleven respondents specifically said that they would not want ever to do a large survey again, and 2 people said that their experiences had put them off all empirical work. Several more were doubtful about the value of team work unless team members were carefully selected for intellectual and personal compatibility. Although quite a high proportion of the comments on what people had learnt were positive in the sense that they could now see ways to do things better, the striking thing about the general tone of the comments was how seldom people reported having gained practical experience of the *right* way to do things; they knew how to do things better next time because they had learnt to avoid what they had so far experienced. This unhappy atmosphere of negative learning suggests that for some, at least, what they have learnt is unlikely to be applied; this, in combination with the lack of permanent research posts or good sabbatical leave opportunities, makes it less likely that a solid tradition of empirical research will be established. There is such a tradition outside the universities, but it is not distinctively sociological and, as some respondents remarked, does not seem to be part of the network of intellectual and personal relationships of academic sociology.

This picture of research in British sociology is not an encouraging one, but perhaps it is already becoming a little dated; it can at least be hoped that, with the institutionalisation of sociology in the universities, and the end of large-scale expansion, the situation will become more stable and research experience will have more chance to be transmitted and cumulated. I would hope that this book might make its small contribution to the improvement of research by encouraging reflection on its organisation and study of the conditions that promote its success.

APPENDICES

A. Research Methods

Those colleagues whom I interviewed for this research gave me very frank accounts of their own projects; I owe them, in return, an equally frank account of mine. In this appendix I give a history of the project, emphasizing those aspects that I have considered in the main body of the book, as well as a detailed account of the methods used.

History

The intellectual origins of this project are described in the Introduction. Its social origin, as a definite research intention, was that I was invited to compile a British version of *Sociologists at Work*,* a collection of accounts of their research by sociologists. I accepted the invitation enthusiastically, although I immediately thought that it would be desirable to give that sort of account of research experience rather more editorial framework. The idea that developed, therefore, was that I would solicit accounts from colleagues which covered a standardized list of topics, and that this would make it possible for me to write something editorially of an analytical and generalizing nature. I prepared an elaborate and detailed list of questions to be answered in these accounts, and took the opportunity of a conference to show it to a number of people and ask for comments on the idea. I found this embarrassing, and felt that it was gauche and impertinent to ask people to write to my orders, especially if they were senior to me or not personal friends. These doubts seemed justified by the reception, which was cool; no one overtly criticized, but everyone somehow thought that is would be better for me to talk to someone else about their research. This does not seem very surprising, since what I had in mind fell awkwardly between a questionnaire and an autonomous essay, combining the constraint of the former with the responsibility of the latter. Without any clear conscious decision being made, my ideas began to change. This was part of a long, vague preparatory period in which I did not know how to start, and was afraid to commit myself to anything specific. (In this state I could hardly have prepared a grant application, if I had wanted to, but in any case I did not want to apply to the S.S.R.C.;

* ed. P. Hammond, *Sociologists at Work*, Basic Books, New York,1964.

182

my previous experience of applying had given me a strong non-rational distaste for the procedure.) I put a notice in *Sociology* in January 1971 partly to force myself to start; this is what it said:

> Jennifer Platt is collecting material for a book on the
> sociology of the social research process for which she
> needs histories of research projects, whether completed
> or not. Anyone who might be interested in providing such
> an account is invited to write to her for further details.

In early 1971 I became pregnant, and it seemed obvious that if I waited until after I had had the baby to start I might never get around to it. I applied to The University of Sussex's Arts & Social Studies Research Fund for a grant of £150 to cover my travelling expenses, and started interviewing in the early summer of 1971. (Subsequently I had another grant from this fund.) I think I regarded this as a pilot, and assumed that the data I collected in unstructured interviews would allow me to develop a more precise plan; imperceptibly, this pilot became the main study.

I did 22 interviews before the baby arrived at the end of September. For the last few, male respondents were clearly nervous that they might be called on to act as midwife; in two interviews with men who took a sympathetic interest in the pregnancy it was noticeable that the sex lives of team colleagues bulked large in the story of their research! For the next few months I could interview only people at Sussex, (sometimes on short visits), in London, or near towns where we could stay the weekend with friends or relations. By the summer of 1972 the baby was weaned, so I could interview intensively again, which I did through the summer and the autumn term when I had sabbatical leave. My husband knows the domestic costs of this, and my absences had to be timed to suit his teaching timetable; had he not been an academic, it would have been impossible without a full-time nanny. The absolute necessity of getting home in time sometimes cut interviews short, or encouraged me not to probe as much as I might otherwise have done.

The interviews were recorded in my private shorthand, developed in previous interviewing experience. Respondents often asked why I did not use a tape recorder, to which one answer is that it did not occur to me. I had never used one before and did not trust my own technical competence, and did not know whether I could get hold of one that would be reliable enough; anyway I did not want to carry any extra weight around when pregnant. I was not initially worried about the accuracy of my recording because I was thinking of it as a pilot; after I had got into practice my own method appeared reliable

183

enough for it not to be necessary to investigate alternatives. For most people I could record almost everything that I wished; for unusually fast or incoherent speakers, or in physically unfavourable circumstances, I would catch the gist and at least some of the actual words used. Since my abbreviations usually left off the end of words, the kind of recording error that is most likely to have occurred is in the tense of verbs, which seldom had substantive importance; in other cases of ambiguity the context almost always makes the necessary word clear where memory could not provide it.

The interviews themselves generated a surprising amount of work. Beforehand, there was the administrative task of getting consent to be interviewed and arranging a mutually convenient time; where possible I arranged several interviews on one trip, which made this more complicated, so there was a lot of correspondence. Afterwards, the interviews had to be transcribed, and this turned out to be an enormously laborious process. I dictated my notes into a dictating machine, and typists typed from this. The interviews normally took well over an hour, which came out as rather less on the tape, but typists usually took a day or more to transcribe one interview. Although the fact that it was all dictation in my voice made it easier, the material was intrinsically harder than the usual dictation because it was colloquial speech with unfinished sentences etc., and often an idiosyncratic mixture of bad language and professional jargon. This meant that there were a lot of errors and omissions and I had to check it very carefully. Like, I now realize, most researchers who do this kind of interview, I enormously underestimated the work of transcription. I was given a further grant to pay to have some of it done commercially when the burden became too much for the University's usual secretarial resources, but the commercial agency was even less at home with such material and did it very badly. In the end it was saved by the fact that a section of the University administration had a typist with failing sight who could now only do dictation, of which her own section could not provide enough, and so she did a lot of it. All this meant that there were a large number of typists, working in different buildings, involved; until I devised a bureaucratic system for keeping track of my tapes I nearly lost some. Obviously a project of this nature really needs its own full-time typist.

There were yet further practical difficulties associated with the transcription. In principle I dictated each interview as soon as possible after its completion. In practice this could not be done. During my sabbatical term, when I was doing a lot of interviews and university typists were busy with routine work (faculty research officially has less priority than all other work), it emerged that there were not enough tapes for the dictating machine. Previously they had been transcribed and then could be used again, but now they were all full; I had occupied the whole stock of tapes of the Arts side of the univeristy! My transcription grant therefore also allowed for the purchase of some more tapes, but by the time these came an overwhelming backlog of dictation had built up. In the following term I returned to teaching, and had a number of coughs and colds; this meant that on many evenings when I had time my voice was too tired for intelligible dictation. Thus the progress of the whole project was considerably delayed by these trivial mechanical factors.

The grants I had from the University set no deadlines for the completion of the research, but a deadline was set by the contract for this book. Not wholly irrelevant to the decision to sign a contract was the fact that the advance would come in very handy for the unexpected expense of needing a new kitchen roof; it is also, of course, reassuring to feel that publication is guaranteed. Having signed, and allowed myself to be persuaded to a deadline that made no provision for contingencies, had consequences for the timetable of the research. I stopped interviewing when I did because by then it seemed urgent to start analysis if I was to get the writing done; as things have turned out, the book is about 8 months late anyway. (But I would probably not have continued much longer in any case.) This is no doubt in part due to my incompetence, but the intrinsic nature of the problems involved in the analysis (which are discussed below) has also contributed; these issues have not been much considered in the methodological literature.

Early in 1974 I had to concentrate on writing a paper for a British Sociological Association conference. I had unwisely let myself be persuaded to give one on sex roles in social research; this was unwise because it was not a salient theme of the project, and the sample did not have a high enough proportion of women to make comparisons feasible. With great difficulty I wrote the paper, and this forced me to structure some of the data in relation to organizing ideas. Although I regret the time spent on a peripheral paper, writing it probably helped to focus my mind. When I got back from the conference I was ready to start writing, and found that some of the earlier problems became unimportant. It seemed natural to make extensive quotations from interviews rather than attempt to construct tables, and the quotations had their own logic that gave a structure to the chapters; occasionally the course of the argument suggested some counting, and generally it could be done.

The reader will judge how appropriate this mode of presentation has been. The first drafts were dominated by quotations, and although to me chapters had some intellectual structure it was no means explicit enough to be clear to other readers; I was so fascinated by the data in all its detail that I could not bear to leave anything out, and the task of imposing an analytical framework on it kept getting postponed. Moreover, I have lived with it so much that the theoretical implications seemed obvious to me, and I felt that it would be crude and almost insulting to my readers to spell out what was self-evident; kind friends who read first drafts disabused me of this idea. As I wrote more, it became increasingly obvious that I could not put everything in, and I became capable of leaving out interesting titbits that could not be fitted into the general argument. I still felt, however, some ethnographic responsibility, given the paucity of other research in this field, to give a fairly full picture of what I had been told irrespective of whether inclusion had an obvious theoretical rationale. The end result is some sort of compromise between these conflicting tendencies. Clearly the fascination with every corner of ones data, which can easily become intellectually almost pathological, is a product of a degree of involvement with it which is uncommon except in participant observation. Sociologically, I was playing the role of the research assistant in the division of labour at a point when dialogue between assistant and director was called for; this is a predictable consequence of undertaking solo research.

When I started on this project, I had not thought of the merits and demerits of solo research; having embarked on it more or less accidentally, I found that they forced themselves on my attention in my own experience, as well as having some light thrown on them by the data. The enormous advantage of working alone is that one is so intimately acquainted with one's data. I did every interview myself, and went through each one again at least 3 times, to dictate it, check the typing, and code it; this means that in some ways coding has been almost superfluous, and I know where to look for instances if a new idea comes. I had no problems at all with the training or theoretical understanding of my interviewer and coder, who knew immediately what I wanted. On the other hand, the enormous disadvantage of working alone is the lack of critical comment, and the absence of any external pressure to make one's ideas explicit. With no formal instructions to interviewers, interviewing strategy may vary in ways that do more than just show learning over time, or sensitivity of response to variations in the situation. With no detailed codebook, one can easily not make clear to oneself what one means by one's categories and so their meaning shifts and blurs as new contingencies arise. One can be so convinced of one's total familiarity with the data that one codes from memory rather than looking at the actual interview again — and sometimes memory distorts. I made most of these mistakes, and know I made them because subsequently I caught myself out; there may well be others that I did not catch. On balance, however, these disadvantages seem to me far less than those which can follow from division of labour. Large-scale survey methods (which are very appropriate to some problems) both require division of labour and are required by it. Where they are not appropriate to the problem, criticism can be had without setting up a team to do it; at the cost of an amount of time probably not proportionately greater than if the work were shared one can possess one's own work fully.

Sample and response rate

There was no sampling frame available which could have been useful for my purposes without adding a substantial introductory stage to the project. To say this, however, is *post hoc* rationalisation; probably the prime reason the sample initially took the form it did was my fear of being refused if I approached people out of the blue. The way I started, therefore, was to place my appeal in *Sociology*, and to write to a few friends or acquaintances who had already shown some interest in the research. I received only one reply through *Sociology* but that was a very helpful one since it came from someone who had been involved in a large project; once I had interviewed a colleague it seemed to legitimate approaching other members of the team, which I did. My first friends and acquaintances all let me interview them, and indeed did much better than that, since they also recruited further respondents for me. I had not planned this, but one person simply suggested that while I was at his university I should see other members of the department too, and himself arranged for me to see everyone there who had done any empirical research. This was so successful that where I knew people in other departments well enough I sometimes asked them to do the same for me; in this way I met numbers of people whom I did not know and whose research I had not previously heard of. The excellent response I got increased my confidence, and I then started writing out of the blue, or on the basis of very slight acquaintance, to authors of recent publications or people whose unpublished research others told me about; early respondents often suggested other possibilities to me. I felt that the *Sociology* appeal provided a convenient way of introducing the subject, and so was useful in that sense despite the low response to it. When I interviewed anyone who had worked in a team, I normally then tried to see the other team members.* In principle I only failed to try when (a) there were a number of members playing the same role in the division of labour in a large team, and I had seen some of them, or (b) when the member concerned appeared to have played only a marginal or short-term role in the research. In practice, a few also got left out because it would have been geographically inconvenient to visit them (but see below). I also looked through university calendars to remind myself of names, and lists of research in progress to find out what was going on. At the beginning I looked for any research fitting my basic requirements that I could find. Towards the end I made a special effort to locate projects that differed in theoretically relevant ways from the ones that I had so far; this meant mainly that I looked for projects that had not been university-based. Among those projects and individuals that I identified as possible ones to approach, the ones that I did *not* approach were usually those that were both geographically inconvenient (in that a long trip would be required for only one respondent) and had as far as I knew no special interest to justify the effort to include them — that is, the project sounded a fairly ordinary university one, or the person came from a team where I had seen other people of the same rank, or other members reported that his role had been marginal or not distinctive. But I did take some trouble to ensure that my sample was not geographically biased, travelling as far west as Swansea and as far north as Aberdeen; the mobility rates of sociologists meant that I sometimes wondered if this was worth while when I found myself in Aberdeen interviewing someone whose research turned out to have been done in Southampton. I managed to see 2 people now working abroad while they were in England on brief visits. For these reasons it does not seem useful to report the geographical distribution of the sample. There were 2 or 3 people whom I did not approach because I was frightened of them, on status or personality grounds; there were also a small number of people who might otherwise have been approached but were not because I could not get hold of an address for them, or they were dead or abroad or having a baby.**

* "Team member" was (implicitly) defined to exclude clerical employees and groups such as interviewers and coders whose roles were limited and who were usually recruited for short periods only. Obviously this is in some ways an unfortunate limitation. However, had I tried to see them, they would have been much harder to trace.

** Some whole university departments were also avoided because another researcher was interviewing in them. We discovered each other's existence fairly early, and agreed that each would keep away from the departments where the other had already started work or planned to do so. Fortunately our plans did not clash.

No doubt there are biases in the sample, but obviously these are hard to identify. Insofar as it consists of my acquaintances and theirs, it has whatever bias this indicates. It probably means that the youngest generation of sociologists are under-represented if they directed research, since there is a greater chance that I will have met people if they have been around longer. If respondents are classified by the extent of my personal acquaintance with them, 21 were friends, 7 past or present colleagues, 24 acquaintances (usually from conferences) and the remaining 69 previously completely unknown to me.* Of those I did not previously know, the ways in which I contacted them were: introduction by friend who arranged the interview for me, 10; response to *Sociology* notice, 2; conference meeting engineered or immediately used by me to make an appointment, 3; letter on the basis of no contact of any kind, 53; and 1 respondent volunteered himself on hearing that I was seeing some of his colleagues. There probably is some bias towards projects regarded as 'interesting', especially in the sense of having suffered mishaps of various kinds, because other people tended to define my interests in this way and hence tell me about the existence of such projects more than others. However, I think the sample does include a high proportion of the strictly sociological projects of any size that fell within my specifications; it was gratifying to note how often, towards the end of the research period, when someone recommended a project to me it was one that I had already included. The major exclusion was earlier projects by the same individual; except in the case of my 2 gallant volunteers, I did not interview the same individual about more than one project.

So much for possible bias stemming from mode of recruitment to the sample. Bias in terms of eventual representativeness of the projects can be checked a little more formally in one respect by looking at the distribution of subject matter. In late 1966, M.P. Carter made a survey of sociological research in Britain, and among the results he reported were the fields into which the current research projects of his respondents fell.**

* I have coded the strongest possible relationship where more than one category might apply; some of those classified 'friend' might be quite surprised to hear of it. The 'respondents' counted are in fact respondent/ interviews; one person was interviewed about 2 projects and another about 3.

** M.P. Carter, "Report on a Survey of Sociological Research in Britain," *Sociological Review* vol. 16, 1968.

The following table compares the pattern that he found with the distribution of my sample; for the sake of comparability I have omitted his categories 'basic theory' and 'methodology':

	Carter %	Platt %
Industrial, sociology of work	23	20
Education	16	20
Local communities	11	7
Sociology of social services, policy etc.	8	13
Religion	6	4
Medicine	6	5
Social stratification	5	5
Political sociology	5	2
Family and kinship	4	4
Criminology	3	5
Mass communications	3	2
Race	1	7
Other	10	5
	101%	99%
	N = 320	N = 55

Carter's respondents appear to have classified their own projects into these categories. I coded the ones in my sample, and found that often it was not clear whether a project should be counted as, for instance, social stratification or industrial sociology, social policy or medicine; I used my judgement to place them in the single category that seemed to fit best. At any rate, the table shows that the broad patterns are similar, and to that extent is reassuring. The higher proportion in my sample of projects in the area of social policy is probably due to my efforts to include governmental and sponsored projects, many of which naturally fall into that area; the higher proportion on race reflects the Nuffield Foundation's grant to the Institute of Race Relations for a survey of race relations in Britain, which led to the commissioning of a number of projects in that field. I detect no bias towards fields in which I have a special personal interest. Five projects that might have been included in the sample were eliminated by 'refusals' (see below) of individuals; from what I know of the projects concerned, there is no reason to believe that their character led to the 'refusal'. Two of them were in the social policy field, one in industrial sociology, one in sociology of medicine, and for the fifth the person concerned and I were going to discuss which of several of his projects should be explored.

In the attempt to get some better check on the representativeness of my sample, I wrote to the editors of the British sociological journals asking if it might be possible to get some data on the distribution of articles sent to them. The editors replied that their records of rejected articles were not in such a form that they could provide the necessary information easily (or at all), and in any case there were doubts about how far it could be given to me without violating confidentiality. This attempt, therefore, could be pursued no further.

Among those people that I approached, the response rate was excellent. There were 2 refusals, both from people unknown to me who refused on the ground that they had only played a marginal role in the relevant project; their colleagues' accounts agreed that their roles had been small, though not without significance. Four people never replied to my letter; of these one was a friend, one a colleague whom I had already interviewed about another project, and 2 people unknown to me who may have left the addresses I had for them. Finally, 4 said 'yes' but were never actually interviewed; of these, 2 simply turned out not to be going to be in convenient places at the right time, and 2 others said they would let me know when they were available and did not. If one takes the most pessimistic possible interpretation and classifies all these 10 as refusals, 8% of those I approached refused to be interviewed. Perhaps such an excellent response rate from a sample of social scientists requires no explanation; even if people were embarrassed to reveal the informal aspects of their research experience (in a situation with none of the anonymity of the usual research interview), this would be counterbalanced by internalized professional norms and the professionally visible nature

191

of a refusal. Numbers of people said that they thought the topic of the research was important and the results would be useful, and co-operated for that reason; their motive was strictly professional, and I hope they will feel that the results justify their expectations. Motives were no doubt complex among those who might have preferred not to take part. I think that some facts about my own position probably helped people not to feel too unwilling: I was neither very junior nor very senior in age or rank, and my name was fairly widely known but my reputation not alarmingly distinguished; it was also known that I had some empirical research experience myself. I think it was also important, having observed my own and colleagues' reactions to questionnaires, that my method was unstructured interviewing, since this provides no specific handle for technical criticism and shows some deference to the respondent, who may if he wishes define himself as an informant passing on his accumulated wisdom. Motives not peculiar to social scientists, such as pleasure in talking about oneself, the wish not to appear to have anything to hide, and the gratification of recounting one's grievances, no doubt also contributed.

The eventual composition of the sample seen, in terms of individuals, was: 96 men, 25 women; 45 research directors, 33 senior research officers and research officers, 33 research assistants, 6 Ph.D. students not elsewhere classified, and 4 clients or administrators. Given the projects included, the population of individuals whom I might have seen — i.e. all those involved in these projects — is defined. It therefore makes sense to look at who I did and who I did not see as a possible source of bias. The table below gives the proportions, by sex and rank, of those in relevant groups on the projects in the sample whom I did *not* see:

Proportions of those eligible who were not interviewed, by sex and rank.

Rank:	Director	Research Officer	Research Assistant.	N*
	%	%	%	
Male	27	25	37	123
Female	25	50	64	49
N*	61	48	63	172

*N is the total number of people in the relevant category.

192

The main reasons for which I did not see people (including 8 miscellaneous ones not in the previous table) can be classified as follows:

	Male	Female
Dead or abroad	7	2
Could not be traced	1	1
Refused	1	1
Geographically inconvenient to see	2	0
Not a sociologist	6	3
Left the project early	3	2
Played small role in project	8	3
Other reasons	13	16
	41	28

The 'other reasons' category needs further explanation. It includes cases where I thought I had seen enough people at that level on that project, which is why it applies particularly often in the case of research asistants. It also covers two cases where I had already seen the person concerned about another project in the sample, and one where a woman was on maternity leave when I would otherwise have seen her. The particular individuals omitted tended to be those who were on the margin of academic life or had left it altogether, for other jobs or for housewifery. In the case of 2 projects, accounting for 5 people not seen, my prime interest was in factors to do with commissioned research in non-university settings on which I thought directors, whom I did see, would be the best informants. The net effect of all these exclusions is that the sample of individuals is skewed in the direction of main-stream university career sociologists. The balance of the book might have been somewhat different had it not been thus skewed, but I suspect it would have made little difference to the conclusions on the topics actually covered.

Interviewing

The interviews took place in a variety of settings. Most commonly it was the respondent's office or home, but by force of circumstance several were done in bars, cafes or common rooms. A few respondents I caught passing through Sussex as visiting speakers or external examiners, and 2 stayed the night at our house to be interviewed. The first half of one interview was conducted while driving from the station to the university and stopping for petrol; my recording of that was less than verbatim! The main practical problem was not so much the setting as the lack of time, since each took up to 2 hours or more and both parties often had other commitments. Three of the interviews were with a pair of respondents from the same project, two of the pairs being spouses; in two other cases the person I was interviewing called in a colleague for part of the time. It was interesting to hear each commenting on what the other said, but each said less than they would have done in a solo interview, so something was lost; each person present for a complete interview has been counted as one respondent, but only the things they themselves said have been attributed to them. Joint interviews were quite often suggested to me, and after early experience I always arranged to see people separately where possible, explaining the value of hearing about events from separate perspectives. Occasionally spouses who had not been involved in the research were present, and made some comments.

My interviewing must have changed in the course of the project, because the later interviews were much longer than the earliest ones. This probably reveals not so much a change of technique as an increasing awareness, created by the earlier interviews, of how many different aspects of a project there are that can be worth asking about. I am sure that it was right to have allowed myself to learn from experience, but the resulting differences among interviews done at different phases make strict comparisons difficult. A related problem arose in interviewing several people from the same project. One could ask better questions after the first interview, but ti was hard to do this without revealing what the first person said, which would have violated confidentiality; moreover, to bring in such knowledge might have distorted the respondent's spontaneity and made interviews non-comparable. In practice I tried to treat each interview as an independent one, and to make use of information from others only when it looked as though the current respondent was not going to cover some point that seemed significant, or on which he might have a distinctive perspective. Sometimes this could be done without revealing that one was drawing on earlier interviews, but when it could not, a verbal formulation that gave little away could usually be devised. (Respondents showed considerable curiosity about what their colleagues had said, and often asked me about it directly; sometimes I seemed like one of the only channels of communication they felt were available to them, and they were really anxious to find out things they needed to know about the project through me. It would not have been proper, however, for me to be very communicative.) To make sure that some of the right questions were asked, it was desirable to bear earlier interviews in mind when conducting later ones. In some ways, however, it was psychologically advantageous not to remember the earlier ones too clearly; one could ask about every aspect of the project with more authentic interest, and there was less danger that the boredom of repetition, or the rationalisation that one knew it all already, would lead to skimping. I tried to discourage later respondents from assuming that they could skip topics others must already have told me about. Inevitably this means that in the data there is some repetition that conveys no new information, although often one learnt fresh things by hearing about a topic from a new angle. (One of the minor points of interest was that several times it happened that I came to a project's recognised black sheep after several earlier interviews; I expected that his version would justify the positions he had taken and condemn other members of the team, but in each case I found that he appeared relatively unconscious of the cleavage in the team and the way in which the others perceived him.)

As these comments indicate, the interviews were unstructured in form, but I always had in mind a list of the sort of topics that ought to be covered. The technique eventually developed was to ask the respondent to take me through the social history of the project in the order in which it happened, probing for amplification as we went along, and then for me to raise any questions that this account had not covered. How people responded to the opening varied considerably; some launched into a complete intellectual and social autobiography, while others initially found very little to say. It was evident that to a considerable extent how people spoke initially depended on what they thought I was interested in, and here there was sometimes a dilemma: they would have liked guidance on what I regarded as relevant, but I was anxious not to mould the data to my preconceptions by giving them any. This produced a few tortured interviews in which an unhappy respondent spoke at length on aspects of the research which it was probably clear, despite my encouraging nods, were not of interest to me, while I suffered agonies of boredom and wasted time but could not see how to turn the subject without being too directive. Both very eventful and very uneventful projects tended to create interviewing problems. In the very eventful ones, there tended to be aspects of such obvious interest that we were both in danger of concentrating on the spectacular bits and forgetting their mundane background. In the very uneventful ones, people tended to feel, with mild embarrassment, that there was not really anything to tell me about because nothing particular had happened; they were of course wrong, but it would take a little while to get them going. Sometimes on this sort of project there were undertones of hostility in the interview, because I seemed to be suggesting that there must have been conflicts and disasters where there had been none. I did not want to do this, yet nor did I want to make it too easy to paper over the cracks if there had been any. One further type of response that made for a 'bad' interview was when researchers, usually quite senior and experienced people, construed their role as that of informant, and told me their own explanations, conclusions and recommendations rather than giving me the raw data on which these were based. This was hard to prevent, because I naturally found it interesting, and such people legitimately felt that they had something useful to tell me. (Although such comments were not always what I wanted, I have frequently made use of my respondents' hypotheses and insights, which were often valuable.) These people and others often had pet theories which they were anxious to pass on to me, and with them there seemed little danger that the nuances of my presentation would affect whether they did it or not. Some, however, had expectations of what I wanted that arose from the wording of my letter or from rumours in the sociological community, and these could give distortions or biases, though I hope these were usually corrected by the end of the interview.

A number of peculiarities in the interviewing situation arose from the fact that I was interviewing my own peer group, and on subjects that we might easily have spoken about in any case. First of all, I knew some of the people already, and would be likely to meet others again; the advantages of this are obvious, the disadvantages perhaps less so. For both parties, the interviewing relationship had a past and, more importantly, a future; though I hope my respondents felt that I could be relied upon to keep their confidences, I would continue to be a member of their colleague group who would know things that otherwise she might not have done. How far this caused constraint I do not know. In at least one case I think I have detected a subsequent coolness in the manner of someone who told me revealing things. (Some people seem to expect me, when we meet again, to start from the point that we reached in the interview, while for others it seems appropriate to act as if the interview had never happened since we meet now in another relationship. I certainly do not feel entitled to treat what I learnt in the interviews as part of my ordinary social experience, but sometimes it is hard to remember whether I learnt something from the interview or from ordinary gossip.) Another person started the interview by saying that he was embarrassed at the prospect of saying unfavourable things about a former colleague with whom he thought I was friendly. My own consciousness of such possibilities certainly affected how I felt during the interviews, although I tried not to let social embarrassment prevent me probing where it seemed necessary. Occasionally almost the reverse effect took place: people did not bother to tell me things that they knew I knew about already, and so in my role as researcher I felt obliged to violate the norms of friendship by pressing for statements that I could write down within the framework of the interview and so make formally available for use. Thus at times some rather conscious playing of the roles of interviewer and respondent took place. One way of easing the artificiality of just sitting there saying "uh-huh" to a colleague talking on matters of shared interest was to join in, and to some extent I did this as a matter of deliberate technique; the social norm of reciprocity could be met, and the sting taken out of hints that things might have gone wrong in their research, by contributing examples from my own research experience.

Another source of embarrassment was that, at least for the purposes of this project, I was not particularly interested in those aspects of other people's research which are normally regarded as the most significant: I did not want to hear much about its intellectual content, except insofar as this could be related to its social history. Most people started the interview by asking me what it was about, and here there was a dilemma: I felt a strong need to justify myself, but could not do so by quoting what I had already heard or by giving a detailed account of hypotheses because the first would have been unethical and the second might have biased the interview. Thus I tended to be very emphatic about the importance and relevance of the research, but rather vague, and thus no doubt unconvincing to anyone not initially sympathetic. I felt a stronger need to appear well in the eyes of my respondents than the ordinary interviewer is likely to have cause for, and this may have influenced the course of the interview, though I am not sure how.

On can only speculate about the ways in which such factors may have affected the content of the interviews. What they were like as an experience for the respondents obviously varied. For some it seemed just a rather lengthy and tiring version of ordinary professional conversation; for a few it was a traumatic reliving of bad times in the past; some called it therapeutic, and there were quips that I should charge for my services; a Catholic at the end jokingly asked me for absolution. My final impression is that most people made a serious effort to tell me the truth as they saw it to the best of their abilities, though that truth is inevitably partial.

Analysis

Originally the analysis was conceived rather vaguely: I just thought that I would identify a series of themes and write about them, and that coding, analysis and writing would be one integral process. Perhaps it could have been like that, but it was not.

There is an innate tension between the interviewing strategy of systematic coverage of standardized topics and that of the open-ended pursuit of whatever themes spontaneously arise. At the stage of analysis this becomes one between a quantitative, survey-type approach and a qualitative one which reports on case-studies and generalizes about the sample only impressionistically. I assumed initially that I would use a qualitative approach, and so devised a system of coding that rested on that assumption: it classified sections of the interview under broad topic headings, and I imagined that I would simply look at everything on one topic and then write. When I came to think about it in detail I was not happy about this, perhaps because my methodological training was very much in the survey tradition, and I started trying to work out precise coding categories to fit the data. Having spent some time on this, I found that I could not use it. It would have entailed coding in the same way, and thus losing the distinction between, an instance where a respondent had initiated a theme himself and developed it with great feeling, and another where the only reference was a passing mention in response to a direct probe. It cannot be assumed that what was said in the interviews was the truth and the whole truth, but to ignore such distinctions would have been to lack respect for the character of the data.

The process by which the coding categories used were eventually decided was that I made a list of headings drawing attention to themes that, in the interviewing, I had identified as significant and recurrent ones; I went through the interviews noting on cards the points at which these themes came up, and added to the list of headings as I came across further themes. This is an enormously laborious and boring process, with great temptations to skimp, because each time a new category is added one has to go back and read through the interviews already coded again.

Even when this decision had been made, the coding still had many problematic aspects. To start with, people speak in different ways, so that verbatim recording of unstructured interviews gives different kinds of material. Those who speak more obliquely, use fewer completed sentences, rely on more taken-for-granted understandings, give less that can be coded literally; one remembers things from the interview that can no longer be clearly identified in the text. Obviously it would not be proper to code things that are not unequivocally there in the text, or one runs the risk of inventing data, but nonetheless one's memories prevent the easy assumption of survey research that what is not on the paper never happened. Both for this reason, and because of the unstandardized nature of the questions asked, the assumption could not be made, as it would have been by counting the number of times items were coded, that people had implicitly answered the questions I might have asked in a standardized schedule. Thus one could not, for instance, assume that people who had not said that they felt guilty that their research had not yet been completed did not feel guilty about it; at most, one could only assume that these guilt feelings were less salient for them than for those who did say so.

In any case, the meaningfulness of counting the times an item appeared in the coding varied with the nature of the coding categories, and here I did not at first fully realize what I was doing. For instance, one of the categories used was 'guilty not finished', meaning that the respondent spontaneously said that he felt guilty that his project was not completed on time. With this type of code, it is in some sense meaningful to count up the number of times it is used and make statements like "x% of the sample said that they felt guilty . . .". But another type of category used was far broader; one, for instance, was 'division of labour', which was used wherever there was any reference to anything that bore on the project's division of labour. With this type of code, it makes no sense at all to count the number of references; all the coding does is to tell one where to find something on that topic, and what that something is and whether it has characteristics that can be counted remains to be seen. A further complication is that initially I tended to note items only when they looked 'interesting', rather than whenever there was any reference to a topic at all; whether this is appropriate or not depends on which strategy one is using. Having decided that it was necessary to note every reference if easy self-deception was to be avoided, I then found myself doing some coding that was clearly redundant, because when there were several respondents from the same project the same purely factual item (e.g. that a certain research assistant left) would get coded over and over again; this created extra work at the analysis stage, when every reference had to be checked, without conveying any extra information. This could have been avoided if I had thought in time more carefully about what I was doing, although at the time irrational and obsessive consistency seemed easier than making rational distinctions.

'Purely factual' items created considerable problems, because only in a few instances had I asked about them systematically in the first place; they seemed of minor importance when I was thinking of the project as more impressionistic and sensational, and as essentially about the perceptions and feelings of those interviewed. When, however, I came to think about it more analytically and look for independent variables, the basic face-sheet types of data on individual and project were sometimes missing. Here works of reference and my personal knowledge of the group interviewed helped, since I could often fill in such points as marital status or rank, and felt no scruple about doing so on factual matters. I now have serious reservations about my own initial tacit methodological assumptions. To have interviews so unstructured that only points regarded by one's respondents as relevant are referred to is, if one has no other sources of information, to rely on them doing one's sociology for one. Perhaps this is more justifiable than it would otherwise be when the sample is of sociologists! But even for them it is clearly insufficient if one wishes to try to construct explanations.

The question of factuality has further complications. Should those interviewed be treated as informants — providers of objective information to be taken at face value — or as respondents — providers of raw data to be interpreted? If one treats the interviewee as an informant, one codes only what he mentions and treats it as fact. Having done this, is it legitimate to supplement the interview data with facts from other sources? And what if two people from the same project give accounts that differ, even if they are not actually inconsistent? On some points it seems only sensible to use them as informants on each other, while on others they must be treated as separate. Cases where the decision on which policy to follow is not obvious are those where, for instance, one team member tells of a quarrel with another member which is seen as having had consequences for the project, while the other member makes no reference to this. Should the quarrel be taken as a fact characterising the project, or merely as part of the perceptions of one participant? In general, I resolved the matter by accepting all participants' reports, but using my judgment to decide how far it seemed likely that their reporting was biased by their position or personal feelings and to try to make allowance for this.

This difficulty is connected with another persistent problem throughout the research, which is whether the unit of analysis is the individual respondent or the project. The obvious answer is that they both are, but they cannot both be simultaneously. In coding, some categories clearly apply to the one or to the other, but some are relevant to both. I found it necessary to have one set of cards for projects and another for individuals. Originally I hoped to classify projects in terms of such things as the basis of legitimation of directorial authority, but the task of devising a formal strategy for translating the relevant data given by separate individuals into something that could be taken as true of the project seemed almost impossible; this was especially so given that varying numbers of individuals were involved in the projects, and of these I had seen varying proportions, which made comparability dubious. Thus in the end most of the items coded on the project cards were either very simple factual ones (how many members did the team have?) or ones where on the basis of incomplete information I made a judgment. Some chapters have become primarily about projects, and others concentrate on the individual and his experiences, though a central theme of the book is the nature of the interaction between the two.

In the end there were some things that could meaningfully be counted, and I have counted them and report the results. This represents an aspiration (seldom reached)towards the strengths of both survey and purely qualitative styles of research. Interpretative insights are of value, and my natural membership of the group studied means that some of the usual difficulties in achieving the understanding that would justify interpretation do not arise. But just for this reason my interpretations may be liable to subtle biases from my established habits of thought — I had gone native before the research even started. In any case, insights are only insights and should where possible be systematically checked; to miss the opportunity to do so is to show more faith in oneself than the critical reader should be expected to share. I have attempted, therefore, to give the data on which my interpretations are based, and to check them numerically where this can be done. I am not immune to the temptation to claim wisdom rather than indicate knowledge, but I hope that it is clear when I am doing so.

One final problem arose from the need for anonymity. In the very earliest stages of thinking about the research the idea was that the projects studied should be identified — indeed this was seen as part of the value of the enterprise, for it could provide background data on projects that readers already knew about from other publications. It would indeed be more informative if one could relate the data I have to the intellectual outcomes of the projects in this way, but in practice that turned out not to be feasible. (In any case, many of the projects have not yet reached their main publication, and a few never will; to have confined the sample to those which had already made their main publication would have limited it unduly, and would have ensured that the typical project included was older and less fresh in participants' memories.)

People often told me things that they would not have bee prepared to see published in ways that could identify them, or that could have harmed or embarrassed them or other people. If all such things had been omitted, their accounts would have been falsified and much interesting data would have been lost. On balance, anonymity seemed a price worth paying. A consequence, however, has been the sacrifice of one of the strengths of my original data: its story line, and the sense it gives of the ways in which different aspects of a project are interrelated and influence each other. The changing of some details in what is reported also inevitably blurs the outlines, and has forced me at times to make anodyne abstract and general statements instead of presenting the richness of concrete data that lies behind them.

Having made the decision to present the material anonymously, problems still remain about how to do it. Since many likely readers are members of the peer-group of the respondents, they could have an idea who some of them might be even when names have been changed; this has made it necessary to choose quotations and change details very carefully. (One amusing minor problem was that on several occasions I had to decide not to change a male to a female because, had I done so, the behaviour reported might have been construed as typically feminine, and therefore explicable by the sex of the person.) Despite my precautions, there may still be some temptation to try to spot individuals and projects. To prospective spotters, and those uneasy about the danger of spotting, I would like to make two points. Firstly, the reader might well be surprised to find out how many cases there are analogous to ones he already knows something about; it would be rash to assume that, because some features of one described here sound familiar, it has been identified correctly and one can assume that other information presented here can be taken to refer to that instance. Secondly, if a reader *can* identify a case correctly (and it would be hard to *know* that he had done so) I do not think that is because I have violated anyone's anonymity: it must be because he already has the necessary information from another source.

The prime danger is that immediate colleagues might be able to identify each other, and thus learn things that they would not have said to each others' faces. Thus there is even a case for attempting to shield respondents' anonymity from themselves, since if they could clearly identify themselves it would sometimes follow that they could identify other respondents as former colleagues. In those few instances where this might occur, my aim has been to report nothing said that the interviews did not suggest the others already knew in broad outline.

When the book was completed I sent round a circular to the

respondents saying that I was prepared, if necessary, to let them see the quotations from their interviews that I had used, so that they could ask for any they did not wish to appear to be cut. I asked them, however, to avoid making use of the opportunity if possible, since to indicate which quotations came from their interviews would in some cases make it certain that they could identify colleagues. (It is less likely that they could do so otherwise, both because some details have been changed and because after a lapse of time it is very unlikely that they remember the exact words they used.) Nine people asked to see their quotations, and one asked for one passage (referring to an episode in his private life) to be deleted. A number wrote to say that they were prepared to rely on my discretion. At this stage, however, another issue came up. One respondent replied to my circular objecting to the proposed anonymity, on the grounds that this was not what had originally been planned, and was inconsistent with the understanding on which he had agreed to take part. Although my personal reaction to this was that the changes in the original plan were a legitimate response to the research situation as it developed, I could understand why he should feel like that, and thought it possible that other respondents who had not written about it nonetheless felt the same. I therefore sent round a second circular asking if anyone else would positively like identification. The whole way in which the book had been written made it now inappropriate to identify particular passages as coming from named individuals or projects, so it was decided to give only a separate list of projects, which appears as Appendix B. Only 3 further respondents asked for their projects to be named, so I have padded the list out with a number more where those concerned did not mind whether it was mentioned or not.

B. List of Projects

Listed below are some of the projects in the sample studied. Where a book has been published, the project is listed by that title, and where it has not the title is that of the project as a whole. The appearance of a title below does not necessarily indicate which, or how many, of the participants in the project were seen. A title is only given, however, when all those seen gave their consent, and the interests of other participants who were not seen were unlikely to be affected. The projects listed account for 36 of the sample's individual respondents.

Aberdeen Child Development Project (Directors: Raymond Illsley, H.J. Birch, Stephen J. Richardson)

The Cloistered Elite, John Wakeford (Macmillan, 1969)

Education and the Working Class, Brian Jackson and Dennis Marsden (Routledge & Kegan Paul, 1962)

Institute of Race Relations' Programme of Research on Race Relations in Britain (Director: E.J.B. Rose; Assistant Director: N.D. Deakin)

Organizational Behaviour in Context: The Aston Studies (Director: Derek Pugh)

The Orientation to Work and Industrial Behaviour of Shipbuilding Workers on Tyneside. (Director: Richard Brown)

The Origins and Recruitment of the British Army Elite, 1870-1959 (Director: Christopher B. Otley)

Power, Persistence and Change: A Second Study of Banbury, Margaret Stacey, Eric Batstone, Colin Bell and Anne Murcott (Routledge & Kegan Paul, 1975)

Students in Conflict: LSE in 1967, Tessa Blackstone, Kathleen Gales, Roger Hadley and Wyn Lewis (Weidenfeld & Nicolson, 1970)

"Survey of abortion patients for the Committee on the working of the Abortion Act", Ann Cartwright and Susan Lucas (Vol. III of the *Report of the Committee on the Working of the Abortion Act* (HMSO, 1974)

Varieties of Unbelief, Susan Budd, Heinemann, forthcoming.

C. Letter to Respondents

This is the letter that was sent inviting prospective respondents to be interviewed, and the document enclosed with it. It will be noted that the document describing the research suggests a rather different kind of book from that which has eventually emerged. Relatively late in the interviewing I realized that this had now become misleading, and made some minor changes to bring it into line with my changed ideas.

> Dear
> I am writing to ask if you might be willing to help me in some research that I am doing. You may possibly have seen in *Sociology* that I am collecting histories of research projects with a view to writing something systematic on the sociology of the social research process . . .
> [There would then be a short passage about why I would be interested to see that particular person, and what I hoped to talk to them about.]
> Could you spare the time to talk to me some time? I don't have anything like a formal questionnaire, so my interviews are unstructured except by the occasional probe; this makes it rather hard to say how long it might take, but general experience so far suggests probably up to two hours. I realise this is quite a lot to ask, but it would be very valuable to me if you could manage it.
> [A paragraph about possible practical arrangements for meeting.]
> I do hope that you'll be able and willing to arrange something. I enclose a duplicated statement which tells you rather more about the research, and of course I should be happy to explain further on any point.

Statement

Towards a Sociology of Social Research — Research Proposals

All of us who have engaged in empirical research know that things take place, and have consequences for the nature of the end product, which do not fit into the textbook recipes; they may directly violate textbook prescriptions, but often simply arise from contingencies which textbooks do not mention. It seems desirable that some attempts should be made to systematize the folklore informally transmitted among social researchers, and to apply sociology in a constructive way to the activities of sociologists. There have been some interesting efforts of this nature recently, mainly by American sociologists: a number of citation studies and discussions of journals' editorial policies, arguments about funding of research and its implications, P. Hammond's *Sociologists at Work*, G. Sjoberg's *Ethics, Politics and Social Research,* and Julius Roth's fascinating and important article, 'Hired Hand Research'. However, these works have been concerned, insofar as the treatment is systematic, only with a few stages in the process of research. By starting from empirical accounts of what happens in the research process, rather than the normative account of what 'should' happen given in textbooks, it is hoped that some steps may be taken towards the development of sociologically realistic and relevant normative suggestions. This does not mean, however, that I am not interested in model projects in which everything went by the book! Indeed the inclusion of such projects is necessary if one is to be able to begin to specify what circumstances facilitate such success.

The general plan is to collect a number of accounts of the history and development of research projects. The difficulty of devising a sampling frame rules out the possibility of attempting to get a random or systematic sample; I am trying, therefore, simply to include a reasonable number of projects, and within that number to include as much diversity as possible of subject matter, method and institutional setting. (Abortive projects too, and the reasons why they were not completed, will be of interest). The hope is that this will provide a provisional basis for the formulation of hypotheses and methodological caveats.

My aim is not only, however, to work towards generalisations, but also to make available information, of a kind not usually published in any detail in a research report, about well-known empirical work. Such information can often add enormously to our understanding of the particular work and its development. It also gives great assistance to the attempt to see how the details of the research process affect the nature of the end product if one can refer to an 'end product' which is a familiar published work.

Thus I hope that my research will result in a book which contains relatively extended case studies of the progress of a number of projects, generally ones which have been published and become fairly widely known, plus a larger number of accounts of limited aspects of other research projects selected for their bearing on the issues which emerge as most significant. This will not, however, be a reader; it is hoped to collect at least the case study data primarily by means of interviews with those involved, hopefully more than one of them in the case of team research; for the rest written accounts built around a framework of informal questions, will be solicited, to be edited and used as eventually seems most useful. Appropriate acknowledgments will of course be given, where preferred anonymity of individual and/or project will be ensured. (In the latter case the advantage of being able to relate the account to published work will of course be lost, but I have reason to believe that some relevant data could only be collected under such conditions). Where any questions might arise factual accuracy and the fairness of editing or partial quotation will be checked with those concerned.

D. Social Science Research Council Procedures

Although the S.S.R.C. is a relatively modest source of research funds in the social sciences, indeed very modest in comparison with some Government Departments such as the Department of Health and Social Security*, the Council plays an important role in the overall pattern of research funding in many social science subjects. Sociology relies heavily on the S.S.R.C. for funds for empirical research related to academic interests rather than directly related to, or dictated by, policy considerations. Some fairly detailed account of the way in which the Council operates, therefore, seems appropriate and this appendix is intended to provide background against which accounts of the social research process given in the main text of this book can be evaluated.

The Funding System

The S.S.R.C. is one of five** research councils in the UK which draw the bulk of their funds directly from Government, in the form of a grant-in-aid from the Department of Education and Science. Part of the total vote at the disposal of the D.E.S. is referred to as the 'science budget'. This is a block of funds set aside to finance the five research councils and one or two smaller bodies with a concern for UK science (e.g. the Royal Society receives a grant).

Following the publication of the Rothschild and Dainton Reports***, which reviewed the arrangements for publicly funded research and development in the U.K., an Advisory Board for Research Councils

* It is difficult to get accurate estimates of the D.H.S.S.'s research budget for social as opposed to biomedical problems, but it seems likely that at least one fifth of their annual £25 million research budget goes on research related to the social services and social security. This compares with S.S.R.C.'s total annual expenditure of some £3 million spread across all the social sciences.

** The five are Agricultural Research Council, Medical Research Council, Natural Environment Research Council, Science Research Council and Social Science Research Council. Each is an independently chartered body with the same basic function of supporting research and intellectual development within its given disciplines.

*** *A Framework for Government Research and Development*, Cmnd. 4814, HMSO, London 1971.

(A.B.R.C.) was established, on which the Research Councils are re-presented, principally to advise the Secretary of State for Education and Science on the allocation of the science budget between the various bodies (the A.B.R.C. succeeded the Council for Scientific Policy, which formerly discharged this function).

The Research Councils submit annual budget estimates to the A.B.R.C. covering a five-year period — these are called 'five year rolling forward looks', and they are made in the context of guide-lines suggested by the A.B.R.C. The A.B.R.C. considers all the forward looks together and on the basis of the respective cases makes it recommendation on the allocation of the science budget for the coming financial year. Once the budgets are allocated the Coun-cils are, in theory, able to spend them freely within the agreed broad headings of research, postgraduate training and administration.

In practice, of course, this freedom is limited by a variety of considerations. One of the most important, in terms of the way in which the S.S.R.C. can perform its functions, is that of accounta-bility. The Council's accounts are subject to the attentions of the Exchequer and Audit Department (E.A.D.), and as such have to bear close scrutiny. In particular, the Council's Secretary is desig-nated as the Accounting Officer and as such is personally answerable to Parliament for all expenditure incurred on the Council's behalf.

This is the system within which the S.S.R.C. operates, and from this stems the need to be able, if necessary, to explain the reason for every penny of expenditure, and for the whole panoply of standar-dised procedures and formal conditions which our clients frequently find tiresome and inexplicable. It does, indeed, sometimes have re-percussions beyond this level, in that the Council may find it diffi-cult to justify expenditure on some ill-defined enterprises which might possibly have a high pay-off in intellectual terms, but appear more likely to be unsuccessful. An example of this is support for the 'thinking time' which goes into the formulation of a research pro-posal. The risk that no proposal or a very indifferent one, might emerge at the end of three or six months has so far deterred the Council from this kind of venture.

S.S.R.C. Research Grants

As this book is concerned only with the research process, attention will be confined here to the S.S.R.C.'s annual budget*. In fact, of

* In 1973/74 the budget of £5.6 million was spent as follows:
    Research £2.4 million
    Postgraduate training £2.8 million
    Administration and general expenses £0.4 million.

course, the S.S.R.C. also supports research through their own Research Units, but as these funds are not generally available to the academic community at large no attention is paid to this aspect here.

The general principle followed by the S.S.R.C. is to spend a lot of time preparing research proposals for decision, to scrutinise them severely and judge them by high standards, and then to interfere as little as possible with the investigators once a grant has been made.

Ideally, prospective grant holders contact the Office for some discussion while they are still at the stage of formulating their projects, and probably some 50% of grant applicants do this. Although the staff do not claim to be experts or specialists in the particular fields, and can give little help of this kind, they do know the criteria which the decision-making committees apply to applications and also give advice on more mundane matters of costing. Advice usually centres on the way in which the proposal is presented, and on straightforward costing such as subsistence rates. The most common faults are failure to spell out clearly the aims of the project, lack of an adequate account of the actual research which is to be undertaken, and over-ambition in the scope of the project. Advice is usually acted on to the best of the applicant's ability, but it is obviously difficult to judge how far such advice helps, or indeed hinders, applicants' chances of success. However, the majority do express gratitude for such help. Office staff may in fact find themselves in slightly vulnerable situations from time to time in that, although they can offer advice in the light of their own experience, they can promise nothing and have no influence on the actual decision on the particular applications. They consequently run the risk of being blamed for failures by disgruntled applicants who took their advice.

Applications are categorised into three groups, each of which is processed somewhat differently. Those under £6,000 are dealt with on a continuous basis outside full Committee meetings. Those between £6,000 and £50,000 are dealt with at thrice-yearly meetings for which deadlines have to be observed; those over £50,000 and research programmes are taken once a year only. These limits, which were adjusted to their present level in January 1973, are fixed somewhat artificially, but the reasoning is: first, to have a category of smaller grants on which relatively quick decisions can be made; second, to have a middle range of grants allocated on a thrice-yearly basis so that money can be set aside at the beginning of the financial year for each of the 'tranches', thus avoiding a first-come first-served syndrome; and third, to enable the Council to take an annual overview of the very big applications and to ensure that these do not absorb too large a share of the annual research budget.

When the formal application is received at the S.S.R.C. the first step is to allocate it to one or more of the subject committees. There are now thirteen of these committees, each of which consists of a dozen or so academics and others who can together span the broad specialisms of a discipline or field of application. Most of the committees are chaired by a member of the Council. The rationale for having committees of this kind is that grants are made on the basis of judgment by peers of the scientific merits of proposals. The allocation of applications to committees is made by the Head of the Research Grants Division.

Current thinking is to minimise the number of applications seen by more than one committee, as reconciling different views on the same proposal can be tedious and lead to unsatisfactory outcomes. Contrary to popular view, these are not necessarily unfavourable to the application, as there is a distinct tendency for compromise, so that proposals given a high 'award' priority by one committee and a 'reject' by another may end up with a 'medium' award priority. Nor does the procedure affect applications' rates of progress through the decision making machinery, as decisions on multi-disciplinary applications have to be ratified by Council on the same date (3-4 weeks after the committee meetings) as those on single-subject applications.

Preparing applications for decision by the committees consits mainly of scrutinising them for glaring costing and, in some cases, substantive anomalies and sending them out to referees.

Costing can be a difficult matter, as investigators are all too well aware, but realistic budgeting is important for two reasons. Firstly, it gives committees insight into investigators' planning capabilities and thus into their competence to conduct research. Secondly, the Council needs to know from the outset the full financial commitment which is being undertaken, in order to budget ahead.

The S.S.R.C. does not fund anything which should normally be met from the University Grants Committee support for universities. The U.G.C. is supposed to provide basic and continuing support, including accommodation and salaries for the teaching and research functions of academic staff. This should also include provision of supporting staff, library and computer facilities, standard office and laboratory equipment and some free funds to enable academic staff to undertake a limited amount of individual research of their own choosing. Once any items of this kind have been sifted out of an application the remaining costs are examined for overall reasonableness in relation to the work to be carried out. This is by no means always easy to establish. Even in relatively straightforward matters such as numbers, levels and salaries of research staff there may be hidden pitfalls, in that different universities often have their own internal scales for research staff to which the Council has to conform. Other items can be extremely difficult to estimate and check, particularly travel for interviewing purposes, and equipment where investigators claim to need a special kind of tape recorder or video machine. Sometimes applicants may artificially deflate all budget headings in order to apply for a grant in the category which does not have to observe deadlines. The general rule followed has to be to seek explanation and justification of items which appear outside the broad ranges currently operative, but this is usually left until after a decision has been made in order to save time sorting out queries on applications which will not eventually be transformed into grants. Clarification may, however, be sought immediately on more substantive aspects of the application which the Committee Secretary knows the Committee will want to know about — for example, intended sample sizes or frames may not be clear, or there may be no curriculum vitae or no reference list.

Referees (usually three or four) are selected by the Committee Secretary in the light of her or his own familiarity with the various fields, supplemented occasionally by that of committee members. The system is based on goodwill, and to retain this some stress is laid on confidentiality, as the S.S.R.C. does not believe that referees would continue to furnish frank views on projects if they thought that these might start prolonged academic wrangles. In addition to academic referees, the views of relevant Government Departments and other official bodies are sought when proposals either require access to Government-controlled data, or are particularly pertinent to Departmental policy. The Council is by no means constrained by adverse Governmental comments, but refusal to allow access to data or people is obviously a serious block to the research which has to be taken into account in making decisions.

In formal terms, decisions to award are taken by the full Council, acting on the recommendation of subject committees. In practice, the real decisions taken by Council are on marginal applications, where funds are low and a choice has to be made between applications recommended for award, and on the very large £50,000 plus applications. Applications are graded into four 'award' categories, reflecting the degree of priority which committees attach to each application, and two 'reject' categories. The main purpose of the 'award' gradings is in fact to give indications to the Council of the relative importance which committees attach to seeing awards made.

Committees look at applications in terms of the declared objectives of the research, the methods tò be used to accomplish these, the way data are to be analysed, and the applicant's qualifications, including research experience, and capabilities. Although some subjects will obviously tend to see proposals favouring particular methodologies, e.g. nearly all the proposals the Social Anthropology Committee are asked to consider use particpant observation, generally speaking the committees do not have preferences for certain kinds of approaches. However, given that the Council's support is confined mainly to the provision of research assistance and research support costs [c.f. page 211, para 6], and that it is difficult for S.S.R.C. to pay for the time of established academic staffs*, there is a tendency for applications to the Council to veer towards empirical work involving data collection. The general rule which committees follow is to check that methods are appropriate to the stated research objectives, and that proposed staffing is adequate for the size of project. For example, experience has taught them that, in the case of large research programmes, the management and research skills, and level of commitment, of the research director are of crucial importance.

Sometimes an award may be recommended on certain conditions, for example that one aspect of the research be brought forward or delayed. Probably the most common form of amendment is for reduction in the scope of a project; other recommendations might concern methodology, such as a larger or smaller sample, or use of a different sampling frame. The committee may ask for referees' comments to be sent to a successful applicant for his general guidance, and this is done anonymously. Applications may be rejected with or without encouragement to submit revised versions, depending on the committee's view of the potential worth of a project; in the former case the committee's comments are passed on to the applicant as broad guidelines for revision. Generally speaking, the committees tend to lean over backwards to enter into fruitful dialogue with applicants in the hope that this will result in improved applications and better research.

Once a decision to award has been ratified, the Office sorts out the financial and other queries and issues the formal grant letter which sets out the agreed budget. Financial control of ongoing grants is fairly tight, again for the obvious reason that the Council has to

* In July 1973 a new Personal Research Grant scheme was introduced which does in fact provide a limited number of grants which pay for the full time of academic staff for one year, but this is quite separate from the normal Reseach Grant scheme.

know the exact extent of its commitment at any given stage in the financial year. Over-expenditure must be approved in advance, and only very limited transfers can be made between budget headings by investigators without prior approval. All money supplements and time extensions have to be argued and justified on their merits. Although there is, of course, no justification required for inflation beyond the fact that it can be shown to have occurred, quibbles might arise over a request for supplementation to compensate for inflationary rises in, for example, survey costs if an investigator had deliberately delayed a major survey for a year beyond his original plan, thereby incurring an additional 25% on the cost; full explanations of all requests for supplementation, whether these are due to inflation or not, are therefore required. The exception to this is the case of nationally agreed salary awards, which are met by the council if there are insufficient funds in the grant, although it is hoped that some of the additional costs will be met out of savings under other headings.

Major changes in research design must also be specifically approved, as otherwise the grant is spent on a different project to the one originally seen and liked by the Committee. The most usual reason for wanting change is because a particular approach proved impracticable or even impossible once the research had started. An example of major change would be a proposal to move from using a survey approach to particpant observation or from analysis of census data to collection of fresh data, or a complete re-structuring of the conceptual framework. Committees are usually sympathetic to such changes, where they are clearly justified. Sometimes a grant holder may actually set such changes in motion without seeking prior approval from S.S.R.C. These inevitably come to light sooner or later, usually because there are concomitant financial changes for which reimbursement cannot be made without S.S.R.C. approval, and they always present problems. In theory, the Council can withdraw a grant on six months' notice, although this is clearly not desirable since it entails losing the investment already made in the project. In practice, a solution is usually negotiated between the investigator and the committee. In some, fortunately rare, instances major changes may not be discovered until the final report on the project is presented. The relevant committee would take this into account when assessing and evaluating the outcome of the project, and also in the event that that particular investigator applied for an S.S.R.C. grant at some future date.

When investigators want to make relatively minor changes, or find

214

minor problems in keeping to their original proposals, they are encouraged to include them in their annual progress reports and in the final report on the project which is submitted at the end of the grant, as committees find these very educative and build what they learn from them into the continuous process of refining criteria for judgment and evaluation.

Chronic problems relating to research management have been identified through their constant appearance in a succession of final reports. Examples of these are the difficulty of conducting successful multi-disciplinary research, and the problem of possible hiatuses between pilot studies (which are increasingly favoured as sensible preliminaries to many larger studies), and major studies. It is, unfortunately, rather easier to identify many of these problems than to remedy them. It is obviously not possible for the Council to contribute much to the solution of communication problems between individuals of different backgrounds in a given research team. Some effort can be made to 'bridge' the gap between the end of a pilot study and start of a main project, but this carries certain difficulties. The Council cannot simply pay the salaries of a research team which has no work to do during the two or three months that it may take for a decision to be reached on whether the pilot has shown that a major study would be useful and worthwhile. Therefore, each time some question arises of carrying a pilot study on into a larger project, there has to be forward planning and negotiation in order to ensure that the timing of the pilot study fits in with the timetable for a decision on the fresh application. If this involves a short extension of the research period for the pilot study, every effort is made to be accommodating.

From time to time, there is some clearly identifiable development which does stem directly from committees' cumulative experiences with research applications and grants. One example is the 'Guidelines to Applicants for Research Grants in Sociology and Social Administration', which the Sociology and Social Administration Committee has just compiled and made available. After eight years of operation, the Committee has learnt enough from the applications and reports which have gone through their hands to be able to issue a short statement outlining the points they have found the most important indicators of the likely success of a research project. This may not be spectacular but it is progress.

Stella Shaw

INDEX

Aberdeen Child Development
  Project, 204
Abortion patients, survey of, 204
Access, problems of, 44-51
Administration, who done by,
  69-70, 74-5
Allocation of rooms and its
  consequences, 37-8, 40, 132,
  142
Analysis of data, (see also *Realities
  of Social Research,* Writing)
  of qualitative data not done,
  177
  who done by, 69-70, 74-5
Anonymity of respondents, 7,
  201-3
Aston Studies, 204
Authorship (see also Writing,
  Contracts)
  allocation of, 80
  disputes over, 149-50, 155
  understandings on, 97
B.S.A. : see British Sociological
  Association
Banbury study, 204
Batstone, Eric 204
Bell, Colin, 7, 204
Bernstein, B., 95n
Blackstone, Tessa, 204
Breakdowns: see Stress
British Sociological Association,
  (B.S.A.), conference 185
  Summer School, 40
Brown, Richard, 204
Budd, Susan, 7, 204
Bulmer, Martin, 156n, 180n
Burns, Tom, 94n
Careers, (see also Job choice,

Status of researchers, Women's
  work) consequences of
research for, 156-65
destinations of researchers,
  107-12, 154
effects of grant system on,
  104-7
in research, beliefs about, 104
in research, insecurity of,
  104-5, 110
in research, lack of promotion
  chances in, 106
in research, opportunities for,
  109-110
& moves into teaching, 111-2
needs of researchers, 48-9,
  147
plans for, 118, 124-6, 158-9
problems of in independent
  units, 22-3, 104, 105
and research topics, 115-8
Carter, M.P., 189-90
Cartwright, Ann, 204
Changing ideas, 31
Charismatic leaders in research,
  39, 115, 117
Cicourel, Aaron, 145
Clients (see also Government
  departments) and action on
research findings, 61-3
affect research decisions,
  56-61
conflicts of interest with,
  47-9, 50-1, 55-6, 65
motives for commissioning
  research, 51-4, 63
relations with, 19-20, 64-5
researchers thrown out by, 47-51

217

ethos of, 74
Empirical research,
    criticism of, 30-1, 39, 180
    disillusion with, 180-1
Ethnomethodology, 21
Family situation (see also
    Spouses)
    demands of conflicting with
    research, 121-2, 126-7, 169-70,
    183
    effects of research on, 166-70
    effects on job choice, 118-9
    and women's work, 123-6
Firms (see also Clients)
    industrial, research on, 44, 52,
    56, 57-8
Foundations (see Funding agencies,
    Nuffield Foundation)
Funding agencies (see also Nuffield
    Foundation, Research grants,
    Social Science Research
    Council).
    assumptions made by, 26, 37
    constraints on, 14, 32
    for projects in sample, 12
    procedures of, 14, 15, 22,
    209-15
Funds (see also *Realities of Social
    Research,* Research grants)
    and bad costing, 18
    shortage of, 15, 18-22
    too great, 22
Gales, Kathleen, 204
Gender: see Sex
Glaser, Barney G, 95n, 140n
Goffman, Erving, 39
Government departments (see
    also Clients, Commissioned
    research, Funding agencies),
    as source of funds, 12
    liaison with, 59, 64
    motives for commissioning
    research, 51-2, 54

research vetting procedures
    of, 60-1
    rivalry among, 63
    special problems of, 25, 56,
    60-1, 63
    use of research findings, 53-4,
    62-3
    veto survey questions 45-6,
    56, 63
Hadley, Roger, 204
Hammond, P., 182n
Hierarchy (see also Directors,
    Egalitarianism)
    ambiguity in, 82-7
    consequences of, 88-9, 93-4,
    175
    directors' policies on, 76-80,
    89
    in general, 76-89
    legitimacy of, 83-5
Husbands: see Conjugal roles,
    Family situation, Spouses,
    Women's work.
Hypotheses,
    absence of, 28, 93-5
Identification: see Anonymity
Illsley, Raymond, 204
Independent research units,
    financial problems of, 22-5
Institute of Race Relations, 191,
    204
Intellectual careers and research
    topics, 113-4, 118, 165-6
Interdisciplinary work,
    consequences of, 16-17, 39,
    40-42, 159-60
Interviewer training: see
    Division of Labour
Interviews: see Depth interviews,
    Division of labour, *Realities
    of Social Research,* Surveys
Isolation of researchers, 37,
    39-40

219

221

Social Survey, 46
Sociometric tests,
    objections to, 45
Solo research,
    characteristics of, 186-7
Sponsors : see Clients
Spouses (see also Family situation)
    careers, 123-4
    help with research, 122-3
Stacey, Margaret, 204
Stalker, G.M., 94n
Statisticians, 25n, 40-41
Status of researchers, 37, 46,
    74-5, 140
Strauss, Anselm L., 95n, 140n
Stress in research, 127, 145, 167-9
*Students in Conflict: L.S.E. in
    1967,* 204
Student unrest,
    effects of, 28, 33, 163, 165
Successful projects,
    characteristics of, 177-9
Surveys (see also Division of
    labour, Questionnaire design).
    and division of labour 72-3, 187
    interviews done by, 69-70, 74-5
    and project type, 73
    reasons for use of, 25, 42, 176-7
Symbolic interactionism, 31
Teaching,
    effects of research on, 164-5
    interference of with research,
    33-6
    moves into from research, 111-2
    reasons for researchers doing,
    141-2
Teams in research (see also Division
    of labour, Hierarchy)
    composition of, 98-9
    conflict avoided in, 134-5
    hierarchy in, 76-89
    operational definition of, 66
    organisation of, 67-8

ranks found in, 66, 72-3
size of, 66-8, 72-3, 101-2
social basis of cleavage in,
    136-7
social relations in, 128-40,
    156, 194-5
types of, 67-8
Tests,
    and project type, 73
    errors in coding, 177
Thompson, J.D., 90n
Time,
    not enough for research, 33
    spent on other commitments,
    35-6
    and university terms, 28, 34-5
Timetables,
    advantages and disadvantages
    of, 29-31
    consequences of breaking, 32
    constraints on, 27-8
    difficulties in planning, 28-9
    in academic projects, 26 et
    seqq.
    in commissioned research, 25
    in independent units, 22-3
    mistakes in planning of, 27
    and pilot studies, 26
    university attitudes to, 24, 29
Unfinished projects,
    reasons for, 15, 26, 77, 81,
    82, 83, 98, 101-2, 128, 131,
    141, 148, 177
Universities, studies of,
    constraints on timing in, 28
    problems of access in, 45, 65
University expansion,
    consequences of, 33, 37,
    179-80
University projects,
    characteristics of, 42-3, 101-2,
    172-3
    late completion of, 26, 101-2

222

timetable problems of, 26
Varieties of Unbelief, 204
Vetoes,
    on publication, 47-9, 51,
    57-61
    on questions: see Government
    departments
Vetting of publications, 57-61
Wakeford, John, 7, 204
Willmott, Peter, 170n
Wives: See Conjugal roles,
    Family situation, Spouses

Women's work (see also Family
    situation, Spouses), 108-9
    123-6
Woodward, J., 73
Writing (see also Authorship,
    Division of labour)
    and direct contact with the
    data, 75n
    and participant observation, 98
    who done by, 69-70, 74-5,
    79-80, 97-8
Young, Michael, 170